AARON'S RECKONING
A TRUE STORY
BY HOWARD B. HERSKOWITZ

AARON'S RECKONING

A TRUE STORY

by
HOWARD B. HERSKOWITZ

Copyright © 2024 Howard Herskowitz
Aaron's Reckoning
A True Story
Published by Pierucci Publishing
P.O. Box 2074, Carbondale, Colorado 81623, USA
www.pieruccipublishing.com

Cover design by Magno Rodriguez
Edited by Sand Sinclair and Russell Womack
Written by Howard Herskowitz

Ebook ISBN: 978-1-962578-13-4
Hardcover ISBN: 978-1-962578-14-1
Paperback ISBN: 978-1-962578-95-0
Audiobook ISBN: 978-1-962578-25-7

Library of Congress Control Number: 2024931588

All rights reserved. Except as permitted under U.S. Copyright Act of 1976, no part of this publication may be reproduced, distributed or transmitted in any form or by any means, or stored in a database or retrieval system without the prior written permission of the copyright owner. The scanning, uploading and distribution of this book via the Internet or via any other means without the permission of the author is illegal and punishable by law. Thank you for purchasing only authorized electronic editions, and for withdrawing your consent or approval for electronic piracy of copyrightable materials. Your support of the author's rights, as well as your own integrity is appreciated.

Pierucci Publishing books may be purchased in bulk at special discounts for sales promotion, corporate gifts, fund-raising, or educational purposes. Special editions can be created to specifications. For details, contact the Special Sales Department, Pierucci Publishing, PO Box 2074, Carbondale, CO 81623 or Publishing@PierucciPublishing.com or toll-free telephone at 1-855-720-1111.

For contact purposes please email info@aaronsreckoning.com. For further information about the book or the author, please visit our website, www.howardherskowitz.com.

DEDICATION

As a young child, I sensed that there was something different about me compared with the rest of the youngsters on the block. I often observed the close loving relationships the other children in the neighborhood enjoyed with their grandparents. I asked my mother why I didn't have any grandparents. Not even one. My mother then told me the sad truth: my paternal grandfather had died before World War II, but all three of my other grandparents were murdered in Hitler's gas chambers at Auschwitz.

My mother, Helen Herskowitz, a survivor of Auschwitz, knew that she and my father could never replace the grandparents that had been taken from us before my siblings and I were born; but our parents did everything they could to extend their love and nurturing to my siblings and I so that the loss of our grandparents was cushioned to allow us to enjoy happy and healthy childhoods.

I dedicate this book to the memory of my grandparents whom I never knew.

> In the humble rustic Hungarian town of Gérjen in 1944, the synagogues lie vacant and ransacked, as do the Jewish shops and homes. A late-war Hungarian compliance with Nazi madness has been cruelly effective. There are no Jews left alive in Gérjen—until later that year, when two reappear in a most unlikely form: as conquerors and dictators with absolute power.

Aaron Herskowitz
(1914 - 2003)

AUTHOR'S NOTE

"So Dad, how many Nazis did you kill?" was the question I always asked my father as a young boy.

He often kept me spellbound with stories about his incredible struggles and fantastic escapes from his enemy assassins, so it was the most natural follow-up question for a boy to ask. But he never wanted anyone to know that he had killed anyone, not even those who committed crimes against humanity. Somehow, Dad always avoided the answer. He would manage either to waltz out of the room or to skillfully change the subject.

It was puzzling to me when my father would suddenly say at the end of an exciting story, "I wouldn't go back there for one hour, not to that scare, not for a million dollars." Why wouldn't one want to go back and relive such larger-than-life adventures, striking back at those who deserved it, always surviving to fight another day, no matter the circumstances? I longed to go back with him to experience those adventures and did so often in my dreams. It wasn't until many years later that I had a better understanding of the full dimension of the horrors of World War II.

I also found myself plagued by another question that has puzzled many historians and observers for decades about the plight of the European Jews during the Nazi occupation: Why didn't they fight back? I was haunted by the black-and-white TV images of concentration camp Jews marching to their slaughter without resisting. Why was my dad one of the only Jews who fought back and got justice against the Nazi criminals? One of the answers, never spoken aloud, has been kept virtually secret for decades, and is at last revealed in this book.

Now an adult and a practicing lawyer, I still maintain a feeling of empathy for the innocent underdog in a conflict, whether on behalf of individuals fighting for their rights denied by large entities, or on behalf of an "outcasted" person experiencing discrimination against seemingly insurmountable odds. I have also experienced the same sympathetic passions in my study of history, where innocent or outnumbered people in a conflict manage to overcome overwhelmingly superior odds and achieve victory. Drawing upon my historical and family roots as the son of two survivors of the twentieth century's greatest tragedy, I have striven to become a champion of the underdog.

In 1990, long after World War II, Aaron Herskowitz—at age seventy-five—did return to visit the Eastern European town that had been home to his murdered family. On this occasion, I finally convinced him to begin telling me about his wartime experiences more fully, including anything he had thought was inappropriate for me to hear as a child.

And so, after decades of talking with my father about the events of his youth, I videotaped, audiotaped, and took extensive notes in a series of private interviews with him which lasted years. He was already known as a captivating storyteller within the family and local community; one who could enhance his testimony by impersonating the facial expressions and voices of characters in his story. He retained an incredible memory of the very conversations he had with these people more than fifty years earlier. As he began to tell his story, it quickly became apparent that all the hours I'd spent listening to him as a boy had not prepared me for the full breadth of the horror, madness, and triumph he had endured.

AARON'S JOURNEY 1939 - 1945

Aaron's journey took him from his home in Bielka Czechoslovakia, to the Russian battlefront at Voronezh; then back by foot to Päks and Gérjen in far west Hungary.

TABLE OF CONTENTS

Dedication 1
Author's Note 3
Prologue 8
Chapter 1 How Did This Come About? 9
Chapter 2 A Nation Betrayed 15
Chapter 3 A Secret Deal 24
Chapter 4 Moving a Mountain with a Teaspoon 32
Chapter 5 A Jacket And A Shoe 47
Chapter 6 Withholding Prayer 53
Chapter 7 A Legless Doll 54
Chapter 8 60
Chapter 9 Death-Fight for my Watch 71
Chapter 10 Horse Master 85
Chapter 11 A Bitter Meal 104
Chapter 12 109
Chapter 13 Sax 120
Chapter 14 Escape from the Nazis and Hungarians 127
Chapter 15 From Slave To Master 147
Chapter 16 Blood Rage 165
Chapter 17 Escape From The Russians 192
Chapter 18 Once The Powerful, Now The Powerless 217
Chapter 19 A Chance Wedding 230
Chapter 20 Aaron Returns To His Faith 241
Chapter 21 A Final Reckoning 245
Chapter 22 Whatever Happened To Sax? 246
Historian's Commentary 250
Index of Photographs 255
Index of Maps (Per Footnotes) 277
Acknowledgements 296
About the Author 299

*To assist those readers who wish to follow the geography of Aaron Herskowitz's journey during World War II, footnotes have been provided at the bottom of certain pages to include references to maps connecting historical events to the geographical terrain where Aaron Herskowitz was located during the war. These maps are located in the rear of the book, courtesy of Col. David Glantz, U.S. Army, ret., who is considered a leading expert on the conflict between Germany and Russia. Col. Glantz has written The Historian's Commentary (See Table of Contents).

PROLOGUE

I am Aaron Herskowitz, beloved son, father, grandfather, brother, husband; a farmer, horseman, patriotic son of Czechoslovakia, soldier, Jew, lover of God; slave laborer, hater of God, Russian partisan, persecutor, assassin; survivor. In my life, I was both reaper and sower of the crops on my family's farm, and victim of the hellish fire that consumed that farm and everything else I knew and was and loved. I was an unwilling participant in the great cauldron of the twentieth century; I survived it, as did Europe. I was stained by it, as was Europe. This stain I have carried in secret for many years, and I reveal it now, as the new century begins and my own time on Earth dwindles. I share it with pain that wells up from long-buried memories, but without apology. I ask only that you hear my testimony before rendering judgment, and ask yourself: What would you have done in my place?

CHAPTER 1

HOW DID THIS COME ABOUT?

IN THE CRAMPED DANK cellar of a farmhouse in Hungary, three men in simple, ill-fitting farmer's clothes huddle together and listen intently, as the farmer who owns the house is being interrogated upstairs in a language they don't understand.

They can make out only one word, and it is repeated often—*"Deutchen!"*—Germans!

The three men in the cellar are Nazi soldiers.

It is November 1944, and the farmhouse is near the town of Gérjen—pronounced *Géryen*, a once-peaceful farming community now on the frayed edge of a global war in its final violent spasms. At great personal risk, the farmer had agreed to hide these men.

The door above suddenly swings open and light shines down upon them. A boot appears on the top stair, and the barrel of a submachine gun held by a short man dressed in civilian clothes is pointed at the three men crouched below. A harsh command comes down in clear German: *"Sie sind festgenommen!"*—You are under arrest!

An SS lieutenant in the cellar quickly orders his two privates, "Men, it makes no sense to resist; the entire area is swarming with Russians. We have no choice but to surrender. But don't say anything to them."

The three soldiers begin climbing up the narrow cellar stairs with their hands raised, the lieutenant leading his two privates. At the top of the stairs, they are stopped by the short man shoving his weapon into the lieutenant's chest. The captives are alarmed by the authority with which he points his submachine gun at them, and the anger in his piercing blue eyes.

Moments later, the floorboards inside the farmhouse groan as if under great strain, and another man emerges at the top of the stairs, a hulking brute well over six-and-a-half feet tall with an expression of searing rage. His reddish skin is tightly drawn around angular features set off by a black stubbly beard, but his dark eyes are curiously lifeless. This man is also clad in simple civilian clothes. The submachine gun he clutches is dwarfed by his huge hands. He frisks the soldiers with great force, until he finds no weapons on them.

The short man barks at them in German. *"Wo sind Ihre Waffen?"*—Where are your weapons?

The lieutenant gestures to the opposite end of the cellar. The tall man rumbles down the stairs and after a few moments, reappears carrying three submachine guns and ammunition.

The short man orders, *"Draussen!"*—Outside!

The short man and the tall man push the German soldiers out into the yard at gunpoint.

The Nazi soldiers wonder: *Who are these two? Where are their commanding officers?* By the deference shown to them by a squad of Russian soldiers now surrounding the farmhouse, the short man seems to be in charge—but both appear to be civilians. They each have the weathered toughened look of the Russian partisans the Germans have battled over the last few years. But what would partisans be doing in Hungary, a German ally?

The short man yells again in German.

"Wo sind Ihre Uniformen?"—Where are your uniforms?

The German officer shrugs his shoulders. The tall man aims his weapon at the officer's head. The short man repeats himself, this time raising his voice.

"Uniforms!"

The Nazi officer replies in German that they no longer have possession of the uniforms; they had given them to the farmer as "souvenirs" for his sons.

When the short man calls for the farmer to come out of the house, he points his submachine gun at him, demanding the uniforms.

The farmer replies, "These Germans never gave me any uniforms, sir."

With that, the short man turns to the lieutenant, yelling, "Lying Nazi pig!" He moves in and slams his submachinegun butt against the Nazi lieutenant's face, turning it black-and-blue. The tall man then smashes the lieutenant in the mouth with his weapon, as blood and a tooth dribble down his cheek and neck, the blow from the tall man knocking the SS lieutenant to the ground.

The SS officer, uttering involuntary guttural sounds of pain, gestures to a patch of dirt in the barnyard nearby, admitting that this was where their uniforms are buried. He and the other two prisoners are given shovels and are ordered by the short man, "Dig!"

Soon the German soldiers unearth three now-filthy uniforms, and the short man orders, "Now put on your uniforms! Now!"

The three Germans quickly strip and put on their dirty uniforms, shaking with fear.

The short man then interrogates them about the location of other German and Hungarian troops who might be hiding nearby. The short man says, "If you cooperate with us, we'll put in a good word for you with the Russians and they won't harm you any further. You'll just go to military prison. But if you refuse, they'll torture you and kill you."

When the Germans deny any knowledge of other Axis troops in the area, the tall man grabs one of the privates by his ear; then the tall man tears the soldier's ear clean off his head, his blood splattering profusely.

Watching his comrade bleeding and whimpering in agony, the lieutenant reveals, under prodding from the short man's submachine gun at his battered head, the location of two other groups of German and Hungarian soldiers, one hidden in a nearby hayloft, another in a barn.

"There's one more thing," says the short man to the Nazi lieutenant. "I need to know your commanding officer's plans for military defense against the Russian army."

The lieutenant refuses, defiantly telling the short man, "You'll never get that information from me. I'm a proud SS officer loyal to my Fuhrer, and I will never give up any intelligence, no matter what you do to me."

"Oh you won't?" says the short man, as he begins smashing his weapon against the lieutenant's head, turning his already bludgeoned face into a bloody pulp.

The tall man then moves in and grabs the Nazi lieutenant by his nose, twisting it until it breaks. Then he grabs the German's nose by the nostrils and rips his nose out from his face. The SS man's nose is literally hanging by remaining tissue from his face, which has become a virtual bloodbath.

The Nazi lieutenant, now writhing and screaming in pain, capitulates to the short man, "Okay, okay, I'll tell you whatever you want."

The lieutenant answers all of the short man's questions obediently, including the location of the Axis military defenses, the numbers of Axis soldiers and tanks, and everything he knows about how they plan to combat the expected Russian offensive.

The short man then barks a command to the Nazis, *"Achtung!"*—Stand at attention!

Now armed with vital information, the two "civilians" take off with three Russian soldiers in a motorcar, leaving the Germans to stand at attention under the watchful gaze of the remaining Soviet troops for an uncomfortable length of time.

At last, a Russian sergeant arrives, and the prisoners are marched at gunpoint to the center of Gérjen by the Russian soldiers, their hands on their heads. Near the town square, they are joined by a dozen other prisoners, about half of them Hungarian, wearing similarly soiled uniforms, also with their hands on their heads while being prodded by Soviet guards. Where are they being taken? They still have not encountered any Russian officers, only the two civilian-clad men who had interrogated them earlier. Some of the prisoners begin to whisper. The German lieutenant can make out a few words.

"Juden!"

Jews? In this town? There are no Jews here. The lieutenant's SS security detachment had spent the last month or so in Gérjen, and with the Hungarian-Nazi Arrow Cross, had been quite thorough in liquidating the Jews. But perhaps a few have survived. Would there be reprisals?

Fear shoots through the lieutenant. Would there be confessions under torture? Knowing that the SS would surely receive the harshest treatment, he tries surreptitiously—but unsuccessfully—to disfigure his uniform to conceal his identity. He already knows that he will stand out from the others as a result of the brutal bloody carnage to his face, but his main concern is his SS uniform.

The ragtag group of prisoners is finally brought to a halt before the town hall, now a command post with Russian guards posted outside. There they are made to stand at attention, shoulder to shoulder.

Finally, a car stops in front of the building. At last they will meet the Soviet commanding officer. But out steps none other than the two men they had seen before: the strange couple—the tall and the short one.

"Juden!" whispers one of the German prisoners from the second group. Now the lieutenant understands what seemed incomprehensible: Two Jews are in command of the town and in charge of at least a platoon of Russian troops. How did this come about?

The prisoners grow increasingly nervous as the two men walk up the line, inspecting their catch. They pause before the SS lieutenant, who begins to tremble, then suddenly breaks free and tries to flee.

In the panic that follows, the prisoners scatter into the streets. The guards open fire, and the scene quickly disintegrates into mass confusion, screaming, gunfire, and bloodshed.

One of the privates who had been hiding in the cellar is the first to go down. His war ends on the cobblestones of Becsi Street, face-down in a pool of blood. The second of the privates, the one who had his ear ripped off his head by the tall man, makes it only a little farther, finding an end to his anguish on nearby Szüret Boulevard, after crawling almost a hundred feet riddled with bullets in his arms and back.

The lieutenant lasts the longest. He slips into an alley behind the shops on Hödi Street, and even manages to prepare a tourniquet for the bullet wound in his thigh, which has left a telltale trail of blood all the way from Town Hall. As he drags his way down narrow back streets and alleys, he can hear the shouting and footsteps of the Russians hunting him, but soon enough, those sounds recede.

The lieutenant reaches the end of an alley and realizes that his only hope is to slip into the crowd. He waits to catch his breath before stepping out into the daylight, only to see the short man aiming a submachine gun directly at him.

"Hands up!" he orders.

The lieutenant complies and hobbles forward slowly, then stops abruptly.

The tall brute appears beside the short man, aims his weapon at the German, and opens fire. His bullet-riddled body lands face down in the alley off Nógrádi Street.

The short man and the tall man move forward to inspect the corpse. The rumors are true; they are, in fact, Jews. They'd endured untold hardship on the Russian Front, all the while refusing to bow to the will of the Germans, the SS, and the Hungarian death squads. They had refused to give in to five years and a thousand miles of brutality and privation of natural and manmade perils, of cold, disease, torture, and starvation.

They had endured, and it is clear to anyone watching the Russian troops arriving to remove the lieutenant's body that they are the absolute masters of this town. The journey of the three Nazi soldiers in the cellar has come to an end at their hands, but the retribution of the short man with the piercing blue eyes and the tall brute whose most eloquent utterances came from the barrel of his gun, was far from over.

CHAPTER 2
A NATION BETRAYED

IN THE FALL OF 1938, a handsome young man steps off the train in Bielka—pronounced BEEL-ka by the locals—a small rural Czechoslovakian town (a/k/a Bilky) on the eastern edge of the Carpathian Mountains. His five-foot-two-inch muscular frame fits neatly into his well-pressed army uniform, and he has an energetic quickness to his movements that complements his bright, optimistic, slightly mischievous blue eyes.

Hoisting his knapsack onto his back, Aaron Herskowitz begins his walk into town—and notices that Bielka, a community of small farms, dirt roads, struggling merchants, and hand-stitched clothing, has changed very little since he's been gone.

When Aaron was born in September of 1914, Bielka belonged to the Austro-Hungarian Empire. But after World War I, he lived in a different country, though in the same town: the new democracy of Czechoslovakia, formed in the ruins of three empires destroyed by war. Bielka was accustomed to regime changes—it had already lived and thrived under the control of Ukraine, Poland, Russia, Austria, and Hungary. The townspeople speak a mix of these languages. Many also speak Yiddish and Hebrew, for nearly a quarter of Bielka's four thousand residents are Jewish. Relationships between Jews and Christians are peaceful, and Aaron has close friendships with many Christians, most of whom are of Ukrainian descent.

But conflicts rage within him. Should he remain in this idyllic village of his youth? His three older brothers had successfully immigrated to the United States. Aaron, too, has longed to travel to distant lands, as there is little to keep an adventurous young man in Bielka.

Aaron had done it all and done it well. He'd been an outstanding student at the university in nearby Münkach and fluent in at least ten languages when he volunteered to join the Czechoslovakian army over the threat of invasion from neighboring Nazi Germany. His name in the Czech language is *Arnost Herskovic*. He is an expert with horses, thanks to his father, Jacob, a horse trader. Aaron is an exceptional rider, his natural ability enhanced by his relatively small size.

Since his father was constantly off to buy, sell and trade horses, Aaron became an expert farmer, helping his mother and brothers run the family farm. Once the last of his older brothers had left home, Aaron was left solely in charge of running the farm—or so he would have liked to believe. In truth, his mother, Paula, has a mental and physical toughness that makes her assertive, and the two become partners. Aaron is very much like her, and the toughness she instills in him later proves to be key to his survival.

There are good reasons for Aaron to leave Czechoslovakia in that fall of 1938.

After joining the army in 1936, Aaron serves with enthusiasm and achieves success. The top marksman in his unit—nicknamed "Eagle Eye" by his comrades, he is promoted to corporal and given men to command. That he is diminutive in size and Jewish makes no difference—the Czechs give anyone who works hard a chance to succeed.

But Aaron's military career is cut short on September 29, 1938, due to the machinations of another army's one-time corporal—Adolf Hitler—with the complicity of the distinguished heads of state for Britain and France. By the spring of 1938, Hitler—in violation of the peace treaty ending World War I—has seized Austria and the Rhineland. The British and French, allies of Czechoslovakia, condemn the Nazi aggression but fail to take any military action opposing the dictator.

Hitler then turns his attention to the Sudetenland—a mountainous region on Czechoslovakia's border with Germany with a large German-speaking population. He threatens war unless Czechoslovakia rips out this region and cedes it to Germany. The Czechs refuse, and it is for this conflict that Czechoslovakia prepares itself and has formed alliances with the three most powerful nations/empires in Europe: Great Britain, France and Russia.

Morale amongst Aaron and his compatriots is high. The Czechs are confident they can hold off the Germans at the high ground of their Sudeten Mountain frontier, expecting their British and French allies to attack Germany from the west, while their Russian allies would attack Germany from the east. This would put an end to Hitler's dreams of world conquest and the elimination of the Jewish people once and for all.

Unfortunately for the Czechs, Hitler's promise of peace is more enticing to Neville Chamberlain of Britain and Edouard Daladier of France, rather than confronting the dictator's pattern of deceit. At the infamous Munich conference of September 29, 1938, they agree to accomplish with the pen what Hitler had threatened with the sword. The Allies coerce Czechoslovakia to give up the Sudetenland and disband her army in exchange for Hitler's promise of no more territorial demands. Without even an invitation to the Czechs to attend the Munich conference to determine her fate, the Sudetenland is sold out from under her by her "allies," and with no more armed forces to defend herself from invasion, the country now lies naked and defenseless against further attack or invasion.

Aaron and his comrades burn with a sense of betrayal by their "allies." With that betrayal goes Aaron Herskowitz's hopes and ambitions to one day rise in the ranks of the army, bringing honor to his family and his country.

Now that Hitler is free to do whatever he wishes against Czechoslovakia, Aaron knows this is not going to be good for Jews. His spirit longs to flee the place, but there are other considerations that weigh heavily upon him, starting with his younger sisters: Hannah, a girl of eighteen, Rachel, sixteen, and Leah, a girl of twelve, who shriek with excitement upon seeing him at the front door, each wearing a dusting of flour on their cheeks from preparing food for the Sabbath. Once his younger sisters smother Aaron with joyous hugs, his three remaining considerations appear: his mother, and his two older sisters, Bela and Sarah. Each erupts with joy, as do other loved ones Aaron hasn't seen since entering the army (Aaron's father had died two years earlier).

Suddenly, Aaron feels a hard whack on his back. He turns to see Max Zelmánovic, his trusted childhood friend and confidant. Max and Aaron had volunteered together to join the Czech army in 1936, but the army quickly dismissed Max because of his slight build. Despite his rail-thin physique, he was strong and healthy, so the army's loss became the Herskowitz family's gain. While Aaron has been away, it is Max who's run the farm looking after each family member as if they are his own—and they consider him one of the family.

"Thank you, Max, for taking such good care of my family," says Aaron, embracing his old comrade. They are more like brothers than friends.

"They are my family too, Aaron," Max replies with a grin. "Besides, I had some help." He points to Bundy, the family dog Aaron and Max had trained to defend the family and farm when they were boys.

"Bundy!" cries Aaron in Russian. *"Fäs! Barého!"*—Attack! Get him! Bundy is older now but still manages to lift his tired head and wag his tail for Aaron. With that, the men break into a hearty laughter, thankful to be in each other's company again.

The cold winds blowing in from Germany cannot penetrate the stout walls and warm kitchen of the Herskowitz farmhouse that night. After a joyous Sabbath dinner, the family sits around the glowing fireplace singing folk songs, as Aaron accompanies them on the mandolin, his sister Sarah on the violin. As Aaron gazes upon the faces of his family in the firelight, he contemplates again the prospect of flight from this place. His destination of choice would have been Palestine, but it is now under British control—and they bar entry to Jewish refugees in order to gain favor with the oil-rich Muslim countries. Aaron knows he can evade the British and make it to Palestine with his two younger sisters.[1]

But what about his mother and his older sisters who have young children of their own? He has already written to his brothers in New York to help settle them in America. But by now, the rabidly anti-Semitic U.S. State Department has virtually closed America's doors to Europe's Jews, and President Franklin Delano Roosevelt approves of this racist policy. It will require substantial sums of money and endless red tape to bring Aaron's family to the US.

Aaron realizes the path his life has taken to that point—the youngest son who had to grow up faster than the older ones. Alone among Jacob Herskowitz's sons, he is not allowed to follow his dream to distant lands, but has become the family patriarch, burdened with responsibilities beyond his 24 years. He feels trapped, bound to the soil in ways his brothers had never been.

As the fire turns to embers, Aaron lets go of his dreams to flee. He lets them dissipate and rise with the smoke to be scattered by the wind, free as he would never be. In the darkness by the dimming fire that night, Aaron decides that no matter what the future holds, he will stay and protect his family. His fate will be bound with theirs.

As he closes his eyes that night, a haunting old memory rushes in:

Aaron sees himself walking through the Carpathian hills on the outskirts of Bielka on an impossibly brilliant summer day back in 1934. The air is thick with the scent of fresh mountain flowers. His father is still alive, his brothers have gone to America, and he is touched by both the possibilities and the dangers of the future...

"Hitler means to wipe out the Jews—worse than any other time in our history," says a young Zionist man from Palestine (Israel) who has come to the Carpathians to organize Jewish youth. "The Nazi army will be here before you know it."

These Zionists, veterans of combat against Muslim terrorists in Palestine, are aspiring to re-establish a Jewish state in their ancient homeland of Israel. They see the ominous trends in Europe and want the Jewish people to be fully prepared. Nineteen-year-old Aaron Herskowitz and some of his friends welcome and admire the Zionists; they eagerly begin to learn the art of guerilla warfare. With the help of these Zionist friends, they will be ready to fight the Nazi threat to annihilate the Jews, and hopefully immigrate to the Promised Land and fight Arab terrorists, if necessary.

Aaron learns Jujitsu and other hand-to-hand combat techniques, as well as sabotage. The Zionists are not allowed to bring weapons into Europe, so they train with sticks and clubs. Aaron quickly learns how to use his bare hands to remove a weapon from an enemy and overtake him. He is the most skillful fighter of them all, and he soon becomes Bielka's Zionist leader, recruiting and organizing the young Jewish men in town. They hear tragic stories about the mass murders of Jews for centuries in Europe, from Poland, from Russia. They will not allow massacres of Jews in Bielka.

Aaron recruits almost thirty members for his group and arranges simple military-style uniforms for his comrades. He designs an eagle insignia that his mother, a skilled seamstress, sews on the front of their caps. They have an identity now and it unites them. They admire Aaron and are inspired by Aaron's fighting and leadership skills, thriving under his patient training, looking up to him as a role model.

In their new uniforms they feel like soldiers. Aaron appoints best friend Max as second-in-command in his group along with, surprisingly, some Jewish girls. In Palestine, the Zionist women fight in the underground military, and Aaron models his unit after them. Aaron heaps generous praise upon both his female and male recruits whenever they perform well, as they grow closer together as the kernel of a Jewish fighting group united in a common cause.

A pretty teenage girl whom Aaron has recruited named Miriam displays such extraordinary fighting and leadership skills that he appoints her as the leader of the young women's unit. Miriam, a high school student, is so overcome with joy and gratitude, that she says with a jubilant smile, "Oh Aaron, I don't know how I can ever repay you for believing in me!"

Aaron smiles back, "Don't worry about that, Miriam. I'm just lucky to have you in my group."

To Aaron's surprise, the Czech government supports the Zionists' training programs. The only resistance and eventual roadblock to their activities ironically comes from the town's rabbi.

One day, as the young Zionists pass by the local synagogue, Rabbi Naftali Weiss approaches them in his black hat and long coat, beard and peyis – the side curls of an orthodox religious Jew. He is flanked by similarly attired elders of the synagogue.

"Aaron!" cries the rabbi. "What are you doing? You should be in shul—[synagogue]—not learning how to fight like animals. Look at you. Why do you have a uniform instead of a prayer book?" The rabbi's eyes continue to bore into Aaron's. He reaches forward and abruptly knocks Aaron's cap off his head and into the gutter. "This is not God's way. Jews do not fight. The Jewish way is to pray."

The head Zionist replies to the rabbi, "The Jewish way is to open the eyes that God gave us to see that the Nazis are the gravest threat to killing Jews in history. It's time we learned from our past mistakes."

Rabbi Weiss doesn't even look at the Zionist and speaks only to Aaron. "It will be God who saves you. It is He who will send the Messiah to deliver us from danger to the Promised Land, not these Zionist thugs." The rabbi is referring to ancient scriptures generated from earlier prophets which rabbis handed down over the centuries, declaring that Jews are forbidden not only from fighting their enemies, but also from immigrating to Palestine until the Messiah leads them there—but this mysterious "Messiah" is never mentioned in the Bible nor the Torah (Hebrew holy scrolls), so these preachings are now considered obsolete and invalid by the Zionists.

Within minutes, dozens of religious Jews emerge from the synagogue and stand in solidarity behind the rabbi with rocks in their hands. Fearful of the rabbi's wrath, most of Aaron's group begin to withdraw. Only Aaron, Max, and Miriam continue to stand with the two Palestinian Zionists. The five of them would have remained steadfast if the war of words would have remained only that. Unfortunately, it does not.

The first rock—thrown by one of Rabbi Weiss's followers—takes one of the head Zionists by surprise, striking him on the cheek.

"No!" Aaron cries out.

Quickly though, more rocks follow, hurled by angry followers of the rabbi. They find their mark, bloodying the two Palestinian Zionist leaders, who try fending them off.

"Jews don't fight, Rabbi?" cries Aaron. "Except against other Jews? Is that God's way, Rabbi Weiss? Is that..."

Aaron's voice is suddenly stilled by a rock striking him on the jaw. He falls to his knees as the crowd of Jews behind the rabbi surges forward and scrambles past him, giving chase to the Palestinian Zionists.

Later, when Aaron catches up to his wounded Zionist comrades, he asks rhetorically, "We are not yet fighting anti-Semites, but instead are at war with our own people?"

The older of the two Zionists replies, "The rabbis—they feel threatened."

"How?" Aaron asks, incredulous.

"They know we're trying to convince the Jews to leave Europe for Palestine, where we have a fighting chance. But these rabbis have decided never to allow any radical ingrates like us to lead their flocks astray. Now we have a civil war, and it's not against the anti-Semites, it's between Jews. And this is going on throughout Eastern Europe."

"What would they have us do?" Aaron asks.

"They want us to wait."

"Wait for what? For the Nazis to come and kill us?"

"They're waiting for their Messiah to come down from the heavens and lead them to the Promised Land. And the local Jews do whatever they say. I hope this Messiah does come, but in case He doesn't, I think we need to be ready to take care of ourselves; even if the Jews can't make it to Palestine, we can fight the Nazis here."

In Bielka, the power struggle goes on for weeks, but the outnumbered Zionists from Palestine are finally chased out. Their influence, however, lingers on.

On a seemingly ordinary day, Miriam from Aaron's group runs up to him. "Did you hear, Aaron?" she says. "The cantor's son ran off to Palestine. His father is disowning him!"

Among the rabbi's ardent followers is Bielka's cantor, one of the most powerful leaders in the religious community. Today, in a somber funeral ceremony, the cantor has declared his eldest son, Samuel Zvi, dead—but has refused to recite the traditional Kaddish—the mourner's prayer—because he considers his son an "unbeliever"—worse than dead.

Samuel Zvi is a friend of Aaron's—a fellow Zionist fighter who apparently is drawn more to Palestine than the rabbi's preachings—or even his father's. *The cantor apparently is willing to disown his own son in a public ceremony to set an example and a warning to others from ever violating their fanatical orthodox beliefs—so that if anyone else ever decides to immigrate to Palestine, they, too, would be declared dead.*

"Aaron," says Miriam, smiling, "I'm going to escape to Palestine, too. Would you like to join me?" Although Aaron doesn't know it at the time, Miriam has by now developed a large crush on him, secretly hoping that he will someday ask her to marry him.

"All the way to Palestine!" says Miriam. "Did you hear me, Aaron?" Miriam removes her head scarf and shakes out her long brown braids.

When Aaron finally opens his eyes, the moon has faded into sunlight, and it is no longer 1934. He knows that nothing can stop the German troops occupying the Sudetenland that fall of 1938. They are now poised to sweep over the border and seize the rest of Czechoslovakia.

Reflecting on his dream years later, after so many Jewish people had perished, Aaron began to believe that the murder of millions of Jews was at least partially the result of the orthodox rabbis' edicts, discouraging any type of resistance amongst the Jewish people against the Nazis, forbidding them to flee to safety in Palestine, instructing them instead to pray for God to send the Messiah.

He couldn't help but wonder—had the rabbis completely misunderstood God's message? Were the Palestinian Zionists the messengers sent from God to lead the Jewish people out of danger? Were they the real Messiahs? And had the rabbis defied God by refusing to follow these Messiahs?

---

1 See the maps on pages 282 through 286 (Europe 1871 through Jewish Escape Routes to Palestine).

CHAPTER 3

A SECRET DEAL

ONE NIGHT IN MARCH of 1939, Aaron is startled by a groundswell of vibrations that rattle him awake. When he opens his eyes, he finds himself in the hayloft of the barn, where a short nap has seamlessly segued into a long night's rest, now rudely interrupted by what is undoubtedly an early spring thunderstorm.

Yet, when he peers out the window, there is no storm, just the clear night sky lit by a full moon. The disturbance comes not from the sky but from the dirt road near the barn where a procession of shadowy figures file past on horseback, accompanied by horse-drawn artillery and supply wagons. The men are wearing dark uniforms and the moonlight glints off their helmets. Somewhere in the darkness, a commanding officer barks orders. Have the German invaders finally come to occupy the rest of Czechoslovakia? The procession soon recedes, and Aaron observes scores of horses grazing on his land. He quickly notices that overnight, much of the vegetation has been eaten by the horses. He decides to report his family's loss to the officer in charge in order to secure compensation—the standard procedure from his experience with the Czech army. Aaron is nervous though, fearing that the German army would not be so sympathetic to his plight. He speaks to some of the soldiers in German, trying to locate their commanding officer, but to his surprise, they react with confusion. As they chatter amongst themselves, he understands why. They are not German after all.

The Hungarian army has arrived.

This is not necessarily bad news. As Czechoslovakia had been part of the old Austro-Hungarian Empire only twenty years earlier, these men would presumably be friends, perhaps even allies, a bulwark against Nazi Germany.

Eventually, Aaron locates the commanding officer—an imposing man in full dress uniform, perched atop his horse and barking orders to his subordinates. Aaron boldly declares to the officer, "A lot of damage was done here."

Before he has a chance to request reimbursement, however, the officer pulls out a whip and cuts the air around Aaron's head with a sharp crack that stings his ears. The commander's face has turned beet red. "Are you complaining? We control you people! You are now under Hungarian rule!" The whip cracks again, accompanied by shrieks of *"Jidi!"*—the derisive Hungarian word for "Jew." The Hungarians already know which lands are owned by Jews.

Aaron stands at attention, terrified—implying a respect he doesn't feel. From his training with the Czech army, he knows that if an officer raises his voice, one does not talk back. The whip snakes around him again as the officer baits Aaron with the lash, waiting for even the slightest move that would allow him to retaliate by striking Aaron. At last, as if in response to Aaron's forbearance, the commander waves him away. Realizing that he is lucky to be alive, Aaron is puzzled by the fascist and anti-Semitic remarks from a would-be ally.

On this particular day, news is announced by the booming voice of the town crier, who makes his way through Bielka's neighborhoods, proclaiming that Bielka's wayward journey from one nation to another will continue. The town is now officially part of Hungary. This explains the arrival of the Hungarian troops the night before. Czechoslovakia has been dissolved by German decree—in violation of the agreement reached in Munich just months before, and Hitler's Nazi army attacks the remainder of Czechoslovakia from the new German/Czech border. The Allies had promised the Czechs that if Hitler should ever dare to invade Czechoslovakia after signing the Munich accords, they would come to the aid of the Czechs with military intervention. And yet, despite Hitler breaking yet another peace treaty, once again the cowardly "Allies" do nothing. The feeling of betrayal spreads anger amongst the Czech citizens.

Czechoslovakia is now being overrun by German troops in the west and Hungarians in the east. The new fascist Hungarian government has thrown in its lot with Nazi Germany, in the hope of reclaiming territory lost in the First World War, and Bielka and its surrounding Carpathian province have been ceded to Hungary as part of a secret deal, a token of German appreciation. In return, Hungary's obligation is to provide Germany with the Hungarian army—if Hitler should ever need their help in his military campaigns.[2]

The townspeople seem to believe a Hungarian occupation will be better than a German one, though based on Aaron's experience that morning, he is not so sure.

The German menace posed to Jews seems more real than the potential threat of their Hungarian junior partners. Many Jewish men from Bielka, including Aaron's father and uncles, had fought valiantly for the Austro-Hungarian Empire during World War I and were decorated for bravery, some even achieving officer status. Not only were Austro-Hungarian Jews spared the cruelty suffered by Jews for centuries in more hostile countries like Poland and Russia, but the late emperor, Franz-Josef, had been kind to the Jewish people, as being one of the first monarchs to emancipate them to become citizens. Aaron's father revered the emperor and had displayed his portrait in their home. Unfortunately, it is Aaron's initial encounter with the Hungarian army—not the kinder, more sympathetic experience under Franz-Josef—that proves to be a harbinger of the future.

Indeed, sinister rumors soon begin to circulate about these "new" Hungarians, and the most dreaded of these rumors is confirmed when one day, as Aaron is picking beans alongside his field hands, several Hungarian gendarmes (police officers) in fitted olive-green uniforms enter the fields. Aaron doesn't stop working and only nods politely. Since Aaron appears in charge, the head policeman approaches him. Aaron wears no beard, side-curls, or black hat, so the policeman doesn't think he is Jewish.

The officer apparently concludes that Aaron is a Christian, employed by a Jewish landowner.

The officer speaks with bravado. "One day these farms are
going to be taken away from the Jews, and we'll give their lands to *you* people." Aaron simply nods as though he is Christian, hoping

to learn more about this plan to steal from the Jews. He listens as the policeman curses the Jews: "Lazy swine ... money-grubbers... Christ killers." Aaron wonders just how much longer his own family will be allowed to keep their farm.

Thus begins the first wave of anti-Semitism, patterned after what the Germans have been doing since the early 1930s. Soon enough, the harassment escalates. Hungarian soldiers patrolling the streets gradually persuade the townsfolk to cease associating with Jewish businesses or entering Jewish stores or homes. Fewer and fewer of Aaron's Christian field hands show up for work. The Hungarians begin to scapegoat Jews for the townspeople's poverty, just as Hitler had done in Germany. Fear erupts amongst the Jews, but they have only two options—to fight or to flee—and neither is open to them. In order to escape, they need a place to go, and there are no places that will take them. The option to flee to Palestine has closed, as the British blockade in the Mediterranean Sea ends virtually all Jewish immigration to the holy land, as a gesture to the oil-rich Muslim countries to keep their oil supplies open to the Allies. And the option to flee to other countries has dried up by virtue of intentionally high immigration fees, quotas, and red tape levied upon Jews that only the very wealthy can afford.

While the outside world conspires to keep the Jewish people from fleeing, it is a fatal flaw from within that stops them from fighting *or* fleeing. For centuries, Jews have had no secular or political leaders. Only the local rabbis had served as revered leaders and mentors, and they refuse to permit any other type of Jewish authority. The rabbinate wields extraordinary power in nearly all Jewish towns and communities of Eastern Europe, and Bielka's Rabbi Weiss, a descendant of a famed rabbinic dynasty, is practically a god.

With the arrival now of the Hungarian Jew-hating fascists and their Nazi-like oppression, Aaron approaches Rabbi Weiss respectfully, but urgently. "Rabbi, the time has come," says Aaron, as he sits across from him in the rabbi's study. "The enemy is here. It is almost too late. I beg of you—let me organize a resistance."

"You need me, Aaron? To 'let' you?"

"Yes, with your approval, people will listen and rally 'round us," says Aaron. "We need only your word because we can be ready to defend ourselves. There are other men like me, who served in the Czech army, and our skills are still sharp. Our fathers and uncles fought for the Hungarians in the First World War, and they know how to use weapons. But it will soon be too late, because it's only a matter of time before Hitler invades the rest of Europe."

Aaron continues, "If we organize now, we can still fight here to protect our Jewish communities. You are one of the most revered rabbis in Europe, Rabbi Weiss. With your blessing, we can organize a network of Jewish resistance throughout the continent and help defend every Jewish community that comes under attack."

"You have nothing to fear, Aaron," the rabbi says quietly. "The Hungarians are not out to destroy us. We've never had a *pogróm* [mass murders of Jews] under their empire. They're just trying to impress their German friends. This will pass."

"With all respect, Rabbi—the Empire no longer exists!" Aaron replies, incredulous. "Emperor Franz-Josef has been dead more than twenty years! I've heard their fascist gendarmes talk about taking our farms away. And that's just the beginning—"

"You think you can fight off the entire Hungarian army, Aaron? Or the Germans if they come here?"

"No, Rabbi, but the Zionists showed us how to survive in the wilderness, as they do in Palestine when the Muslims attack. We would melt away and fight the enemy on our own terms."

"The Zionists! Those ingrates again?" Rabbi Weiss is furious at the mere mention of their name, but then calms himself as he piously counsels, "And when you begin your rebellion, Aaron, what will happen to our women and children, or the sick and the elderly? Will you try and hide them all in the woods?"

"If we must, we will do so, Rabbi. That's what they do in Palestine—they take the entire community."

"Nonsense! How long do you think they would survive out there?"

"How long will anyone survive if we don't fight to defend ourselves?"

"No, my son," says Rabbi Weiss, trying to end the conversation abruptly with a wave of his hand. "The Jewish people do not fight. We must leave this to God."

Aaron is incredulous. "Rabbi," he says, "Isn't our history full of true stories of heroic Jewish uprisings? Didn't David slay Goliath? What about Judah Maccabee's revolt giving us Hanukah? And didn't Samson use his strength and power to lead his outnumbered Jews to victory over more formidable enemies? Didn't these stories we learned as youngsters in Hebrew school mean anything?"

"Of course they do, Aaron," says the rabbi. "But since the Middle Ages, our prophets have been preaching to us that we can no longer shed any blood or engage in combat against others. They consider such actions a sin. If the Jewish people are in danger and we pray to God, He will send the Messiah down from the heavens to lead us out of peril to the Promised Land."

Aaron feels his pulse involuntarily quicken, and he grows ever more angrier and impatient with the rabbi's refusal to confront the imminent dangers of Nazism and Hungarian fascism with action, instead of stubbornly adhering to the ridiculous scriptures of medieval prophets to pray and wait for this mysterious Messiah to rescue them.

With blood rushing to his brain, Aaron literally is seeing red. In one of the rare instances in his life when the usually coolheaded Aaron loses his temper, he stands up and points to Rabbi Weiss, raising his voice, shouting, "Your Messiah will never come! He doesn't exist! He's not even mentioned in the bible, not even in the *Torah* (holy Hebrew scrolls). He's nothing more than a fantasy dreamed up by your phony Medieval prophets! You are still living in the Middle Ages! You are a fanatic! You are a traitor! You are no longer my rabbi! I am finished with you!"

Aaron stomps out of the rabbi's study in defiance, while the rabbi is stunned into silence by Aaron's shocking attack against him. Although Aaron is too angry and overwrought to realize it at the moment, when he goes to sleep later that night, he prays to God, asking forgiveness for committing a grave transgression forbidding such harsh behavior and rhetoric directed against a member of the Jewish clergy. Contradicting a rabbi is tantamount to defying God.

Although Aaron's belief in God remains unshakable (at least through this point of his life), he no longer believes in the orthodox rabbis, who have by now been in power for centuries, and who have hijacked the Jewish religion into a meek flock of cowards who refuse to fight against their mortal enemies. Aaron feels the belief in any so-called "Messiah" to be pure rubbish, but with the head of the Jewish community refusing to fight or take flight, most of Bielka's Jews would do neither. And the same outcome holds true in countless towns and cities across Eastern Europe, where few people are bold enough to defy the rabbinate, the repository of all wisdom.

Thus, Aaron and his family endure, struggle on the farm, try to help others when they can, and wait for the appearance of this illusory Messiah.

In May, Aaron does receive a visitor—but it isn't the Messiah. It is a man in a government uniform. "Aaron Herskowitz?" he asks, delivering a letter to Aaron which states that all able-bodied Jewish men who had served in the Czech army are now drafted into the Hungarian army. Aaron needs to report in three days' time and can expect the same pay and uniforms as the Hungarian soldiers. Aaron ponders: *But for what? To serve as soldiers for a nation that now curses us?*

The ominous winds that have blown in from Germany and Hungary that day linger into the evening; they sweep up the smoke from the chimneys of the town, dispersing it across the darkening corners of the European continent, where, in hundreds of towns and villages like Bielka, the decree of the rabbis leaves the fate of the children of Israel in God's hands alone.

The Jewish people waited for the Messiah as Germany re-armed; they waited for the Messiah as the German government established laws that told Jews where they could live, what they could do and what they must wear. When Hitler threatened war with Czechoslovakia over the Sudetenland, the Jews thought the Messiah had come—but he proved to be England's Neville Chamberlain, altogether mortal, who willingly surrendered Czechoslovakia in exchange for Hitler's lies that everyone knew to be lies. The Jews waited for the Messiah when the Czech army, in which Aaron served with honor, was disbanded and Hitler's allies, the fascist Jew-hating Hungarians seized control of his town, threatening to do to the Jews under their rule what Hitler had done to those under his.

For a thousand years, the Jewish people populated Bielka and its surroundings; for fifty generations they gave birth and died. They suffered through the upheaval of the First World War, many of them decorated for their service in the Austro-Hungarian army. No matter what, the Jewish people endured and had continuity in life and community.

Now Aaron's generation would taste something new. In the last week of May 1939, Aaron Herskowitz, the only son remaining on the farm that his family had owned for generations, a hard worker and good citizen who counted both Jews and Christians among his closest friends, a man who did no one intentional harm and broke no laws, a loyal soldier of the nation that had nurtured him which was now gone—now bade goodbye to his mother and sisters at the train station in Bielka. He would embark on a journey that would test much more than his ability to survive—it would test his capacity to remain human—to resist becoming one with the pestilence of barbarism and savagery that had blown in like a huge dark cloud over Europe, poisoning everything and everyone that it touched.

---

2   See   the   map   on   page   287   (The   Partition   of   Czechoslovakia   1938   –   1939).

CHAPTER 4

MOVING A MOUNTAIN WITH A TEASPOON

THE NEXT DAY, AARON reports to the regional Hungarian army headquarters. As he recalls the medal he'd won for marksmanship in the Czech army, Aaron finds himself at the head of the line, where a Hungarian soldier pushes a uniform into his hands and barks an order for him to move on.

The uniform is not what he'd expected. It is a yellow band of cloth.

"What is this?" he asks the soldier.

The soldier gestures for him to tie it around his upper arm.

"But where is my uniform?" asks Aaron, astounded.

Instantly, he feels the butt of a rifle shoved against his ribs. He turns to see another Hungarian soldier prodding him onward.

"Munka Tábor," grunts this soldier, words that startle Aaron. *"Munka Tábor!"* the soldier yells again and pushes him through a doorway that leads to a wide parade ground where hundreds of Jewish men with yellow armbands mill about. They are being guarded by Hungarian soldiers with rifles. One does not, Aaron knows, guard new recruits with rifles. Prisoners, yes, recruits, no.

The real meaning of *Munka Tábor* becomes clear very quickly. Instead of uniforms, Aaron and his Jewish compatriots are to wear civilian clothes with the yellow armband. Instead of rifles, they are given shovels and pickaxes, and rucksacks with tools. Instead of rations, they are given a mere chunk of bread per day. Instead of the pay they were promised, they are heaped with scorn and physical abuse.

They are slave laborers. They move rocks, hammer spikes, cut tunnels, lay track, build railroads and airstrips. The Hungarians beat them with clubs and whips if they move too slowly.

On one occasion, when Aaron is pushing a wheelbarrow full of rocks, a young lieutenant grabs his arm and suspiciously looks him over. "Why isn't your coat buttoned?" he barks.

Aaron immediately stands at attention—a vestige of his military training that will save him on more than one occasion— and calmly replies, "It's the only coat they had left, sir."

The lieutenant's response is to slap Aaron hard across the face. Aaron doesn't flinch and continues to stand at attention. The officer is new to the battalion and rumors of his explosive temper have circulated among the slaves. Aaron has seen him brutally beat other Jews who had objected to his demeaning or abusive behavior. Apparently, Aaron's forbearance does the trick, because the officer snaps, "Go to the quartermaster and get another coat with buttons. Go! Now!"

As Aaron once more takes hold of his wheelbarrow, a sergeant who has witnessed the exchange stops him with a grin. "Why didn't you fight him, Jew?" The sergeant laughs and moves on. Aaron keeps out of the soldiers' way and finds himself a new coat. But his lack of response doesn't mean he isn't silently seething with rage: *One day I will get even with them—all of them.*

By the summer of 1940, Hitler has conquered Northern and Western Europe,[3] including France, Czechoslovakia's erstwhile ally. Now Hitler begins to turn his attention eastward, and the slaves are given the task of building a road through the Carpathian Mountains, whose purpose—although they don't know it at the time—is to provide an attack route for Germany's impending invasion of Russia. With no machinery or explosives to move the massive formations of earth and rock, it is like trying to move a mountain with a teaspoon.

For months, they labor in futility. The Carpathians prove to be too much even for their taskmasters, so the slaves are finally dismissed to go home. Aaron looks to the sky to thank God that the ordeal is over.

The sergeant who had taunted him earlier when slapped by the hot-headed lieutenant walks by, smirking, "Seems like your prayers worked, Jew."

The slaves eagerly set off for home on foot. Aaron's unit is soon joined by scores of others. As he trudges onward, he contemplates the many chores that await him, wondering how he could ever repay Max for running the farm again. At that moment, he hears a familiar voice in the crowd.

"Aaron!" cries Max.

"Max! Is it really you?"

The two men hug. "What are *you* doing here, Max?"

"Digging a roadbed into the Carpathians. You?"

"I mean," says Aaron. "I thought you were running the farm."

"I was. They called me up."

"But you never served in the Czech army," says Aaron.

"A few months ago, they took the rest of us," Max replies. "The Czech army thought I was unfit, but the Hungarians were eager to take me. They're taking everyone. The rumor is, they're going to be taking our fathers and grandfathers, too."

Aaron shakes his head. "My own father is beyond their reach," he says at last.

"I wouldn't be too sure," says Max. "You know, they've restricted our travel, too—closed the borders on us. No chance of escaping to America or Palestine. Jews are not even allowed on trains!"

"Listen, Aaron," Max says sheepishly. "I don't mean to make things harder for you, but I have a chance to marry this nice girl from Khust and take over her father's leather business. What do you think?"

Without hesitation, Aaron replies, "Are you joking, Max? Take it. You're entitled to some happiness."

"I'd be leaving you in the lurch again. Maybe I can delay things and help you out just this year, 'till you find someone else."

"I wouldn't let you. You must take the chance while you have it. It's time you had a wife. And besides, there's no future at my farm, especially with the Hungarians patrolling. You'll have a better chance in leather. There's always demand for that skill."

The two men force smiles, hug, and go their separate ways.

When Aaron arrives at his farm in Bielka, his mother and his two youngest sisters, Leah and Rachel, are cultivating the fields with two old Jewish men. Their reunion is joyful but brief, as Aaron quickly joins them at work, taking on the hardest jobs himself.

Unfortunately, in less than two months, Hungarian gendarmes come through the neighborhoods, announcing that all Jewish males between the ages of sixteen and fifty are to report to the train station the next morning. Max was right. Now they are taking everyone—the young and the old. The nightmare is beginning again—this time more awful than before. The bearded orthodox Jews get the worst of it. Targeted for special abuse, the Hungarians viciously rip out their beards and side-curls, and then savagely beat them. Other Jews who show even the slightest hint of defiance or hesitation to obey their taskmasters are beaten to the ground until they are unconscious and then carried away.

In time, conditions for Jewish families at home grow into a state of despair. Food becomes scarce. A shortage of customers means little income for Jewish merchants who are having trouble feeding their families. Farm families like Aaron's, without any capable field hands, can barely feed themselves.

Realizing that his own family's predicament is becoming desperate, Aaron starts taking desperate chances. Whenever the slave labor camps are close enough to Bielka, he slips out at night and works his farm while his comrades in the labor camp cover for him. His mother and sisters are terrified that the Hungarians will kill him if they find out and urge him not to take the risk. But Aaron makes sure that his family is taken care of before himself. Fortunately, the Hungarians, unlike their German counterparts, are not sticklers for detail, so he is never caught. Aaron carefully notes this Hungarian ineptitude, which will prove to be crucial to his survival later on.

The slaves are released yet again from the labor camps in October 1942. This time, however, they know their freedom will be short-lived—war is in the air. Hitler had enjoyed enormous success with his invasion of Russia the year before, and Stalin had offered the entire Ukraine and the Baltic states to Hitler in exchange for peace by the fall of 1941. Stalin offers the Ukraine again to Hitler during the great German offensive of 1942, but Hitler refuses any treaty less than complete unconditional surrender, as he intends to enslave the entire Russian population.

Hitler's armies in Southern Russia are now on the verge of seizing the vast Russian oil fields of the Caucasus, which will surely mean final defeat for the Soviets; Hitler likewise needs more oil to continue his world conquest. However, he commits a crucial error by diverting the German Sixth Army to conquer Stalingrad, instead of using that army to help secure the oilfields—he is obsessed with seizing the city that bears the namesake of his mortal enemy, Joseph Stalin. However, the Sixth Army is stalled by fierce unexpected house-to-house fighting there, delaying Hitler's conquest of the oil fields.[4]

Needing reinforcements to deliver the final knockout blow to destroy Russia, Hitler calls upon his Axis allies: Hungary, Romania, and Italy—to provide all their available forces for the Russian Front. The Hungarians mobilize their army, and within two weeks, Aaron will be shipped off with his fellow slaves to serve the Hungarian and German troops at the front lines.

While walking through town, Aaron learns that those Jews in Bielka who had no documents to prove that their ancestors were subjects of the old Austro-Hungarian Empire have been deported across the Russian and Polish borders, where they are raped and slaughtered by Nazi and pro-Nazi assassins. Hungarians are given possession of their homes. The ugly rumors of a Hungarian influx are apparently true.

When Aaron sets eyes on his property, he is shocked at the abandoned condition of the fields. Two of the front windows of the house have been smashed and hastily boarded over. When Aaron opens the gate, it nearly falls off its hinges. As he kneels to repair it, he hears footsteps approaching and looks up. It's his mother.

"Aaron!" she cries out, bursting into a smile of disbelief.

She throws her arms around him and holds on tight while tears pour down her cheeks. "My son, my son," she sighs. When she finally looks at him, she trembles, asking, "For how long?"

"Not long, Mother. They're shipping us to Russia in two weeks. I've got to get busy."

"Yes. We'll knit the warm clothes you'll need to survive."

"I didn't mean that," says Aaron. "I need to make sure you have enough supplies for the winter. I'll take the horse into town now before the shops close."

"You can't."

"Why not?"

"We're not allowed."

"Who isn't?"

"Jews. Us. The Hungarians don't want us in public places anymore. Some of our friends have been beaten."

Aaron is stunned. "I knew this would happen," he says angrily. "I never should have listened to the rabbi when he refused to let me organize a resistance. I should've just done it myself."

"Aaron, don't be foolish. You know Pauli, our neighbor's son? He's just come back from Slovakia on a special work pass and says the Germans there are shooting Jews in the streets. At least the Hungarians would never do that to us."

"I'm not so sure of that anymore, Mother. And besides, how are we supposed to survive if we're not allowed to go to public places? Maybe they'd rather starve us to death than shoot us."

His mother just shrugs. Aaron holds her hands in his and says, "I just got back from the labor camp, remember? I don't know any better. I'll be right back."

"Please, Aaron—don't take chances. Not after we've waited so long." The look in her eyes shows the toll that the last few years have taken.

Aaron's eyes twinkle as he smirks, "Don't worry, Mother. The horse isn't Jewish—I'll just be going along for the ride."

As it turns out, Aaron secures the necessary supplies with little difficulty, and then decides to take the longer way back home through the farm of his long-time army friend, Wolf Lazárovic. As he approaches Wolf's farm, he can see his old friend in the distance wearing a heavy overcoat and laboring mightily on the fence at the edge of his property.

Hard labor had never suited Wolf, who is from a large orthodox family. He and his brothers are so devout that some of them had aspired to become rabbis. When Wolf was drafted into the Czech army, he was a lost soul, arriving at headquarters in his beard, side curls and dark religious clothes. No one could communicate with him because he only spoke Yiddish and Hebrew. His commanding officers tried everything; they brought in soldiers who could speak the different languages of the country: German, Czech, Ukrainian, Russian, Hungarian, Polish, Slovakian. But no one could get through to Wolf, and he became the laughing stock of the whole division. He couldn't even put on a uniform and refused to eat non-kosher food. He was relegated to the most menial tasks, cleaning the toilets and sweeping the floors.

Aaron had laughed at Wolf along with the rest of the soldiers until he saw him one day sitting alone in the barracks, his head down, deeply depressed. Aaron's heart went out to him, and he felt guilty for laughing at the humiliating ridicule of a fellow Jew from his hometown.

"Listen, Wolf," he said. "I want to help you." From that point on, Aaron taught him everything he could: the Czech language, how to dress properly, how to salute. Within a few months, Wolf fit right in. He was proud of himself and looked up to Aaron as his savior, begging that he be allowed to do something, anything, to express his gratitude. Aaron told him not to worry about it.

But Wolf knew that Aaron had taken considerable risks on his behalf. Under pressure from his peers to let Wolf fail, Aaron had courageously risked his own military career, and Wolf never forgot it. Wolf promised to one day introduce Aaron to one of his sisters, assuring him that they were all beautiful and that any one of them would make him a good wife. But Aaron, recalling a scrawny thirteen-year-old girl named Helen whom he'd seen hanging around Wolf's house during their army days, always found an excuse to avoid such an encounter, telling Wolf that he was not yet ready to settle down, especially with a war coming.

As he approaches Wolf on his farm, he sees him struggling mightily to remove a fencepost from the semi-frozen ground. Slave labor has evidently been very hard on Wolf, for he seems smaller and thinner than Aaron remembers.

Aaron approaches him from behind, stealthily riding his horse, sprinting between bushes and trees, concealing his advance. Wolf is so engrossed in his work that he doesn't turn around.

"That would be much easier if you had a horse," says Aaron at last, smiling.

Startled, Wolf turns around. To Aaron's surprise, it isn't Wolf at all. Instead, a slender young woman of about nineteen stands before him, whose beautiful features still shine, regardless of the dirt and sweat on her brow. Her long dark hair is tied back loosely, and she wears a rugged overcoat.

"I don't *have* a horse," she says.

"You're not Wolf."

"No," she says, and then turns back to her work.

Aaron swings down off his horse. "If you don't have a horse," he says, "you could use a man to help you with that."

"I don't have one of those either," says the woman without turning.

"They're useful to have around."

"I've heard they're more trouble than they're worth."

Aaron smiles. "You should give one a try."

"Why should I, Aaron?"

For a second time, Aaron is surprised. "Have we met?"

The young woman turns around to face him. She is even more beautiful up close.

"Yes. You don't remember?"

"I think I would if we had."

"I'm Helen, Wolf's younger sister. My brother invited you here to meet my older sisters. They weren't home, so you ended up teasing me instead. In fact, you scared me, doing those tricks on your horse with your riding whip. You weren't very nice to me, Aaron."

Aaron is astonished. A notorious practical joker all his life, he suddenly recalls an incident several years earlier when he apparently made the then thirteen-year-old Helen the victim of one of his pranks, mischievously whipping his riding crop in front of her while teasing her.

"I'm sorry about that, Helen, but at the time you were, well…"

"What?"

"What I mean to say is, now you seem *different*."

"I wouldn't know. Haven't you heard? The Hungarians have banned the use of mirrors." She turns away again as Aaron stares at her. Helen's name in the Czech language is *Helena.*

"Pity the mirrors," he says. "Let me help you with that." Aaron takes the rope from her hands and fastens it around the horse's saddle horn, then prods the horse onward, easily yanking the fencepost from the ground.

"Thank you," says Helen, reclaiming the rope as she walks toward the fallen fencepost.

Aaron stops her. "Helen—I'd like to stop by again before I go to Russia."

"Good, there are twenty more fenceposts to move. The Hungarians took forty acres from us and turned it over to Hungarian families."

"I'm really sorry to hear the Hungarians stole your family's land, Helen. It seems to be part of their cruel plan. Although I'd still be glad to help you with more fenceposts," Aaron offers. "But how about a real visit after that work is done?"

She studies his weathered face. "For how long?"

"An afternoon, maybe an evening."

"I mean, how long before you go back? A week? A month?" she asks.

"Two weeks, they told us."

"Why come visit then, Aaron? To what purpose?" says Helen, reflecting a wisdom beyond her years.

Before he can answer, another voice shouts out. This time, it really is Wolf.

"Aaron!" he says gleefully. "And you brought a horse, too! I owe you once again!" Wolf runs up to him and the two men embrace.

"I heard that you were back and hoped you'd come by," smiles Wolf. "I still want you to meet my sisters."

"I'm talking with Helen," Aaron says, gesturing to her.

"Oh, never mind her," says Wolf, taking the rope from her hands. "She's just my *little* sister and she has work to do at the house. She'd want us to catch up, anyway."

Wolf turns to Helen. "Thanks for your help, Helen. We'll take over now."

"But—" says Aaron.

Aaron can't take his eyes off Helen, as she walks slowly down the hill toward the house.

It's a long ride home for Aaron. Thoughts of Helen, the once scrawny girl who has blossomed into an unfathomable beauty, preoccupies him. He wonders how many times over the next two weeks he'll be able to see her, if only to visit and chat.

The next morning, as he works feverishly to prepare his family's farm for the oncoming winter, he realizes he needs more supplies from town. He decides to take a longer route to get those supplies, a route that will take him past Wolf's farm. After a restless night in which Helen's image appears to him numerous times, he needs reassurance that she is indeed real, and not a figment of his imagination.

When he finally approaches Wolf's farm, he is distraught to see Helen struggling with yet another fencepost but delighted that she is alone again. As before, the noise of her hammering drowns out the sound of his approaching horse. When she pauses to take a sip of water and wipe her brow, she is startled by the loud pounding of a mallet. She turns to find Aaron taking over her task.

"Aaron!" she yells. "What are you doing?"

"Helping you," he replies, smiling. "Hard labor—my specialty."

"But aren't you supposed to be—"

"Helping my own family? I am. But I couldn't bear the thought of you working all by yourself." When she smiles at him, Aaron's heart melts all over again.

"Wolf went into town for supplies," says Helen. "I'm grateful for the help."

The two of them work together, finishing the remaining fenceposts, as they laugh and share their hopes and dreams, despite an uncertain future.

When at last they pause to rest, Helen says, "I have a little secret to confess, Aaron. Ever since that first time you came over here, I'd watch you from the window whenever you rode by the house to visit Wolf. You never noticed me, but I noticed you."

"I wish I'd have known," says Aaron.

"All of us were so grateful about how you helped Wolf in the army. You were our hero. And you were always so handsome in your uniform."

"I think I still have that uniform somewhere," he winks.

She smiles again. "I guess I was infatuated with you."

"Helen!" cries a voice from the hilltop. This time it's her younger brother, Ludwig, a boy of twelve. "We need you. There's a lot of work to be done up here."

Helen waves her brother on.

"Well, one job done, another waiting," says Helen, picking up the mallet.

Aaron takes it from her.

"I have a better idea. Let's go for a walk and let your older brothers do some work."

"Wolf is doing at least as much as I am," says Helen. "And Meyer-Joseph and Hillel have already been taken to Russia."

"Ah," says Aaron, pained by the news. "So soon."

"We haven't heard from them. I hope they're all right. At least they're together."

"I wouldn't worry too much then. I know that Joe is resourceful, and he'll watch out for his little brother."

"Then I'll worry about you," she says suddenly. "In fact, I'm worried that you're hungry. Will you join us for supper? We'll be eating soon. I'll do the rest of my work tomorrow."

"I wish I could, Helen, if only I didn't need to get back to my place with more supplies. But I'm sure I'll be hungry for supper tomorrow."

"Yes!" says Helen, as she lights up the darkening afternoon shadows with her radiant smile.

By the time Aaron gets home, it's already dark. He apologizes to his worried mother and sisters, and the three celebrate his arrival by cooking up a meal with the supplies he's brought. The gloom of the evening lifts quickly, and there is much joy, teasing and laughter, especially after Aaron tells them about Helen and how much she's changed since he last saw her.

"Do we hear wedding bells?" chortles Rachel.

"Wedding bells for Aaron?" adds Leah.

"Will you break the glass for Helen?" asks Rachel.

"That's not all I'll break," says Aaron, chasing the two of them around the room.

The family fun, however, is soon interrupted by a loud whistle outside. When they go to the front of the house, they find a Hungarian gendarme at the gate, announcing that Aaron is to report to the train station the following morning for the journey to Russia, cutting Aaron short of the two weeks promised.

"Everyone back in the house!" orders his mother. For the rest of the evening, the women work feverishly to finish his coat, cap, gloves, and other warm garments that will shield Aaron from the freezing Russian winter. His mother also hands him *tefillin*—prayer implements—to take with him on his journey. This is heavier religious firepower than he has worn in years.

Once his sisters and mother are fast asleep, Aaron pulls on his overcoat and quietly slips out the door. He has to see Helen one last time before leaving. He takes great care to ensure not being caught after curfew by the Hungarian patrols.

When he finally approaches Helen's farmhouse, his spirits sink as if it is completely dark. Deciding that the great forces pulling him east into the conflagration in Russia are more frightening than the prospect of incurring the wrath of Helen's parents, he strides resolutely up the front steps to knock on the door. Before he does, Helen's soft voice speaks from the darkness of the porch.

"Here I am, Aaron."

He turns to see her sitting bundled up on a chair near the door. "I have some bad news," he says.

"I heard. Wolf is already packed."

She gets up and stands close to him. "I was hoping you'd come. I've been sitting here for a while. I didn't want to wake anyone."

Aaron looks into her eyes now caught by the moonlight. Her Yiddish and Hebrew name is *Chaia*—meaning "life," and at that moment, Aaron feels a breath of new life entering his soul. After years of endless dreary agony in a slave labor camp, the contours of Helen's face, the way her long dark hair catches the faint light, the way her eyes look deeply into his, allow him to forget his torments. He holds her hands, and then embraces her gently.

When they pull back, they stare at one another. She is noticeably taller than he, but his power and spiritual intensity seem to increase his stature, making them equals. Aaron knows that Helen is the woman he wants to share his life with. He hopes she feels the same.

"There's so much more I wanted to say before I left. I know I'm asking for a lot, but will you wait for me, Helen?"

"I will," she replies softly. "But the Russian winters are so cruel. And the Hungarians and the Germans are crueler still. We've already heard stories about Jewish slaves dying there." Tears come to her eyes.

Aaron looks at her sympathetically, then takes her into his arms. "Don't worry, my *beschert* [one's destined mate]. I will survive anything. Nothing will stop me now. Not the Hungarians, not the Germans. To hell with all of them!"

They kiss—an act bolder than would be appropriate if these had been ordinary times. But of course, these are not ordinary times. Forces from far beyond their village are about to rip them apart, so they seek to compensate with intensity for the brevity of their short time together.

They have no way of knowing how long it will be before they would see each other again.

"I promise you," says Aaron. "No matter what—I'll be back for you."

"I will wait for you, Aaron. And I will write to you."

The next day, on October 23, 1942, Aaron's mother and sisters tearfully insist on accompanying him to the train station.

"No," he tells them. "You know how dangerous it is for Jews to be seen in public places. Please!" He kisses them all goodbye and tells them once again how much he loves them.

But as he walks to the station, he turns to see his mother following behind him. He warns her again that she must turn back and go home. With tears in her eyes, she nods her head. Yet she continues to shadow him, walking behind other people so Aaron wouldn't notice her. But he does see her—and it is heart wrenching; his once-vibrant mother, now a broken-down old woman, trying to savor her last moments with her son.

At last, as Aaron is about to board the train, he sees tears streaming down his mother's face as she cries out, "I know I'm never going to see you again!"

Aaron's heart breaks. His voice cracking, Aaron promises, as they embrace each other, "Mother, I pledge on my soul, I will come back to you." Years earlier, Aaron had promised himself that he would never abandon his mother. Circumstances and events beyond his control have forced him to break that promise. He cannot afford to break another one, so to himself he says, *I'll stay alive—just to see her again.*

Nodding, his mother pulls something from her pocket and places it in his hand. For an instant, Aaron recoils as if he has seen a ghost. He had—it is his father's wristwatch, a prized object that had fascinated him as a child. Although it is neither fancy nor expensive, any watch is considered "priceless" in a community of dirt-floor houses and dirt-poor farms. Aaron hasn't seen it since his father died and had assumed it was lost in the confusion of events surrounding his death.

"Why are you giving this to me now?" he asks.

"He always wanted you to have it. I was waiting for the right time to give it to you. Now that time has come. Wear it, Aaron, so you will remember not only your family, but your faith."

Aaron touches the watch and trembles at the sudden and unexpected connection he feels to his father, and to his ancestors before him. He promises his mother to always remember her words.

Then he watches his mother shudder with sorrow. What had she done to deserve this agony? She had shared her beautiful voice, singing in the fields and in town festivals; she had shared life, love and friendship with the townsfolk, both Jewish and Christian. Aaron wishes he had the power to take these agonies from her, to be her balm. He realizes there is only one way he can do that—survive. He decides at that moment to survive against all odds; to see her again, and return to Helen, no matter what.

At last, with tears drying on his cheeks, Aaron boards the train. As it pulls out of the station, he stares out the window and watches his mother, dressed in her *babushka* and shawl, become smaller and smaller until she finally disappears.

That image would haunt him for the rest of his life.

---

[3] See the map on page 288 (Axis Europe July 1940).
[4] See the maps on pages 289 through 292 (Axis Europe June 1941 through Peak of Axis Power, October 1942).

CHAPTER 5
A JACKET AND A SHOE

AARON ENDURES AN ETERNITY of darkness in a dreamlike state in a crowded cattle car for thirteen days. When at last there is light, it comes from a Hungarian soldier who throws open the door, introducing the men within to the white Russian winter in the town of Novyi Oskol.

Stumbling blindly out of the darkness along with the others, Aaron is stung by a freezing cold that rages against his skin as fiercely as the sunlight assaults his eyes. When his eyes slowly adjust to the light, he beholds a landscape of pristine snow stretching to the horizon and interrupted only by a humble collection of bombed-out buildings left from a once thriving town.

Soon enough, Ivan, the Hungarian major who had been commander on the train, appears with a contingent of soldiers and orders the slaves in Aaron's company to form two lines. The major leads them for inspection to a small building which promises at last to provide shelter from the cold.

The promise proves short-lived. The building, which turns out to be a former schoolhouse, has no doors or windows. Part of the roof has been blown off in an explosion which, judging by the acrid smell of charred wood, occurred not too long ago. The men are herded into a large classroom with no furniture except for an ornate desk at the front of the room. Seated behind the desk is a sharply dressed officer of the Hungarian SS, flanked by other SS men. There is not a wrinkle in their uniforms and their boots are spotless, despite the snow and mud outside. They wear revolvers, and heavy wooden clubs hang from their belts. Modeled after the German SS, these Hungarian Nazis comprise the most fanatical fascist wing of the Hungarian security forces, meant to bring order and oppression to those lesser beings they choose to target—Jews.

Aaron looks over the SS men, then glances at the blackboard behind them. From the fragments of text in the Cyrillic alphabet, he judges they are standing in a Russian elementary school classroom.

After they stand in silence for a few minutes, the head SS man barks a command for the Jews to strip naked and wrap all of their belongings inside their blankets. After a momentary shock at the absurdity of the command, the men quickly comply.

Aaron lays out his blanket on the floor, peels off his clothing and places it on top, then folds the blanket around it. Among his effects are the *tefillin*—the prayer implements his mother had given him—and his father's watch, which he hides within the folds of the blanket.

As soon as all the slaves in the company are naked, the SS commander orders them to bring their belongings forward, one at a time. The first man steps forward nervously and sets his blanket on the desk, whereupon three Hungarians throw it open and inspect its contents. They quickly confiscate the man's warm clothes, tossing them into a pile next to the desk. They throw the blanket back to the man and then order the next man to step forward. No matter how measly each individual's belongings might be, the SS men find something to steal.

The largest of the SS men throws open the center of Aaron's blanket, and three Hungarian Nazis feast on the items Aaron's family has sacrificed to give him. His heavy coat, extra shirts and pants, socks, and warm gloves all end up in the pile of confiscated items. When the inspection is complete, all he has left are a shirt, a pair of pants, and his shoes, like the Jews who preceded him.

The large SS man begins to shove the blanket back to Aaron but stops when the *tefillin* fall out. There is a momentary pause as the three Hungarians stare at the object. Aaron starts to pull his blanket away when the big Hungarian stops him and picks up the *tefillin*. Aaron can visibly see the edge of the watch just beneath another fold in the blanket. His heartbeat quickens in fear of what punishment might await him if they accuse him of concealing something of value.

The SS commander examines the *tefillin*, fascinated. "We could use this for something, maybe shoelaces," he says, tearing off the laces and the leather, then throwing them on the pile of stolen goods while discarding the boxes of parchment inscribed with prayers. He then tosses the scrunched blanket back to Aaron and barks for the next man to come forward. Aaron feels the watch still in its fold and says a silent prayer of thanks.

Suddenly, the relatively quiet atmosphere is interrupted by a dull thud and a scream of pain. Aaron turns to see an SS officer clubbing the head of a man two rows away. Then more sickening thuds and screams break out as other SS men begin swinging their clubs savagely, crying out, *"Dirty Jews! Dirty Jews! Dirty Jews!"*

When one of the slaves falls to his knees and begs for mercy, he is bashed over the head until he falls silent. As more and more slaves are subjected to this "inspection," the room becomes a blur of purple bruises and bloodied noses from an unholy chorus of pounding clubs and cracking bones amid screams of anguish. Spurts of blood splash through the air.

Aaron waits in silence as the terrifying sounds draw closer to him. At last, the tall SS man looms directly before him, and beats him in the face. Aaron lifts his arms to shield himself while his assailant screams, *"Go to hell, Jew!"* then has his cohort hold Aaron's arms behind his back while he bludgeons his nose, which breaks under the savage pounding.

As quickly as it came, the torrent of violence passes, and the room falls silent, except for the sounds of tortured breathing and soft moans of pain. Aaron breathes a quiet sigh of relief through his mouth and watches as the SS men assemble in two rows leading to the door of the room.

The commanding officer announces that the prisoners will now be allowed to exit, one at a time. The sense of relief in the room is palpable. Several of the men begin to pull on their clothes, until one of the guards orders them to stop. The commander points to the nearest Jew and barks, "You! Now!"

The man quickly pulls his blanket and belongings together in a bundle and hurries toward the door. Before he exits, the SS men begin swinging their clubs, beating him savagely. As the remaining prisoners watch aghast, the victim stumbles and falls under the blows, dropping his blanket. Still, the clubs rain down on him. When the beatings turn to the next slave in line, somehow, he manages to pick up his belongings and stumble out the door.

So it is with each man—having to run this insane gauntlet. Several fall and do not get up; their crumpled bodies serving as further impediments to those who follow.

Aaron watches in horror as he moves closer to the front of the line. He quickly comes up with a plan, and when his turn arrives, he stumbles slowly to the door, as if mortally injured, clutching his belongings close to him while the SS men scream for him to move faster. Then, just as he gets within reach of their clubs, he sprints past them to the door. A few savage blows land on his head and shoulders, but by then the next man is already behind him and they turn their attention to him.

Aaron stumbles into the icy darkness, shocked that he's made it out alive, and then he feels the sudden onslaught of cold. He staggers to the other survivors, all of whom are bleeding; some whimpering, others too weak to even put their clothes on. Aaron quickly yanks on his own clothes, realizing that he has suffered a broken nose, which is bleeding profusely. But worse, he is missing one shoe. He quickly rechecks his steps from the doorway, but his shoe is nowhere to be found. He has dropped it inside.

As the cold snow bites into his bare foot, Aaron realizes that this is a death sentence. He observes several Hungarian soldiers—those who had herded the slaves off the train—now with shocked expressions on their faces. Ivan, the Hungarian major and commander on the train who had led the Jews to the schoolhouse, comes up to Aaron.

"I didn't know this was going to happen," he says. "I have no authority over these SS men. I can't do anything for you people."

Some of the other slaves look at the major skeptically, but Aaron takes hold of his arm. "You can help me," he says. "I'm freezing, and I have only one shoe." He points to his bare foot. "I'll die. The other shoe I lost inside."

"If you go back inside, they'll kill you."

"I know," says Aaron. "Can you find it for me, sir?"

"No," says the major. "I'm sorry."

As the major begins to turn away, Aaron makes one more attempt. "I understand," says Aaron. "Hungary has changed. The army has changed."

The major stops and turns to him angrily. "What do you mean by that?"

"My father and uncles, they fought for Emperor Franz-Josef. At the Isonzo, in Italy," says Aaron.

"The Isonzo?" says the major, repeating the name of the river over which the Italian and Austro-Hungarian armies had fought many bloody battles in the First World War.

"And at Caporetto," adds Aaron. "Very proud soldiers. Decorated." Aaron points to the schoolhouse, "No thugs back then." The muffled sound of clubbing and cries of pain can still be heard.

The major nods, glaring at the schoolhouse.

"Different now," says Aaron. "I understand, sir. I will somehow find another shoe." Aaron begins to hobble away but the major stops him. Aaron's desperate move has worked. The major goes into the schoolhouse. When he reappears with the shoe, Aaron thanks him profusely and quickly pulls it on. The other slaves in the vicinity are astonished, and immediately begin to press the major for more favors, but he brushes them off and heads away.

When the last of the surviving slaves stumbles to bloody freedom outside the schoolhouse door, the Hungarian major orders everyone to reassemble near the cattle car. He says that some of the slaves will not be rejoining the company—they did not survive the beatings.

While Aaron and his wounded comrades await further instructions, columns of other slaves pass before them.

Suddenly, a familiar voice cries out, "Aaron!"

Stepping out from a passing column is none other than Max, his beloved best friend. They stare at one another as if they have each met an apparition from another world, and then they fall upon one another in a warm embrace.

"The Hungarian SS beat us," says Aaron. "Stole all my clothes."

"Aaron, you're going to die out here in this freezing cold without your coat." Max is wearing a warm shawl that he pulls from his shoulders. He has evidently missed the brutal SS officers in the schoolhouse.

"Aaron, take this shawl before you freeze to death."

"No, Max. You need it."

"I have an extra coat, Aaron."

The two argue before Max finally says, "If you don't take the shawl, I will never speak to you again."

At last, Aaron accepts the shawl with gratitude.

The two men embrace again tightly, before the Hungarians order them back to their companies.

CHAPTER 6
WITHHOLDING PRAYER

AARON WAS WITHOUT HIS tefillin. Some Hungarian thug was probably using them as shoelaces, or maybe as a souvenir. As far as Aaron is concerned, they seemed better suited to either of these uses than for their original purpose. For the rest of his days on earth, Aaron would never again wear tefillin. Once they were taken away from him by the enemies of his people, he could not bear to wear them ever again. They had become soiled. Stolen by the SS, they had lost their sacred power and had become a reminder of how God and the rabbis had forsaken the Jews.

In the darkness that evening, Aaron's prayers to God ceased and anger took their place. How could God allow those innocent Jewish men in the schoolhouse to be killed? Do not misunderstand—Aaron relates these things not to build a case against God, but in his own defense for what he would do later—long after the slave labor, the cattle car, and the fourth-grade classroom in Novyi Oskol.

As his body throbbed with pain, it became increasingly clear to Aaron that he was alone, in mortal combat against monsters. He withholds prayer until he can see evidence of its worth.

CHAPTER 7
A LEGLESS DOLL

A FEW DAYS AFTER the beatings in the schoolhouse, Aaron's company begins marching eastward—all the rail lines leading to the front have been bombed. Blizzards become a routine part of life, and when the snow blinds them, each man marches in the footsteps of the one in front. Losing sight of the others in the Russian wilderness means certain death.

Far to the southeast, on November 19, 1942, the Russian army launches a massive counteroffensive surrounding the entire German Sixth Army in Stalingrad—three hundred thousand men. The Russians now lay siege to the Germans in the City, who, with no more supply lines, eventually must eat their horses to exist.

The German High Command wants the Sixth Army to break out westward to the safety of the rest of the Axis forces and finish off the Russians in the spring. But Hitler adamantly refuses. "No retreat! Not one step backward!" is his command. His top generals regard this as pure military suicide, but Hitler, like a dog without a bone, is obsessed with holding Stalingrad, the city bearing the namesake of Soviet communism, which he hates nearly as much as he hates the Jews.

While the Sixth Army tries to hold on to the ruins of Stalingrad, other German forces, together with the Hungarian army, are trying to establish a new defensive line from the city of Vóronezh on the Don River, southward to the Black Sea. Aaron and his fellow slaves march onward toward the Vóronezh front.[5]

As they march, some of the Jews look to the sky and pray to God. But no help from above is forthcoming. "Damn fools! Idiots!" mumbles Aaron to himself.

In the days that follow, Aaron and his new friend Eisler chat away in Yiddish as they march. Eisler is a schoolteacher from Irshava, a town near Bielka, where Aaron's sister Hannah and her family lived.

Aaron could tell that Eisler is a kind man by the way he would grip Aaron's arm when he stumbles. The conversations seem to provide warmth on their long marches, even before the sun begins to shine and the air warms up. But with the sun, as with everything else, it seems that whatever gift God might bestow with one hand, He would take away something with the other.

On another day of bright sunshine, Eisler poses a question to Aaron.

"Do you speak Russian?"

Aaron smiles—for Eisler has asked him in Russian—so Aaron replies affirmatively in fluent Russian, at which Eisler smiles back.

"Of course, most of the people in Bielka speak it," says Aaron.

"In my town, too. It will come in handy, and soon I hope," sighs Eisler, speaking quietly.

"No need to whisper," says Aaron. "The Hungarian soldiers don't speak Russian. And the Hungarian Jews—none of them know Russian *or* Yiddish, let alone Hebrew. I've tried it for years with them in the labor camps, but most of these Jews here are 'deep Hungs.' They became so assimilated under the kindness of Emperor Franz-Josef, that all they speak is Hungarian."

"You're right!" says Eisler. "How much longer do you think it will be?"

"That we march?" asks Aaron.

"Before we run into some Russians."

Aaron ponders, "Soon, I think. It's been eight days. I overheard the Hungarians say we're headed to the front at Vóronezh on the Don River. If we find ourselves in the South China Sea, we've gone too far."

Eisler laughs and says, "The question will be, how do we get over to the other side before the Hungarians or Germans shoot us?"

Aaron shakes his head. "We'll have to watch carefully for our moment. We must be patient. It will come, my friend."

Their moment of optimism is interrupted by a high-pitched whine coming from the sky. The Hungarian soldiers order the company to halt as three stubby aircraft appear on the horizon. Everyone—soldiers and slaves alike—strain to make them out.

"Take cover!" shouts the Hungarian commander, his voice tinged with panic. "They're Russians!"

Everyone scatters. Flashes dance off the noses of each aircraft and instantly the snow is riddled with machine gun bullets. Several men cry out in pain.

Aaron grabs Eisler's hand and leads him to a shallow ditch on the side of the road, where the two dive in and cover their heads. The planes roar low overhead, the red stars of Soviet Russia glaring from their wings, the air reeking of burnt engine oil and cordite from the guns. When their deafening sounds recede, they are replaced by the anguished cries of the wounded.

Aaron and Eisler scramble to their feet and find two slaves sprawled on the ground, writhing in agony, their blood splattered on the pristine snow. With proper medical attention, their wounds might not be fatal, but in the cold desolation of the Russian steppes, with no hope of even a bandage from their Hungarian masters, the men are clearly doomed.

"Pray for them!" says Eisler. "We must give them comfort." He kneels by one of the dying men, and Aaron, watching him, reluctantly does the same. As Eisler begins uttering a solemn prayer, the commanding Hungarian officer orders the slaves to get back in formation, while soldiers prod them with rifles. Aaron tugs at Eisler's arm. His friend has managed to cover the two men with blankets before joining the line.

"We're not even at the front and already they're attacking us," Eisler wails mournfully after another particularly vicious strafing from the air. Then he shrugs. "What's the difference? The sooner we're killed, the better."

"No!" replies Aaron. "Don't...think that way! We've got to survive and get back to our homes, our families. We've got to see this through. We still have a chance."

Eisler sighs and thinks of his wife and children. "Alright," he mutters.

Soon enough, though, the sound of the planes return—nine this time. Soldiers and slaves scatter instantly. Aaron looks around and spots a deep ditch near a tangle of debris on the far side of the road.

"Come on!" He grabs Eisler's forearm and the two run for their lives as machine gun bullets start churning the snow around them. Aaron sprints low and fast and finally dives into the ditch. Turning, he sees that Eisler has fallen halfway across the road. Aaron beckons him forward and Eisler manages to get up, but just as he begins to run, there is a terrific roar from above.

Everything goes dark and silent for Aaron. He doesn't feel cold. He doesn't feel anything. He cannot see anything. *I'm dead,* he ponders to himself. *I didn't make it after all.* Yet his mind is still working. And gradually he starts to hear again—the dull crump of bombs exploding on the snow-covered ground; the screams of agony from the wounded. He remembers the rabbi telling him once in Hebrew school that a dead man hears but cannot talk. *That old rabbi was right after all.* Then he begins to see more clearly: a deep darkness, then red and black. It is blood on black dirt. The bombs have racked up the soil under the snow and the dirt had gotten in his eyes. He shakes his head and blinks the dirt away, realizing that he is still among the living—but barely, and for how long? The dull thud of machine gun bullets striking the earth continue to rattle him. The aircraft engines roar; bombs continue to explode, tossing ice, dirt, and bloody body parts his way. An unholy chorus of screams arise from the wounded, along with plaintive cries for lost limbs and loved ones.

At last, the sound of the planes recedes. Aaron lifts his head and scans the sky. It is clear. He looks at the ground nearby now littered with the dead and wounded. He sees Eisler struggling to get up on his hands and knees. Aaron heaves a sigh of relief.

"Eisler!"

Aaron rushes to him and sees that Eisler's face is white as chalk.

"Aaron!" he rasps.

"My God," Aaron whispers. Eisler's legs had been blown off—one below the knee, the other at the thigh. Blood is pouring into the snow.

"You see what happened to me?" says Eisler, his voice trembling. "Look at me." He shivers. "I'm cold."

Aaron kneels by his friend. "Eisler—what can I do for you?"

Eisler pushes his torso up on his hands. "Take me into a house, Aaron. I'm freezing to death."

"Where?" says Aaron, as he looks into the distance beyond the carnage. "There are no houses. There's nothing here." The land is a frozen plain stretching to the horizon, not even by a single tree. "I can't take you anyplace, Eisler, and you can't walk."

Eisler nods—or perhaps it isn't a nod, merely a death spasm. His head begins to sink lower as if he doesn't have the strength to hold it upright. He shakes once again, then falls over like a broken, legless doll. The look of shock leaves his face and is replaced by a strange look of serenity.

Men are still screaming and sobbing all around him, but Aaron ignores them and simply stares at his friend. At last he gets up and runs to the supply wagon now turned on its side, dead horses still hitched, with the Jewish wagon master lying motionless nearby, his eyes wide open, reins and whip still clutched in his hands.

"I need a shovel and a blanket," Aaron says to the wagon master, who doesn't respond.

As Aaron draws closer, he can see that most of the man's torso has been blown away. Frantically picking his way through the supplies in the wagon, Aaron grabs a shovel and a blanket, then heads back to Eisler.

The ground is too hard to dig, so Aaron makes a hole in the snow, gently wrapping his friend in the blanket, and then buries him. He kneels, and then, shuddering with spasms from both the horror and the deadly cold, lips quivering uncontrollably, he recites the *Kaddish,* the Jewish prayer for the dead. Afterward, he says to himself that this would be the last time he would ever utter those words.

Aaron found himself in the woods that night while everyone else was asleep in an abandoned farmhouse. Twelve hours after his legless friend spoke his last words, the light outdoors seemed to grow stronger. Moonbeams cut through the branches of a tree to shine off the earth's icy crust. Aaron pondered: Is this where God is?

Impossible, Aaron's mind tells his soul. What happened that day proved there wasn't any God. The God of Aaron's childhood was kind and benevolent, but by now he knew He didn't exist, or if He did, He was very cruel. Nothing else was possible. How could the Almighty have allowed Aaron's only friend to be mutilated and die so young, while beasts like the men in charge of the schoolhouse were warm, well-fed and full of cruel laughter? This couldn't possibly be Aaron's God.

Soon enough, clouds overcame the moon, and in the dim light Aaron began screaming. "Have You betrayed me? Have You forsaken us?" Silence is the only response. But Aaron would not allow God to ignore him so easily.

"You don't want to help me? You, who did nothing to stop a beast from turning sacred tefillin into shoelaces? You, who let Eisler's legs be blown off? You, who allowed all those slaves to be killed, innocent Jewish men who trusted in You and praised Your holy name?" The moon emerged again from the clouds, and its light shone brighter as if to mock Aaron. "Leave me alone, God! I don't need You! I don't want You around me! Be someone else's God! Don't be mine!" Tears poured from Aaron's eyes.

Everything was frozen—the ground, the underbrush, the few trees. Aaron's tears began to freeze into tiny icicles on his face. Aaron waited for God to answer, but he heard only the wind. Nothing from the heavens told Aaron he was wrong. "How could You allow Your people to die this way?" More wind. "I'm going to save myself in spite of You. Because from now on—I believe only in myself!"

---

5   See the map page 293 (Russian Front November to December 1942).

CHAPTER 8

"RETREAT!"

UNBEKNOWNST TO AARON AS he laments Eisler's fate and ponders the fate of Helen and his family, the swarm of Russian aircraft wreaking havoc upon his miserable column of slave laborers is a harbinger of far worse things to come. Surviving the merciless air attacks, Aaron's column continues marching stoically eastward under the Hungarian Second Army until they reach the Don River front in December 1942, ostensibly to bolster the German lines south of the city of Vóronezh.

The German High Command, facing the annihilation of their Sixth Army surrounded at Stalingrad to the southeast, continue to try in vain to persuade Hitler to allow their besieged Stalingrad forces to break out westward and withdraw to more defensible lines. One German rescue mission to relieve the Stalingrad garrison launched in December from Southern Russia has failed. But the Führer refuses to cede control of the city named after his mortal enemy, Joseph Stalin. Therefore, the German High Command considers it vital to hold the Don River line to avoid another catastrophe along the rest of the front. Thus, as he had just done with his Sixth Army at Stalingrad, Hitler orders the Axis armies holding the front at Vóronezh: "No Retreat! Not one step backward!"[6]

"This morning we escape—over the Don." It's Foeldish, a Hungarian Jewish doctor from Debrecen, who's been helping Aaron pull camouflage netting over a German tank in the predawn darkness. It is January 13, 1943. All along a lightly wooded stretch, an army of intermingled slaves and Axis soldiers work hard at digging fox holes and trenches in the snow, as exhausted slaves wheelbarrow supplies and ammunition to the front-line troops. The slaves are given rucksacks to strap over their shoulders to store their tools, including a small work knife. Any slaves who are observed by the Germans or Hungarians as working too slow are brutally beaten by their taskmasters to set an example for the rest of the Jews. Those slaves who are severely injured requiring medical attention are left for dead and removed to the rear, as Jews on the Russian battlefront are denied medical care.

Any slaves who are observed by the Germans or Hungarians as working too slow are brutally beaten by their taskmasters to set an example for the rest of the Jews. Those slaves who are severely injured requiring medical attention are left for dead and removed to the rear, as Jews on the Russan battlefront are denied medical care.

"Through the woods is a field," whispers Dr. Foeldish to Aaron, pointing furtively through the stand of trees before them. "On the other side of the field is the river and the Russians. The river is frozen—we go just before dawn to join them before they attack."

At the Vóronezh front, the Russian army and the German army—the latter augmented by elements of the Hungarian army—eye each other warily across the frozen Don River. It is the first realistic chance the slaves have to defect to the Russian side.

"We need you," says Dr. Foeldish. "You speak Russian."

Aaron shakes his head, drawing on his military training, "The Germans are preparing a surprise attack, too. Rumor has it that after they smash through the Russian defenses across the river, they intend to head southeast to rescue their Stalingrad garrison. So don't do anything yet because we could get caught in the middle of it."

"All the more reason—we should go before either army attacks—before dawn."

"It's not the right time. It's a mistake. If the Russians attack first, they'll kill us, just to get us out of the way. Be patient."

Just then a Hungarian officer arrives and orders the slaves to pick up shovels from the supply wagon. Aaron and the others labor on into the night, digging slit trenches in front of the German tanks. It is not lost on Aaron that the slaves' trenches are placed well in front of the German and Hungarian foxholes—making the Jews cannon fodder for whoever attacks first.

Dawn is fingering the eastern sky when Aaron is awakened in his trench by a low rumble. He lifts his head above the edge of the trench just in time to see a series of artillery shells bracket a German gun position fifty yards away, sending the gun skyward in a ball of earth, ice, twisted metal, and flame.

The attack is certainly underway, but it is not a German attack. The faint light in the eastern sky is suddenly darkened by the arrival of Soviet aircraft. The first wave of nine planes roars in low, raking the trenches with machine gun fire, then releasing bombs as they pass. Aaron and the others hunker down as bullets tear up the snow and the bombs rip apart trees, equipment, and men. The chorus of machine guns, artillery, and bombs is quickly joined by the cries of the wounded in two languages intermingled: German and Hungarian.

Soon there is another sound as well—an oddly musical whistling that seems to speak in multiple voices, rising and falling in discordant scales like a hellish pipe organ. The sounds reach a crescendo, then erupt into a bone-jarring ripple of explosions. The Axis forces are being treated to a dose of "Stalin's Organ," as the Russian *Katyusha* rockets are called.

Aaron continues to hug the earth, enduring a rain of hot metal, broken tree branches, and bloody body parts. Another volley of rockets manages to hit an ammunition dump forty yards behind him, turning dawn into bright daylight in an explosion of small-arms ammunition. Shortly thereafter, a gaggle of bloody, burned slaves stumble through the snow and dive into Aaron's trench, some screaming in Hungarian, *"Yoj, my hásam! Yoj, my lábam!"*—Oh, my stomach! Oh, my leg! Others whimper in pain and fear. One man, still on fire, rolls in the snow to douse the flames. The snow itself, pristine at dawn, is now soiled and running with rivers of blood and ice. Aaron feels a hand on his shoulder and turns—only to see that the hand is not attached to anyone. He tosses it away, then hunkers down again and waits. He knows if he lifts his own hand from the ditch, he probably won't get it back.

The bombardment abruptly stops and an eerie silence washes over the woods, broken only by the crackle of flames and the faint cries of the wounded. Aaron lifts his head to see Dr. Foeldish lying next to him, trembling, blood trickling from his ear and down his neck. He looks farther down the trench and sees others in the same condition—their eardrums punctured by concussions from the explosions, blood running down their necks. Aaron thinks, *Did that account for the silence? Am I deaf?* He rubs his ears and neck with his hand and looks at it—as of yet, no blood. The bombardment has indeed, for some reason, ceased.

"Why?" shouts Dr. Foeldish. "Why did the guns stop?" He stares at Aaron with a look of shock and terror on his face. Aaron reaches out a hand to calm him.

"The Russians must've figured out what the Germans were planning, and the bombardment was a spoiling attack, aimed at disrupting them. Or—"

"Or what?" shouts Dr. Foeldish.

"Or—" Aaron slumps back into the trench. "Or it was the prelude to a Russian attack."

The ground begins to shake. Aaron peeks over the edge of the trench toward the Soviet lines. Through the broken trees and burning wreckage, he can see the open field leading to the Don River, yet the river itself is obscured by what appears to be an avalanche—a line of drifting snow stretching the length of the horizon and rapidly heading their way. A growling chorus of diesel engines and clanking metal tracks float in on the wind, and then the shapes of tanks—the Russians' deadly new impenetrable T-34s, faster and more powerful than any tank the Germans had. Then assault guns and infantry emerge from the clouds of snow.

Dr. Foeldish climbs to the edge of the trench to take a look, then slides back down as machine gun fire zips through the air, slapping into trees, snow, and earth, pinging off equipment, and occasionally thudding into a soldier or slave unfortunate enough to be exposed at the wrong instant.

"Our chance! Our chance to surrender!" cries Dr. Foeldish, trembling. "They'll be here soon."

Aaron shakes his head 'no.' "They'll kill us." As he well knows, again from experience in the Czech army, it is a dirty little secret of war—prisoners are rarely taken during an assault. The adrenalin level of the assaulting troops is too high—they will shoot anything that moves. Besides, each prisoner taken at the front would require a soldier to guard him, and the Russians wouldn't spare the troops. If the Russians reach the trenches where he and Foeldish lay, Aaron knows that slaves and soldiers alike will be mowed down.

"Only one hope," Aaron shouts above a din that now includes gunfire from the approaching tanks. "The Germans and Hungarians have to stop them."

But the Axis troops are oddly silent, and the rumbling of the approaching tanks grows louder. One after another, Soviet cannon fire finds the camouflaged German tanks. One after another, they go up in flames, spewing burning fuel and hot oil into the surrounding woods, spreading more misery and pain.

"Why aren't they shooting back?" cries Dr. Foeldish.

Aaron shakes his head in bewilderment. Perhaps the German and Hungarian officers at the front lines have been killed or too badly wounded to command; or, Aaron supposes, again from his experience in the Czech army, that the German command and control centers are knocked out and can no longer issue orders to fight back. *There is no option left to avoid certain death*, thinks Aaron, because just before the battle, he understood the Germans and Hungarians confirming that they had to obey Hitler's insane orders: "No Retreat! Not one step backward! No matter what!"

The rumbling grows louder and deeper as the earth shakes. Aaron dares not peek over the edge of the trench again, but he can guess, by the fact that small arms fire is now joining the Soviet machine gun fire, that the Russian assault force is within five hundred yards.

"We can run back to the woods!" shouts Dr. Foeldish, his eyes wild with panic.

"The Germans and Hungarians will shoot us, even if we get out of the trench alive. They know we're Jews," says Aaron.

Within minutes, the Russians nearing them will overrun their position and all the slaves will be killed. It appears that Aaron's brief journey on earth will shortly be at an end.

In the fury of the final minutes of the assault, a momentary lull in gunfire catches Aaron's attention. It is difficult to see very far, because of the mist in the air from all the bombs and explosions. He comes up with one last possibility. He abruptly lifts his head above the level of the trench, turns around to face the Hungarian soldiers behind him and bellows with all his might the Hungarian word, *"Viszavonulás!"*— "Retreat!" Almost instantly, all the surviving Hungarian soldiers, taking this pronouncement as a command from one of their officers, scramble out of their defensive positions and flee to the rear, tossing their guns aside.

My God, thinks Aaron. *It worked!* He is shocked.

"Aaron, that was remarkable!" exclaims a stunned Dr. Foeldish, staring at him in disbelief. "For a small man, you have the lungs of an elephant! I've never heard a man yell so loud. Let's join the Hungarians and run for our lives!"

"Not so fast, doctor," Aaron says, peeking above the ditch, then dropping down, his voice sullen. "The Germans are still in their trenches—they don't speak Hungarian. They know we're Jews and they'll kill us."

"What are you going to do?" asks Foeldish.

Without answering, Aaron lifts his head once again, turns to face the Germans, and with all the power and air his lungs could summon yells, "*R*ückzug!"—"Retreat!" in German this time. Within moments, all the Nazi soldiers, thinking their Führer has changed his mind and ordered a withdrawal from the front, begin to run to the woods behind them.

Aaron yanks Dr. Foeldish out of the trench, waves on the rest of the Jews in sight, and the rout is on.

Jews from other ditches cry out to Aaron, "Where are you going? What are you doing?"

"Just follow me!" Aaron exhorts, as waves of slaves from adjacent companies flee as well.

Incoming volleys of machine gun fire rip into the backs of retreating soldiers and slaves in a blizzard of blood and screams. Several Hungarian troops mount a truck only to have it instantly smashed by a Soviet tank round, shattering men and metal and hurling a tire past Aaron and into a fleeing German soldier. The roar of the Soviet tanks is now deafening. Desperate panicked men claw their way through the tangled wreckage of equipment and men, trampling the wounded and the dead.

Aaron runs as fast as he can, bullets zipping by his head, unwilling to even glance over his shoulder for fear that a moment's delay will mean death. But just as the rain of bullets from the rear begins to recede, he can hear the crackle of gunfire ahead, and sees several German and Hungarian soldiers fall.

Diving for cover behind a fallen log, he finds himself sharing a low depression in the ground with two other Jewish slaves.

"Are we surrounded?" asks one of the slaves.

"Military police—German," replies Aaron.

Aaron glances over the log—the soldiers ahead wear the distinctive helmet of the German army. "They're here to uphold Hitler's orders of 'No Retreat.' They have orders to shoot anyone retreating from the battlefront."

"We wait here—for the Russians," adds the other slave.

Aaron is still unsure—is this the time to make his escape? He looks around—a wave of German and Hungarian soldiers fleeing from the battlefront is rapidly overwhelming the outnumbered military police trying to stop them. Meanwhile the roar of Soviet tanks can still be heard.

"No!" says Aaron. "Not here. Not yet. Come with me."

The two slaves refuse. Aaron wishes them good luck and sprints out of his hiding place to continue his frantic retreat just in time to see three Hungarian soldiers overwhelm one of the military policemen and beat him to death with his own rifle.

The sun is well up in the sky and the sounds of gunfire are growing fainter when Aaron at last stops and leans against a tree to catch his breath. German and Hungarian soldiers, intermingled with slaves, plod wearily onward through the forest. Dr. Foeldish appears at Aaron's side and the two exchange the weary smiles of survivors.

"Aaron," whispers Dr. Foeldish. "How did you get the nerve to impersonate the commanders and order the retreat? You saved my life. You saved thousands of us—maybe *tens* of thousands of Jews! And you changed the course of the battle," rambles Foeldish. "Today, the Germans and Hungarians have lost!"

"Yes," said Aaron. "I saw hordes of Jews following me into the woods. But my first instinct is to survive, doctor; though I'm thrilled that I brought the lives of other Jews out of danger. But let's keep what I did today between ourselves," Aaron winks. "We don't want any retaliation from our tormentors."

"Yes, you have my word, Aaron. Your secret is safe with me. They'll hang you for sure if they ever find out," says Dr. Foeldish, still shaking his head in disbelief over Aaron's courageous actions. "But Aaron—I shall never forget what I saw with my own eyes—all those soldiers behind us retreating from their trenches, the 'brave' Nazis and Hungarians both north and south of us running for their lives like cowards—it was a mass exodus!"

"Okay, doctor, I guess I'll have to take your word for it. But by now," says Aaron, "the Russian attack has run its course—they'll pause to regroup. Now is our chance to join the Russian army."

"No, not now," says Dr. Foeldish. "Still too many Hungarians and Germans wandering about. If they see you, turn around, you'll be shot."

"Then I won't turn around."

Dr. Foeldish looks at him, perplexed.

"Debrecen, right?" asks Aaron.

"Yes, I am from Debrecen."

"I'll look you up after the war."

Dr. Foeldish grins wryly. "I'll visit you in Bielka. Good luck, Aaron." He puts a light hand on Aaron's shoulder, then stumbles onward with the rest of the slaves. Aaron watches him go, then starts to follow, but at a very slow pace. Another group of slaves passes him, then another, and then a group of Hungarian soldiers.

Aaron glances behind him—only a few stragglers are left. He begins to walk even slower, barely making any progress at all. A few more German and Hungarian soldiers stagger past, their eyes fixed forward, their thoughts on survival. No one pays any attention to him. As they disappear into the woods, he finds himself alone.

At last, Aaron stops moving forward altogether, and then he begins to walk backward through the forest, slowly and carefully, eyes still trained forward, hands reaching behind to guide him through the underbrush. *Now is the time,* he reassures himself. He will continue walking backward a bit longer to make sure the last of the German and Hungarian stragglers are gone, and then find a log to hide behind, or a hollow in which to conceal himself, and wait. When the Soviet troops approach, he will use his knowledge of the Russian language to persuade them to spare his life, and the worst will be over. At least he hopes so.

He would also offer the Russians his military services. He would fight for them—after all, he knows how to use a gun. He could interrogate prisoners, using his skills to speak German and Hungarian. And if he could hasten the defeat of his enemies, even by a day, an hour, a minute, it would be worth it.

He is still mapping out his future when he comes to a deep hollow in the ground bordered by fallen logs that looks like a perfect place to wait. He is about to crawl into it when he hears the word *"Chekai!"*—Ukrainian for "halt."

Aaron stops. When he overcomes his momentary surprise, he breathes a sigh of relief. He has evidently encountered a Russian soldier from Ukraine, and judging by his Ukrainian accent, one who has probably grown up not too far from Bielka. Aaron is more fluent in Ukrainian than he is in Russian, so negotiating his surrender to the Russian army would pose no problem.

"Obertaysia!" the voice commands, ordering him to turn around. Aaron does so and finds himself facing a young soldier—a teenager whose rosy cheeks have not yet known a razor blade, and with a look in his eyes of utmost earnestness—is aiming a rifle at his chest. But it isn't the soldier's face or his rifle that draws Aaron's attention—it is his uniform.

It is a German uniform.

Aaron has the misfortune of stumbling into one of the Ukrainian nationalists who has defected from the Russians to join the German army. Hitler has promised that if substantial numbers of Ukrainians volunteer to become soldiers in the Axis army, he will declare an independent Ukraine from Russia after the war. The Russians had always been cruel to the Ukrainians. As recently as the early 1930s, Stalin starved to death over three million Ukrainian citizens for no reason.

This soldier's uniform has the markings of the military police. He has obviously been trained by the Nazis and is under orders to shoot deserters from the Axis Army on sight.

"Davai! Ne Strelei!" Aaron cries in Ukrainian, "Hey! Don't shoot!"

The soldier seems surprised that Aaron knows his language. "Who are you?" he asks.

"A prisoner," Aaron replies. "A slave laborer. A Jew."

The soldier stares at him, his rifle still aimed at Aaron's chest. Aaron keeps talking, desperate to make a connection. If the Ukrainian sees him as a fellow human being, a neighbor, perhaps he will spare his life. "I am from the Carpathian Mountains. We speak Ukrainian there. We are friends."

The soldier shakes his head. "You want to be friends, maybe, but I must do my job."

"And you've done your job very well," says Aaron.

The soldier looks at him a moment longer, then glances around. Aside from the faint sounds of battle, the forest is silent and still. He lowers his gun. "Go back to your company. Otherwise, I have my orders. I could already have shot you. Go back and find your company."

"Spasiba—zdorov," Aaron says. "Thank you—good luck."

Aaron took secret delight in watching the vaunted Nazi army and their Hungarian allies run in utter fear for their lives from the Vóronezh battlefront following his "Retreat" command. He felt even greater gratification in saving the lives of so many thousands of Jewish slaves from certain death who followed their fleeing taskmasters into the woods. Yet this joyous feeling soon dissipated during the long dreary retreat through the snows of January, February, and March 1943. The defeated Axis soldiers took out their frustrations on the Jews, shooting slaves for sport, but they wouldn't kill Aaron if he was performing a useful task.

The soldiers themselves had little in the way of rations, so Aaron and the slaves had even less—a piece of bread every three or four days. The Axis field kitchens were either destroyed or abandoned following the retreat from the front. Realizing that he was losing weight and strength, Aaron took the laces out of his boots and tied them around his waist to avoid his pants from falling down. He didn't want to appear weak for fear of becoming a target at the hands of his persecutors.

Aaron realized that without any food, it was only a matter of time that his pathetic life on earth would shortly come to an end, so he began taking big chances: when everyone was asleep at night, he quietly left camp to beg for food from Russian villagers. If their cupboards were bare, he would furtively break into village stores to steal whatever food they carried. He was often fired upon by faraway Hungarian or Nazi sentinels when he would leave or re-enter the outskirts of camp; but his training with the Palestinian Zionists and the Czech army taught him how to quietly elude them. He shared whatever food he brought back to camp with his starving slave comrades.

Aaron has brought you this far through his journey into hell, not to provoke your pity, but rather for you to gain understanding. There was still time for him to turn away from the path he would later take. If there had been a merciful and just God, he and his fellow Jews would not have had to endure what they did, and thus Aaron would not have become what he later became. But there was no God in his world, only hundreds of unrelenting miles of humiliation and barbarism. Thus, Aaron continued to nod "respectfully" as the Hungarians and Nazis heaped scorn, urine, and feces upon him, pushing him to the edge of death.

And so, Aaron endured months of the brutal ordeal of retreat until it finally ended in a small town, or perhaps more of a collection of shacks. Would this be Aaron's refuge, his salvation? Would it be here that the world would show him another face—the face of mercy and humanity?

---

6   See   the   map   page   293   (Russian   Front   November   to   December   1942).

CHAPTER 9
DEATH-FIGHT FOR MY WATCH

AS WORD FILTERS DOWN through the ranks of the Axis soldiers, Aaron and his comrades take covert pleasure in learning of the German surrender at Stalingrad on February 2, 1943. Hitler's insane orders to not allow his Sixth Army to retreat from Stalingrad would prove to be a major turning point of the war. Although the Führer's orders were obeyed at Stalingrad, his orders not to retreat from Vóronezh on the Don River front were disobeyed. Hitler is furious, and he orders an investigation to determine the identity of the traitor who issued the order to retreat from Vóronezh. The initial findings reveal that the retreat order came from an officer from the Hungarian positions, but intense Hungarian interrogations never solve the mystery. Hitler now regards the Hungarians as cowards on the battlefield, and henceforth, their armies are "punished" by being relegated to lower grade assignments from the German High Command.

One can only imagine what Hitler's reaction might have been if he had ever discovered that a lowly Jewish slave had impersonated a German officer, bellowing the command for the valiant Nazi soldiers to disobey their Führer's orders by retreating from a major battle. This action handed the Russians a major victory and the Nazis a crushing defeat, while saving the lives of countless thousands of Jewish slaves, who followed the routed Germans and Hungarians into the woods.

But Aaron's hopes for a complete Axis collapse and an early end to the war are soon dashed. Despite losing an entire army at Stalingrad, and the collapse of another at Vóronezh, the Germans, under the command of Field Marshal Erich von Manstein, key mastermind of the German conquest of Western Europe in 1940, and conqueror of Crimea in Southern Russia in 1942, have just mounted a brilliant counter-offensive, recapturing vast territories and halting the Soviet winter offensive. The Germans are far from finished and the war is far from over.

While the Germans are shoring up their new defensive line in Southern Russia, they withdraw the remnants of the shattered Hungarian Second Army and its surviving Jewish slaves far to the rear, northwest of the Kiev region, where they could refit in relative safety. Following this long retreat, the Hungarians finally halt on March 28, 1943, at the small town of Davidóvka.[7]

Hollow-cheeked and hollow-eyed, Aaron holds the reins of a horse-drawn wagon as it trundles slowly through the rutted, slushy ground of the slave encampment just outside town. Dr. Foeldish, who seems to have aged considerably since the retreat began, sits at his side. This seems less a camp than a scar across the face of the earth—a discolored gash where eight hundred dirty exhausted Jews huddle around fires, shivering, coughing, and clinging feebly to life. Their skin is punctured by hundreds of bites from lice. The faces of many are marked by the dark red rash of the typhus epidemic that has gripped the entire camp.

Aaron stops the wagon near a group of men lying in their blankets by a fire. He and Dr. Foeldish step down and kneel by the men, checking each one, brushing the lice off their faces, muttering words of reassurance to those who are either too delirious or too weak to lift their heads. Dr. Foeldish pauses over one who has no discernible heartbeat. He nods to Aaron, and the two continue on, finding one more dead slave among the group.

Their survey complete, Aaron and the doctor lift the dead Jews to the back of the wagon, laying them next to the dozen or so who are already on board. These dead slaves, under the ravages of starvation and illness—have shriveled to mere skeletons.

Kimlit, an emaciated youth whose face is covered with the typhus rash, stumbles up to them, offering to help.

"You must rest, Kimlit," Aaron tells him. "You need to get well. You need to see your family again."

Kimlit nods and staggers back to a spot near the fire.

"Kimlit is Chaim Leib from Bielka, the eldest son of the cantor," says Aaron. "His younger brother, Samuel Zvi, escaped to Palestine before the troubles."

"Why didn't he take his family with him?" asks Dr. Foeldish.

"His father didn't approve—disowned him for leaving before the Messiah came, then declared him dead, sat *Shiva*— (funeral ritual) for him, but didn't even say *Kaddish,* because Samuel Zvi was considered *worse* than dead—a non-believer. Now it looks like he's got a son he *can* say Kaddish for."

Dr. Foeldish nods grimly. "He has a few days, no more. Unless he gets help."

"He *had* help. We all did. From the Zionists, years ago. We didn't take it."

A big, open-topped truck with a large red cross on it cuts in front of them and grinds to a stop. Two Hungarian soldiers climb out and quickly escort four sickly Jews into the back of the truck where several other typhus-infected slaves sit shivering in their blankets.

Aaron and Dr. Foeldish exchange glances and get down off the wagon.

"Are you here to help the sickest ones?" asks Dr. Foeldish.

The Hungarian soldiers stare at him for a moment.

"Yes, help," says the taller one. "You two—you're still healthy. Get back to work."

"I know someone who is desperately ill," says Aaron.

"There are worse cases than Kimlit," says Dr. Foeldish.

"He's bad enough. Please, can I get him?"

"Hurry," says the tall Hungarian.

By the time Aaron arrives with Kimlit, the truck is full.

"Can you take one more?" asks Aaron.

"Of course," says the taller soldier.

Aaron helps Kimlit up into the rear of the truck, where the others squeeze together to make room for him.

"You'll be okay now," Aaron assures him.

Kimlit grabs Aaron's sleeve as he turns to go. "Give this to my mother," he says, his voice hardly more than a whisper, handing

Aaron an embroidered handkerchief he's kept hidden. "In case I don't make it. Tell her I love her."

Aaron pushes the handkerchief back. "You give it to her yourself, because now you're going to get well, Kimlit."

As the truck drives away, Aaron breathes a sigh of relief and climbs back on the wagon with Dr. Foeldish. Having finished their rounds for the day, they drive to a snowy field about a mile outside Davidóvka, where Aaron stops the wagon near a stand of trees. Once more the two dismount, this time to dig a communal grave for their passengers.

"How do I avoid typhus?" asks Aaron, as they labor side by side.

"Avoid lice," says the doctor.

Aaron smiles, peeling back his sleeve. Lice crawl everywhere on his skin; some drop off into the snow. "What kind do you want? A big one? Little one?" He reaches inside his shirt and pulls one out from under his arm. "How do I avoid lice?"

"You take a hot, soapy bath."

"What's that?" asks Aaron.

"It'll come back to you," says Dr. Foeldish. "You come to Debrecen after the war. I'll take you to Biro's; you'll get a warm bath, a hot meal, and a good night's rest. My treat."

Their task completed, the two gravediggers stick their shovels in the snow and begin placing the stiff bodies in the hollow they have cleared. Aaron goes back to the wagon while Dr. Foeldish kneels at the edge of the grave.

"You do not say *Kaddish* for them?"

"I do not believe in God anymore," says Aaron.

"But you know Hebrew. I don't."

"Then say it in Hungarian."

Dr. Foeldish looks at him, slightly bewildered, then utters the prayer quietly to himself. When he is done, he joins Aaron on the wagon.

"Dinner time," says Aaron.

"Dinner isn't 'till Thursday," says Dr. Foeldish. "This is only Monday."

"I know," says Aaron, urging the horse forward.

"Where are you going?" asks the doctor. "The camp is back that way."

"We're not going to the camp."

"Where are we going then?"

"To get dinner," says Aaron. "Unless you want to wait."

"Where do you think—?"

"Look," says Aaron, pointing toward a distant farm with a windmill. "A windmill means a prosperous farm, one that has enough grain left over to grind and sell. Maybe we will have dinner there. Maybe we celebrate Passover."

"Passover?" Dr. Foeldish repeats, surprised.

"Yes. You've lost track?"

Foeldish is quiet for a moment. "I guess I have."

"Coming with me?" says Aaron.

"The Hungarians will shoot us if they catch us."

"They might. Do you want to go back?"

Dr. Foeldish hesitates. Aaron hands him the reins.

"You go. I'll come back on foot," Aaron says, hopping off the wagon and beginning his walk toward the farm.

"What if they ask me where you are?" Dr. Foeldish asks nervously.

Without turning around, Aaron says, "Tell them I got lost."

Aaron sets off briskly toward the farmhouse. Dr. Foeldish shakes his head and turns the wagon the other way.

As Aaron approaches the woods, he hears voices—many voices. A truck engine growls. Aaron crouches in the bushes, watching as a truck with the Red Cross emblem drive to the entrance of a huge barn, where hundreds of very sick slaves, Kimlit among them, are huddled. A group of soldiers herd these slaves toward the barn, along with the new arrivals from the truck.

Aaron briefly thinks of visiting Kimlit, but knows he'd be risking punishment for being in a place where he is not permitted, when he notices something peculiar. After the last of the slaves is herded into the barn, the Hungarian soldiers close the door and secure it with a wooden beam.

As Aaron watches, a soldier ignites a rag stuffed into the top of a large bottle of liquid and hurls it through the barn window, and then a second one. Within minutes, the building explodes into flames. Aaron hears shouting, the men inside crying out for mercy, pounding on the doors and walls. Quickly, their cries turn to screams of agony. Several times, a man inside manages to push out a windowpane or loose piece of siding and starts to climb through. Each time, merciless soldiers push him back inside. The few slaves who do manage to jump out of the flaming barn are gunned down by anxious guards awaiting them. In the mayhem, a handful of wounded, torched slaves manage to escape to the woods.

Aaron sinks to his knees and watches as the flames climb the sides of the barn and collapse its roof, sending a shower of sparks arcing into the evening sky. The inferno blasts the surrounding woods with radiant heat and bright light, enough to awaken residents of the nearby town of Doroshich. At last the screaming stops, replaced by the roar of fire and the crash of timbers. The smoke carries with it the unique scent of cooked human flesh, and among the ashes floating heavenward are surely those of Kimlit, and the handkerchief that he tried to give Aaron for his mother. The smoke will reach her sooner than Aaron could know, for she would die at Auschwitz, and her ashes would be likewise lofted to Heaven.

Back in the darkness of another farmhouse that night, Aaron stays awake while the other slaves are asleep around him. He does not, for once, wander during the night in search of food, for he has lost all appetite. Being awake, he is the first to see headlights approaching and hear the rumble of a truck engine. When the engine stops, a door opens.

"You!" a voice says in Hungarian.

Aaron stirs. In the glare, he can make out the tall Hungarian who had earlier collected Kimlit with the other sickly Jews, for their journey to the inferno.

"And you and you!" the Hungarian says, pointing to several other slaves just now stirring in the darkness. Among these is Dr. Foeldish, who looks at Aaron in bewilderment.

"Outside! Now!" barks the soldier.

The sleepy men scramble to their feet and stagger into the icy midnight air. Aaron stops short when he sees the Red Cross truck parked in front of the house.

"Onto the truck," says the soldier, herding the Jews with his pistol.

"We are not sick," says Aaron, hesitating.

"Lucky for you," smiles the Hungarian.

The slaves climb onto the truck and the Hungarian soldier joins them, pounding on the roof of the cab to signal the driver to move. The vehicle rattles forward.

"Where are we going if we are not sick?" asks Aaron.

"Your big night. We are going to get some food," says the soldier. "You will load it into the truck. If you're lucky, you may even get to eat some."

The vehicle begins its journey along a rutted road through the snowbound countryside. Aaron gazes at the tall soldier for a while.

"How is my friend, Kimlit?" asks Aaron. "The one I helped onto the truck this afternoon?"

"The little Jew? The one with the big, long sideburns?"

"Yes," says Aaron. "How is he doing?"

The big Hungarian grins. "He is fine, Jew. He is nice and warm. You get sick, we'll make you nice and warm, too."

After traveling many miles, the truck arrives at a supply depot where Aaron and the other slaves bend their backs loading it up with sacks of flour and other staples. They stuff their rucksacks and pockets with food, and then begin their journey back along the lonely road winding beneath a full moon.

Aaron is sitting across from the tall Hungarian soldier when the truck suddenly hits a bump in the road. Aaron reaches for the side of the truck to steady himself, but as he does, the sleeve of his coat inches up, exposing his wrist. The Hungarian's eyes light up.

"Let me see," he says abruptly, pointing in Aaron's direction.

"What?" says Aaron.

"You have a watch. I want it."

"No," says Aaron defiantly. "It was my father's watch. It's a gift from my family. Now it's mine."

"Goddamned Jew. Give it to me! Now!"

The other slaves, astonished by Aaron's defiance, shrink back in their seats to remain as unobtrusive as possible.

The Hungarian leans forward, his face red with rage. He shouts directly into Aaron's face, "Give it to me, Jew, or you're dead!"

Aaron looks at him coldly in the eye. "Go ahead. But if you want it, you'll have to take it."

The Hungarian soldier stands up, towering over his prisoner, smiling. He lunges for Aaron's wrist, but Aaron, summoning every ounce of his remaining strength, resists. The Hungarian begins punching him, but Aaron, relying on his early Zionist training in jujitsu, knows how to fight bigger men, and uses the larger man's weight and his own body to keep the Hungarian off balance each time he lunges.

"Help me!" yells Aaron to the other slaves, but they simply stare, frozen in fear. Even Aaron's friend, Doctor Foeldish, doesn't help him.

"Cowards!" barks Aaron angrily at the Jews on the truck.

Aaron and the soldier violently thrash about, the Hungarian now trying to release his gun from its holster, with Aaron doing everything in his power to thwart him. Even as he struggles, he knows there is no escape—he will be killed by the guard or the driver, or the other Hungarians when the truck arrives back in camp. His whole life's journey has come to this—a doomed struggle to deny this Hungarian thug the one heirloom that connects Aaron to the life he once knew, the people he loved, defining who he is.

Using his short stature to get low and gain leverage, Aaron pushes the Hungarian against the back of the truck. The big man's head and torso are leaning over the edge, as he tries once more to release his gun. Aaron says to himself, *"Now is the time! Push more!"* Feeling a surge of adrenalin charge through his body, he lifts the big man off his feet. As the truck bounces over a rut in the road, the Hungarian flips backward over the edge of the truck, hitting the ground with a dull thud.

The other Jews on the truck look out the rear with astonishment. The soldier's head has struck a large rock, and he lies motionless, sprawled on the side of the road beneath the moon, his lifeless eyes wide open. The truck continues to move forward while the soldier's body disappears from view.

As the adrenalin leaves his system, Aaron collapses into his seat exhausted, and feels for his watch. He looks at the other Jews, who are now staring at him.

"What have you done?" cries the doctor. "You've killed us all!"

"Then why don't you start saying Kaddish for all of us?" Aaron replies.

The truck finally pulls back to camp. "All right, everyone out!" cries the driver without calling for his erstwhile guard. The Jews scramble out the back, and the truck immediately kicks into gear and speeds away. Dr. Foeldish and the other Jews watch its taillights recede in bewilderment. Aaron is already heading for the camp when Dr. Foeldish stops him.

"How long do you think it will be before the Hungarians figure out he's missing?"

"A few hours. Maybe a day," says Aaron.

"God help you when they find out what you did. God help us all."

"Don't wait for God to help you." Aaron turns away and goes inside.

During the next few days, Aaron and Dr. Foeldish go about their business of collecting bodies in the wagon, and the truck with the Red Cross on it continues its business of collecting the sick. Not a word comes down about the dead soldier, and Foeldish says not one word to Aaron, still furious at his friend, as they go about their grim chores in silence.

As the third day dawns without a complaint from the Hungarians, Aaron awakens feeling weak and feverish. He struggles to the wagon, where Dr. Foeldish is already at work.

"You are lucky, Aaron," hisses Foeldish. "You may get away with your foolishness after all; your prideful impulse that put us all in danger. Seems you're becoming something of a hero, maybe a legend. Word is getting around amongst the Jews that they have a champion, a David who single-handedly slew Goliath. God still watches over you, Aaron."

"God didn't help me. I did. The Hungarians don't suspect anything because they can't believe a Jew might actually rise up and fight. How could anyone blame them? And thank you very much for the hero worship, but I can live without it. The more the Jews talk about it, the sooner it leaks out to the Hungarians. Then I'm a dead man. So tell them to be quiet or we'll all be punished."

"And what you did at Vóronezh, ordering the retreat," Foeldish continues. "How many thousands of us did you save?"

"Quiet!" says Aaron. "Never a word about that again. I'll be hanged for sure if the Hungarians or Germans even get a whiff of it."

"OK," replies Foeldish.

Aaron climbs onto the wagon but nearly loses his footing. Dr. Foeldish reaches out to steady him, exposing part of Aaron's arm. It is covered with the telltale rash of typhus. The doctor quickly examines Aaron's neck.

"You'd better learn how to pray again, and quickly. You have a week to live, maybe less. You need to find God again."

"I need to find food," says Aaron.

The moon throws its bright light across the porch of a remote farmhouse as Aaron knocks feebly at the door. An older Russian woman opens it warily. Aaron, gaunt and weak, his face a constellation of red typhus scars, must look like a bizarre apparition to her. It had been a tremendous struggle just to get out of his blanket and make these desperate rounds.

"Please, can you give me some food?" asks Aaron.

"No," the woman says. "Go away. You're sick." She begins to close the door, but Aaron stops it from closing.

"Please—I must eat, or I'll die. Even a crumb."

"I will die, too," she says. "We have no spare food and no money, not even enough to get supplies."

"I'll get better—I'll help you, if you help me now."

"Bring me money, and you eat," the woman says.

Aaron trembles. "I have no money—I have nothing."

The woman closed the door. Aaron begins to shuffle away. The door opens again, and the woman tosses him a crust of bread, and then she disappears inside once more. Aaron consumes the bread and shuffles off into the night.

Aaron knows that the woman was lying when she denied having any food. He notices that her farm has three windmills. He knows from his expertise as a farmer that one or two windmills on a farm means prosperity. A farm with three windmills would produce a plentiful supply of sustenance. But he is too weak to force his way in after she falls asleep to steal her food. Instead, he knows that he will need to do something inconceivable the next night in order to convince the woman to feed him.

The next morning, he awakens too weak to move. "Help me up," Aaron says to Dr. Foeldish. "I'll help you with the wagon."

"You? What will you do to help me?"

The doctor goes outside. Aaron struggles to get up but settles back down. Several other men in the room are in a similar condition—deathly ill.

Outside, the Red Cross truck is approaching. Through the window, Aaron sees it stop and two soldiers get out. They enter the room, stop for one sickly slave, and help him to the truck.

Aaron struggles to get up. He has just made it to his knees when the soldiers return. One of them walks over to him and offers a hand.

"Come on with us, you look very sick."

"No," says Aaron. "I'm fine. I have work to do on the wagon."

The soldiers smile. "What work are you going to do?"

Aaron staggers to his feet, leaning against the wall. "I drive the wagon."

"Okay," says one of the soldiers. "We'll come back for you tomorrow."

Aaron staggers outside, steadying himself against the door sill. His sleeve slides up, revealing his watch. He stares at it briefly, the metal glinting in the morning sun.

That night, Aaron again approaches the same farmhouse and knocks on the door. Again, the woman opens the door, then immediately begins to close it.

"I have something for you this time," says Aaron feebly.

"What?"

Aaron holds out the watch, his hands shaking. "It's a good watch," he says. "Worth money. It was my father's. You can get supplies; you can get help. Please, just give me something to eat."

The woman takes the watch and carefully examines it. She takes it inside and closes the door. Aaron falls to his knees.

The door opens again, and the woman reappears with another older woman. The two help Aaron inside and feed him well. Afterward, they give him a hot bath, and wash and dry his clothes by the fireplace, removing all the lice they can find.

Then the older woman takes Aaron by the hand and leads him to the living room, which is decorated with a crucifix and a large picture of Jesus.

"I want you to pray with me."

"Pray? No, please. It's getting late. They'll kill me if they find I'm here."

"*Znay*," she says gently. "I know. But my husband is dead. My son is in the army. I worry so much about him. Please pray with me."

She kneels before the crucifix and folds her hands. She beckons him down, and he slides to his knees next to her. She makes the sign of the cross and gestures for him to do the same. Aaron finds it unexpectedly hard. True enough, he has forsaken his religion, and true enough, his God is dead, but that demise was recent, and beneath his conversion to a new reality there remain cultural traditions and instincts of his upbringing, and those rivers run very deep. At last, she takes hold of his hand and helps him make the sign of the crucifix on himself.

They kneel there a few minutes, she in silent prayer, until she leads him back to the kitchen.

Before he leaves, the two women stuff his pockets with more bread.

"You come back tomorrow," the older woman says.

Aaron nods as he leaves.

A week later, Aaron is once more digging a grave near a wagon loaded with dead bodies. The rash has gone from his face, the life returns to his eyes, and he resumes the work routine he had always shared with Dr. Foeldish.

"You were wrong, doctor," he says out loud. "I was stronger than the disease, stronger than the Hungarians."

The snow is now turning to slush, the muddy green earth visible beneath it. "I lived to see the spring, doctor. I fought back, and I lived, and now spring is here. I may even live to see Debrecen, visit Biro's, and get that bath."

Aaron walks to the back of the wagon, which is stacked with bodies, and tugs at the one lying on top. It is that of Dr. Foeldish, his face a mass of red scars, his form shriveled, his eyes staring blankly. Aaron gently lifts the doctor's body from the wagon and sets it in the grave.

"I do not say *Kaddish*, Dr. Foeldish. "The ones who do are in the wagon, and they'll be with you soon. So I will simply say goodbye."

With Foeldish gone and no chance of ever finding Max again, Aaron didn't have anyone with whom to talk. Perhaps it was for the best. Talking led to friendship, and friendship led to loss, and loss led to pain.

It wasn't Aaron's physical strength that enabled him to push the big Hungarian soldier out of the truck during the fight for his watch. It was the layers of outrage that had built up, the humiliation and brutality of the SS beatings in the Russian schoolhouse, the predations and deprivations of the long marches, and the cruel trick of the role he'd played in Kimlit's death, and of having to watch him and his other comrades die in the searing flames. It was that which sprang forth from inside him that killed the Hungarian soldier.

Aaron's taste for vengeance was whetted. During the weeks that followed, he tried to make contact with the Russian partisan resistance of whom he'd heard rumors for months; but alas, the slaves were sent marching again. In the meantime, the Hungarians were now bringing the Jews food and vitamins to help end the typhus epidemic. If they let their slaves starve to death, who would do their work? As his health improved, Aaron's strength renewed, as did his mantra to survive. Then when he would make his escape and join the Russian resistance, God help the Hungarians and the Nazis.

7 See the maps pages 294 and page 295 (Southern Russian Front January – March 1943).

CHAPTER 10
HORSE MASTER

ON THE VAST RUSSIAN front, the likelihood of any one person encountering anyone they'd known prior is remote. Aaron is just one easily-overlooked speck of dust in the vastness. Early in May 1943, he finds himself crouched in a narrow trench outside the city of Nezhin, where the Axis soldiers are enduring a furious counterattack by the Russians. Bullets zip through the air above Aaron's head and thump into mud, snow, and an occasional man, the latter usually punctuated by shrieks, then moans of pain.

Aaron makes his way along the trench to a spot that offers better protection from the hot metal knifing in the air above him. A thundering explosion from a nearby mortar hit knocks him to the ground. Before its debris can rain down on him, he quickly crawls beneath a covered wagon parked near the end of a trench.

The wagon seems to be the target of small arms fire despite the large red cross on its side, identifying it as a field hospital unit. Agonizing groans escape from within.

Aaron has little use for field hospitals since the experience at Davidóvka and thinks it best to keep his distance from them.

As he crawls away, he hears a voice that stands out above the other moans, not because it is more desperate or more anguished, but rather, because it is *familiar*...

"Max!" yells Aaron. "Is that you?"

"Aaron! It can't be!"

As Aaron crawls back to the wagon and peeks inside, he is astonished to find Max, his beloved best friend. The hurricane of war has blown these two unlikely specks of dust together again. "Max, how hurt are you?"

"Just bad luck. But my God, I can't believe it's you, Aaron."

"God had nothing to do with it. I'm hoping to stay out of *there*," says Aaron, pointing to the interior of the wagon.

Another wounded Jew peers from behind Max. "Can you pull us to safety?" he grimaces in pain.

"Yes, can you, Aaron?" says Max. "The horses broke free and we're sitting ducks here. Can you pull the wagon down farther?"

Aaron glances at the front of the wagon, where the wheels are askew. "For you, I'll do it, but you owe me, Max," he grins to his friend. He seizes the abandoned yoke and pulls the wheels straight, heaving mightily. The wagon lurches forward, deeper into the trench, where it is sheltered from the rain of bullets.

A faint cheer rises up from inside. Aaron climbs aboard and embraces his old friend. Luck had been kind to Max. At Aaron's prompting, he'd married his fiancée from Khust, in the Carpathians. They already had two children, and Max had taken over his father-in-law's leather business.

As a result, he has spent the last few months in Kiev, working in a leather factory. The Germans and Hungarians need his skills, so he's been sheltered and well fed. Max was being transferred to another leatherworks outfit when his unit came under fire. The medic has tended to him and is due to come back.

"You must be careful of Hungarian medics—they can be deadly," says Aaron.

"They need my skills, or I would've been dead a long time ago," says Max.

"You'll need to teach me that skill," says Aaron. "But watch out for Hungarian field hospitals. I saw them burn one to the ground outside Davidóvka, with hundreds of sick Jews inside it. One of the slaves was Kimlit from Bielka, who'd fallen ill with typhus."

"The cantor's son?" asks Max.

Aaron nods. "His prayers didn't help him."

"Then it's true," says Max. "I overheard some Hungarians and Germans back in Kiev joking about how they were burning field hospitals with dozens, sometimes hundreds of sick Jews inside, throughout the Russian front. I thought it was a rumor."

"Believe it, Max. We're useful to them until we get sick. Then they burn us to death."

Despite this grave awareness, both men take heart in miraculously finding one another in the middle of the vast Russian wilderness. *Now I'm going to make it,* Aaron thinks to himself. *I have Max with me!*

A long line of slaves and Hungarian soldiers trudge eastward along a dusty road in the searing heat of late May 1943. Officers ride on horseback, and an occasional truck skirts by on the shoulder of the road, kicking up more dust. The Axis summer offensive near Kursk is soon to begin.

Near the end of the slave column is Aaron, his back weighted with firepower for that offensive—a heavy machine gun called a *geppùshka*. Next to him walks Max, who has recovered from his wounds. Max carries the machine gun's tripod and barrels.

Aaron and Max seem sturdier than most of the slaves at this point, for they have taken the risk to sneak out of camp at night and scrounge for food amongst the Russian farmhouses. The rations from the Hungarians have now shrunk to the point where starvation looms. Aaron and Max beg for food from Russian farmers and the two men are grateful for any morsels they receive. Whenever the two feel that any of the Russian farmers are lying when they deny having any food, they would break into those homes later that night or break into a store in a nearby village and help themselves to whatever they might find. Aaron's and Max's sturdiness got them noticed by the Hungarian officers, which in turn, soon got them the jobs of doing the heavy lifting.

All along the line, Hungarian soldiers whip the slaves with clubs, urging them to move faster. Aaron struggles to keep up, the weight of the machine gun cutting into his shoulders and back. When he pauses to shift its weight, he is immediately struck on the side of his head with a club.

"Move, you lazy piece of shit!" shouts a Hungarian sergeant, who has spent most of the journey trying to impress his superiors with how boisterous and cruel he can be to the Jews. He strikes Aaron and Max several times with his club, bruising them both.

About noon, a shadow passes over Aaron, accompanied by the clip-clopping of a horse. He turns to see a big, burly captain riding

Aaron has, in fact, heard mystical tales of a secret brigade of Jewish partisan guerillas, but his lifelong experience with the Jewish people's failure to resist anti-Semitic abuse causes him to dismiss the notion. Nevertheless, he groans and gets to his feet and the two creep away, moving from shadow to shadow, quietly dodging one bullet after another from Hungarian and German sentries. Aaron and Max trek on with only the sliver of a moon illuminating their way.

Although Aaron grows excited that Max has learned there may be Jewish partisans about, the rumor is that these fighters refuse to trust anyone. Their need for secrecy is absolute—not only from the Germans, but the Russians, known for a long history of anti-Semitism, whose leader, Joseph Stalin, is too paranoid to allow a unit of fiercely independent Jewish soldiers to spring up in the midst of Russia. But Max is confident that when he and Aaron prove their fighting skills, these partisans will gladly accept them.

When Aaron and Max reach the outskirts of town, they pause at the sight of two dead horses. Aaron steps on the neck of one to see if it is still soft and warm enough to indicate that it is fresh. To Aaron's surprise, the horse raises its head and even tries to jump up, but falls back, injured.

"Oh, I've got to put this poor horse out of its misery," says Aaron as he pulls out a long sharp knife he's been hiding deep in his rucksack that he'd stolen from a farm. He then kills the dying horse.

Max begins to butcher the second horse before realizing that someone has already taken the choicest parts. He and Aaron exchange looks.

"The partisans!" whispers Aaron. He gestures toward two women who are moving quickly away from them, carrying baskets in both hands.

"Partisans eat," says Aaron. "We follow the food supply, and we'll find these partisans at the other end."

Max nods. The two scramble after the women, moving carefully and quietly behind them, gradually catching up. When they are close enough, the men take cover. Then Aaron calls out a greeting in Yiddish. Turning swiftly, the women drop their baskets and pull out knives.

"We mean you no harm," says Aaron, as he and Max emerge from the shadows. "We are Jewish slave laborers. We hate the Germans and Hungarians." Aaron spits on the ground.

"Good for you," says one of the women. "Now leave us alone."

"We want to join the partisans," says Max.

"So, join them."

"We want you to take us to them," says Aaron.

"We don't know anything more about them than you do," says one of the women.

"Where are you taking the food?" asks Max.

"For us, for our families. Go away, you endanger us all."

The two women put away their knives, gather up their baskets and hurry away. Aaron and Max wait a while, then follow at a considerable distance. The women make their way to a shack on the outskirts of town. Aaron and Max watch as they disappear inside, then reappear a moment later without their baskets. The two men wait until the women are safely out of sight before advancing on the shack and calling out to its occupants. When no one answers, they venture slowly inside. They find it empty, except for the baskets filled with cooked horsemeat.

Aaron and Max eat some of the meat, put some in their rucksacks, then wait for the partisans to appear.

They wait while the moon sets, plunging the landscape into even deeper darkness. They wait until the faint light of dawn appears in the sky. No one comes.

"After those women saw us, they must've warned their friends," says Aaron.

"Perhaps on another night we will find them and actually get to meet with them," says Max. "But now we need to get back, and fast."

"Wait!" Aaron listens carefully. Max can hear nothing. He begins to move. Aaron stops him with a gesture, so the two remain perfectly still.

A raspy male voice comes from somewhere outside the shack. "Come out slowly, hands raised."

The voice speaks in Yiddish.

Aaron and Max do as they are ordered, finding themselves in the faint light, face-to-face with a half-dozen armed Jews, dressed in rough peasant clothing. One of them frisks Aaron, then Max. Their leader uses his weapon to prod them back inside the shack, where they are surrounded by gun toting partisans.

"What do you want?" asks the leader.

"To join you."

"You think we want Nazi spies to join us?"

"We are not spies," says Aaron. "We are Hungarian slave laborers. Jews."

The lead partisan pokes his submachine gun against Aaron's ribs.

"You are too well-fed to be Jewish slaves. Didn't your German trainers tell you that? Hungarians don't feed their slaves."

"We escape from camp to forage and steal food nearly every night. Like we are doing now," says Max. "Otherwise, we'd starve."

"How did you get out of the labor camp without being shot?"

"Their sentinels always fire at us," says Aaron. "But we know how to move quietly and avoid their bullets. We were trained by Zionists from Palestine."

"The Germans sent you because you are spies," says the man.

"No!"

"How did you find out about us?"

"We saw your supply wagon in the ditch, and then followed your women carrying your food," says Aaron.

"That's no proof!" says the partisan.

"I have scars!" Aaron begins to shed his jacket. The partisans react by cocking their guns. "I have scars from where I have carried a machine gun for a hundred miles for the Hungarians."

The lead partisan signals for Aaron to continue. Aaron pulls off enough of his shirt to reveal the scars. The partisan then moves away with the others, and they begin to confer in whispers, while one keeps his gun aimed at the prisoners. After a while, the leader instructs Aaron and Max to stand facing the wall with their arms raised, and not to turn around until instructed or they would be shot.

The partisans continue to talk, then fall silent. At last Aaron turns and sees that they are gone. He is devastated.

"We need to get back," says Max. "It may already be too late."

"You go," says Aaron. "I cannot face another day with the *geppùshka.*"

"You can't survive out here," says Max. "You know it. Give it one more day—tomorrow night. You know they have to be suspicious, but maybe we can bring proof."

"What proof?" asked Aaron.

"We'll think of something."

"There isn't *anything*, Max," shrugs Aaron. "If the Jewish partisans won't take us, no one will. This is the end for me, my friend. I can't go back there. Not with hundreds of cigarettes betting against my surviving even one more day."

"Then *I* will take on the *geppùshka.*" said Max.

"No!" says Aaron. "They'll murder you, and then kill me."

"Then give it one more day, Aaron. After that, we escape together."

Aaron reluctantly agrees, and he and Max make their way quickly back to the slave camp, managing to sneak into their tents just as dawn is breaking. Soon after they arrive, the Hungarians awaken everyone and assemble them for the day's march. Aaron, standing next to Max, eyes the *geppùshka*, then waits for the moment when he will be ordered to pick it up again. There is a delay, though, as the sergeant moves among the slaves, accompanied by two soldiers. The sergeant is calling out a name. When he gets close, Aaron can at last make it out: "Max Zelmánovic!"

Aaron's heart sinks. Have they been discovered missing the night before? Will they be summarily shot or tortured first, then hanged? Aaron grips the long knife that he had stolen from a Russian farm hidden deep in his rucksack, intent on putting up a fight.

Max reluctantly raises his hand. The sergeant and his men walk over to him.

"You are the one, aren't you?" asks the sergeant.

Max shrugs his shoulders apprehensively.

"You work with leather?" asks the sergeant.

"Yes," says Max.

"You are needed back in Kiev," says the sergeant.

Aaron and Max utter sighs of relief. They have survived yet another brush with death.

"You were needed an hour ago," continues the sergeant suddenly, eyeing both Aaron and Max. "But you weren't here. Where were you?"

"I—I don't know. I was here," says Max.

"Liar! You were hiding. Trying to escape. The two of you!" The sergeant slaps Max across the face. Aaron has to stop himself from intervening on his friend's behalf.

The sergeant then grabs Max's rucksack and pulls out a piece of horsemeat. "Look," he says to his soldiers. "They've been out stealing meat. It's no wonder the *little* Jew bastard has the strength to carry that damned machine gun."

The sergeant points to Aaron, whose spirits now sink. "So, this is how you've tricked us, *Jidi?* You think you have nine lives?" He pulls his pistol from his holster and cocks it. "I made bets and I'm not going to lose cigarettes over some stinking yid."

He then aims his pistol at Max. "Do you know what the penalty is for trying to escape?" he asks. "Death!"

The other slaves stare, holding their breath. Aaron wonders if he can throw himself at the sergeant and kill him with his knife before Max is killed.

"However, *you* are lucky," says the sergeant to Max. "You are valuable to us. At least for now. Too bad your friend is not."

The sergeant now aims his gun at Aaron.

Max steps forward. "If you kill him," he says. "You'll have to kill me first."

The sergeant ignores Max and pulls the trigger.

For reasons that may at first seem inexplicable, Max throws himself in front of Aaron and takes the bullet. They've been lifelong friends, it's true; brothers would better describe them. Still, does that justify a suicidal act?

Aaron's family had taken Max in and treated him like one of their own. In his gratitude, he would have done anything for any one of them. When Aaron became patriarch of the family, he treated Max as his equal, trusting him completely to run the farm and look after his family while he was away in the Czech army. Max had regarded this investiture as a special gift from Aaron, an honor. And their forced separation under horrific circumstances followed by their recent improbable reunion, has only served to strengthen their bond.

Thus, when the sergeant pulls the trigger, Max's instinct for self-preservation is eclipsed by his need to protect his friend. For Aaron, Max jumps into harm's way, and then crashes to the ground as his blood begins to spill from the gunshot wound.

The bullet enters Max's chest, missing his heart by a few inches, and lodges into his shoulder blade.

"Max!" cries Aaron, whose instinct to comfort his wounded friend now overrides his instinct to flee.

"Stupid goddamned Jew!" cries the sergeant, furious at Max as well as horrified by what he has done to him. *"Stupid Jidi!"*

The captain rushes to the scene and quickly sizes up the situation. He angrily orders the sergeant and the other troops to carry Max to a waiting truck, where he can be driven for treatment.

So concerned are the Hungarians about keeping Max alive, knowing that their superiors will be angry at them, as his skills are needed elsewhere, that they forget—at least momentarily—about Aaron, who quickly disappears into the crowd.

"Don't give up, Aaron!" Max cries out in pain, as he is carried away. "I have faith in you! You'll make it!"

"Shut your stinking mouth, you Jewish piece of shit," says the sergeant.

The other Jews watch as Max is taken away and put into the truck and driven out of sight. Once again, the two friends from the tiny town of Bielka have drifted apart and are left to work out their uncertain fates separately.

Aaron's sagging spirits are soon matched by his sagging shoulders—burdened again by the *geppùshka*. Apparently, the Hungarians have decided to torture him with the heavy machine gun until he finally meets death, rather than let a quick bullet end it all. Aside from which, there are many bets on his head.

Aaron feels more hopeless and alone than ever before. Rejected by the Jewish partisans, his last hope of escape has vanished. And his remaining source of strength, the one man with whom he had a chance to survive—Max—is taken from him. He staggers onward through the day, the sharp angles of the *geppúshka* cutting into the skin of his neck, digging into his shoulders, crushing his lungs under its pressure. Just after noon, with the sun at its hottest, he finally stumbles and falls.

The captain smiles as Aaron falls to the ground, struggling to get back on his feet. "What are you worried about?" the captain says to Private Miklos. "If God made the world in six days, He can keep this Jew alive for six more. Then you'll get your cigarettes."

Aaron finally staggers to his feet, eliciting a mixed chorus of boos and cheers from soldiers who have placed bets. He rejoins the column, but soon enough, when he glances up at the vast flatness of the land around him and at the long road stretching endlessly ahead, he realizes he isn't going to make it. To get through the day, he will need a miracle.

Unfortunately for the captain and the others with bets on him, he's got one. Aaron's miracle comes in the person of Helen. With the machine gun cutting into his back and his legs weakening beneath him, Aaron looks ahead and sees her. She isn't in Russia. She isn't even in the present. She is in the future, and the future is not vague or formless. It is as sharp and clear as anything Aaron has ever seen. The flat horizon becomes rolling hills and then mountains with crisp, clear cool streams, flowers, and trees. And there is Helen, greeting him with a smile.

She extends a hand; he takes it. The *geppùshka* doesn't seem very heavy now.

"Soon I'll be free," says Aaron. "And we'll be with each other whenever we want, all the time."

She leads him right through a stream. The water cools his hot, tired feet. The sun begins to go down, the air becoming chilly. They draw nearer to the farmhouse—Aaron's farmhouse. By now it is dark but there is a warm firelight, and the sound of laughter coming from within—the laughter of children.

"Aaron," says Helen. "Rest."

"I will."

"Aaron!" calls another voice. This time it is his friend, Shmiel, from camp. "You can rest!"

Aaron stops walking and looks around, confused. He is back to reality with his fellow slaves at a campsite. The sun has set, and the Jews are bedding down for the night. Shmiel stands before him.

"Set that damn thing down. You've been carrying it all day."

Aaron sets the *geppùshka* down and collapses.

During the next day's march, Aaron's stride improves, his pace is quicker. He seems to be gaining more strength.

"You see?" smiles Private Miklos. "He gets stronger. I tell you, it's God looking out for this Jew."

"It's *you,*" barks the sergeant. "You've been slipping him food."

"No!" says Miklos.

"If I catch you, you're the one who will be carrying the *geppùshka.*"

That night the captain, concerned for his bet, works Aaron even later, arranging men in shifts to force him to march around the campsite, occasionally lashing him with a whip. When the last soldier finally retires for the night, Aaron collapses onto the crowded floor of the slave camp.

To his surprise, Aaron is not disturbed by the Hungarians the next morning to carry the machinegun. In fact, the slaves are not disturbed at all until the sun is well up. When Aaron finally arises, he discovers Jews and soldiers alike are gathering at a corral by the edge of the encampment. Here, a new commanding officer for the battalion is reviewing several horses. This commander—a major in rank—has gray hair with a beard and a colorful uniform decked out with medals, ribbons, and decorations, topped off with a feathered fedora—a throwback to the flamboyant Hungarian officers of old. But he is missing one ingredient appropriate to his rank and stature—a big, tall, beautiful horse. Hungarians are known to take considerable pride in their horsemanship—as well as their beautiful horses.

Aaron watches as officers and soldiers, who had been ordered to round up all the horses in the area, bring one mount after another for the major's inspection. He rejects them all—good horses, it seems, are scarce in wartime.

But down near the corral is a beautiful white stallion the major has at last chosen to be his personal steed.

"He seems wild," says Aaron to Shmiel. "I doubt he's broken in yet."

Aaron and Shmiel head down to get a better look. The stallion is the most magnificent horse Aaron has ever seen, and as the son of a horse trader, he has seen thousands. The animal is pure white and muscular, a regal complement to the Hungarian major, an indispensable accessory. But sure enough, it bucks when a soldier tries to saddle him.

The major immediately calls for a volunteer among his experienced horsemen to break in the horse. Several officers come forward. The first one is the captain who has so antagonized Aaron.

Fascinated, Aaron and Shmiel make their way down to the edge of the corral where soldiers have gathered, along with some slaves to watch the contest. The captain approaches the horse carefully, swings himself skillfully onto the stallion's back, then rides him for about three seconds before being violently thrown into the fence, head first. A hush falls over the crowd as the captain lies motionless.

"That horse is your ticket to life, Aaron," whispers Shmiel. "The captain is dead."

After a few seconds, the captain on the ground stirs. The sergeant and several other soldiers help him to his feet. He has been bloodied but manages to limp back to the major to apologize and offers to try again. The major waves him aside and another soldier moves forward to try his luck.

"Tough luck, Aaron," says Shmiel. "Maybe he'll take another shot."

Aaron and the rest of the Jews in the crowd are enthralled, as one soldier after another tries to mount the horse, only to have the magnificent animal rear up and throw every one of them off within seconds. One officer manages to hang on for a full ten seconds, but none come close to taming the magnificent animal.

"I need to try," says Aaron suddenly.

"Are you sure?" asks Shmiel.

"Yes. I can do it."

"You'll be killed if you fail."

Some of the other slaves have overheard and warn Aaron against it, citing anger from the Hungarians against the Jews.

"I was raised with horses. I know how to do it," says Aaron.

He starts moving toward the gate of the corral. Shmiel follows.

"They won't let you. They'll just shoot you."

"The captain is going to kill me soon anyway. This may be a chance to get out."

Before Shmiel can protest again, Aaron has slipped to the front of the crowd and faces the major.

"Sir," he says. "I'm a master horseman. Please let me try."

A chorus of angry shouting wells up from the soldiers at the outrageous audacity of a slave confronting their commanding officer. The major looks at Aaron's five-foot-two-inch frame dressed in tatters, and then smiles as he summarily dismisses him with laughter and a wave of his hand, as if to gesture that the little Jewish slave couldn't even mount the tall stallion. The soldiers erupt into laughter as Aaron falls back to rejoin the slaves.

"You see, Aaron?" says Shmiel.

"You're lucky they didn't kill you," chime in other slaves, declaring that Aaron had put the rest of the Jews in jeopardy.

But as the last of the volunteers is being thrown off the horse, and without saying a word, Aaron slips again in front of the crowd, this time where the captain stands.

"Sir, please ask the major to let me try."

"Shut your stinking mouth, Jew!" says the captain.

"He might throw me off, or worse. If so, you win your bet."

Private Miklos immediately protests, "That wouldn't count."

The captain snorts at Miklos, "Why wouldn't it?" Then he turns to Aaron. "You want to die, Jew?"

Aaron replies, "If you volunteer me, sir, and I break him in, you get the credit with the major. If he throws me, I could easily get killed. You win either way."

The captain now turns to the major. "Sir!" he shouts, smiling, "The Jew still wants to try."

Laughter again rings out from the soldiers as the captain points toward Aaron, the diminutive, emaciated, ill-clad Jew. The major smiles, but this time he gracefully gestures Aaron to the horse. Aaron climbs over the fence and approaches the stallion from behind. As he draws nearer to the magnificent animal, it seems to grow in size while Aaron seems to get smaller. He stops a few feet from the horse's tail, where he stands for a moment without moving. The Hungarian officers shake their heads in disbelief, and the captain is about to call it off when Aaron abruptly runs forward, then leaps onto the stallion's back. He holds its mane, squeezing with his legs with all his might to stay upright.

There is no saddle, but Aaron grew up mastering bareback horses at the farm. He is out of practice and weak from the ordeal of the last few years, but this is a mortal struggle, so he holds on as the horse bucks wildly. Five seconds…ten seconds…fifteen—he has already exceeded the best efforts of the Hungarian soldiers. He is focused so completely on staying on the horse that the wild cheering from the Jews, and the jeering from the Hungarians, fade from his ears. Several times he is nearly thrown, but each time he manages to keep his balance, and soon he has the familiar feeling of being one with his mount. He strokes the horse's mane and whispers soothingly, as his father had taught him.

"Aaron! Aaron!" cheer the slaves, spurring Aaron on. But just as he thinks he's brought the stallion under control, the animal takes off in a ferocious gallop. Aaron hangs on as the horse jumps the fence and races away from the corral and the noise of the crowd—he is the fastest mount Aaron has ever ridden. The wind and the greening countryside sweep past in an exhilarating blur. Tears come to Aaron's eyes as he tastes freedom for the first time in four years.

Aaron bends forward and whispers into the horse's ear, "Faster, faster, faster!" He wishes he had an apple or a carrot or a cube of sugar to feed him. But onward the stallion gallops, and Aaron does nothing to try to slow him down. The encampment disappears from view, and still they gallop onward.

Aaron thinks of fleeing from his tormentors—is this the right time at last? He could certainly get several miles away by the time the horse tires, and then perhaps soon locate a band of partisans, or join the Russian army. How could they refuse to accept him this time—especially now that he could offer his magnificent steed to their cause? And then somehow, some way, he could arrange to smuggle Helen and his family out of harm's way.

On the other hand, the Hungarian major back at the corral appeared to be an old loyalist to Emperor Franz-Josef, and perhaps he would generously reward Aaron. Further, the idea that a deserting Jew would humiliate a Hungarian major in front of his men would be too much for them. The officers would likely be sending scouts soon to hunt him down—and there would surely be reprisals against the Jews left behind.

As the horse tires at last, Aaron strokes the horse's neck and whispers, "Good boy!" in his ear, then guides him to turn around. When they get back to the corral, he is greeted by a wild cheer—this time from both Jews and Hungarians—as he rides the horse calmly back into the corral and dismounts him before the major. Private Miklos is cheering.

"I told you God is looking out for that Jewish bastard," says the private.

At last even the sergeant and the captain join in the cheering.

The captain steps forward toward the major. "I knew this Jew could do it, sir!" he shouts above the din.

The major nods to him, then watches as Aaron gives the horse some water from a trough. After the horse drinks his fill, Aaron takes a bridle and saddle off the fence and puts them on the horse with little resistance from the animal, then leads him before the major.

"He is yours, sir. He is now safe to ride and will obey all your commands."

The major's eyes light up and he smiles widely as he approaches Aaron and speaks to the troops. "This gentleman," he says, gesturing to Aaron, "is going to be my *Csikos,"*—pronounced *ShEEkosh* (horse master).

Aaron is surprised and brimming with pride to hear the major refer to him, a lowly Jewish slave, as a "gentleman" in front of all the Hungarians. Aaron doesn't try to hide his grin.

The major continues, this time addressing Aaron directly, "Henceforth, your duties will be to take care of my horse: train him, groom him, make him look good for me."

"Yes sir," says Aaron with a bow, as everyone applauds, Jews and Hungarians alike.

And so it was that Aaron came to live a civilized life. He laid down the geppùshka and picked up the bridle, saddle, and horse brush, charged only with the tasks of feeding the stallion and keeping him healthy, grooming, and training him for the major to ride. Aaron was given soap to clean the horse and had plenty left over to wash his own body and clothes. It was not Debrecen, nor Biro's, but he at last felt clean for the first time in years.

The major was generous in other ways as well. A corporal from the major's quarters brought Aaron a fresh set of clothes in place of the rags Aaron had been wearing for so long. For the first time on the Russian front, Aaron no longer had to steal or beg for food. In fact, he had enough to share with Shmiel and some of his starving slave comrades. He made excuses to get out and slip them bread and cheese or whatever else he had in surplus. He suspected the major was aware of this, but he ignored it. The major was from the "old school" of Emperor Franz-Josef's era, when prejudice was overridden by merit, and a man like Aaron who could master a wild stallion was respected, whether he was serf, noble, or Jew.

After a few days of working as the major's Csìkos, Aaron experienced another shock—the major began to speak to him, not in the guttural, vile, abusive language of his other masters, but as a human being. After the major's rides, he would tell Aaron how he longed for the old days, when such things as honor and noble deeds were valued. He spoke of the Jewish men who had served under him with valor in the First World War, and of his frustration and anguish at how the army was now serving at the behest and whims of the crazed Nazi Führer. The major listened to Aaron with keen interest and shook his head with world-weary regret when Aaron told him how his father had so loved the Emperor, that Franz-Josef's portrait had been displayed in Aaron's home long after the new Czechoslovakian government outlawed such allegiances to the past.

But if it was the major who had given Aaron refuge in the middle of chaos and destruction, it was of course, the stallion who had brought him that deliverance. Aaron had a secret name for him—Chillock—the favorite horse of his youth. Chillock seemed to sense Aaron's plight somehow and responded to his commands with sure-footed respect. Through Chillock Aaron found salvation—and a reconnection with the peaceful kinder world he once knew. The major told him that if he were ever transferred to another station, he would take Aaron with him, along with Chillock, of course.

If Aaron had known a merciful God, such things as food, soap, kindness and respect would have been taken for granted, but in the godless world he inhabited, he was given only a glimpse of these things, a taste with the tip of the tongue—just enough to whet Aaron's appetite so that he might suffer even more if the meal was plucked away from him before he could eat of it.

CHAPTER 11
A BITTER MEAL

"You've won and I've lost, Jew," says the captain, silhouetted in the doorway to the stable with the setting sun disappearing behind him.

Aaron is brushing down Chillock, who is sweaty after an afternoon workout with the major. He has been serving two weeks as *Csikos*, two weeks of decent meals and plenty of rest, and the skin of his shoulders is growing back from where the *geppùshka* had scraped it to the bone. Putting down the brush, he stands at respectful attention before the captain, who continues, "I understand you are leaving tomorrow with the major, and with you, there go my cigarettes and the respect of my men."

"I did not mean any disrespect, sir."

"Of course not. You can only disrespect me if you refuse my invitation."

Aaron is perplexed. "Invitation, sir?"

The captain orders Aaron to tie up the horse in the stable, then leads him to the officers' encampment, where copious amounts of liquor are being consumed while the evening meal cooks over a blazing campfire. The officers joke about how easily they've been able to seize as much vodka as they want from Russian homes and stores.

Aaron feels distinctly uneasy and tells the captain that he must return to the stable, as he is under orders from the major never to leave his horse alone for any extended period of time.

At this, the captain angrily reminds Aaron that he would never have attained his position as *Csikos* if the captain hadn't spoken up to the major to allow Aaron the chance to break in the horse. The captain orders Aaron to stay put, or he will shoot him. His masters offer him meat, pretending to treat him like a comrade, and the captain orders him to drink vodka.

Sitting at the edge of the fire, Aaron can discern the staring eyes of the Jews in the nearby slave encampment, who are no doubt wondering how he had found such good fortune while their own plight remained so utterly hopeless. Aaron feels uncomfortable and is anxious to flee.

Around ten o'clock that night, Aaron is at last given leave to return, his balance unsteady from unaccustomed alcohol. He glances at Chillock, then climbs to the hayloft where he quickly falls into heavy slumber, dreaming of riding the horse amidst swirling clouds and the shimmer of leaves in the forest with Helen mounted on Chillock right behind Aaron, her arms around his waist.

"Make him go faster, Aaron!" says Helen—until Chillock brays an anguished-sounding squeal, which suddenly awakens Aaron from his dream.

Now abruptly awake, Aaron feels a headache from too much liquor. He has trouble seeing in the darkness but hears Chillock scream loudly, so he steadies himself and slides down from the hayloft.

A crowd of soldiers, one of them holding a lantern, is gathered around Chillock's stall. Aaron sees the horse rearing up and pounding the walls with his hind legs. One of his front legs is bent at an odd angle, its bone protruding, painfully crippling the horse. Chillock's blood is dripping onto the hay, as Aaron stares in shock.

"Looks like you didn't tie him up right, Jew," smirks the captain. "Looks like he hurt himself bad."

"Hurt *himself?*" mutters Aaron, still in shock. The horse is writhing and kicking in agony.

"We've got to kill him before he hurts somebody," says one soldier.

The major walks into the barn after hearing all the shouting.

"This Jew was too busy getting drunk to take care of your horse, sir," says the captain. "It's injured bad. We need to shoot the horse; and you should shoot the Jew as well, sir."

"It's not true, sir. The captain lies!" cries Aaron. He immediately feels a rifle butt smash his head.

As he falls to the ground, Aaron instantly knows what has happened. The captain wants his slave back, and he wants to punish Aaron for gaining the major's favor over himself; the horse stands in his way.

"Explain this, Herskowitz," barks the major, in an angry tone that takes Aaron by surprise.

"They have tricked me, sir, and *they've* done this terrible thing," says Aaron, gesturing to the horse.

"Listen to him lie, sir!" hisses the captain. "He's drunk! Smell his breath! You trusted him, and he's just a drunken, lazy *Jidi* swine!"

"Please, sir," says Aaron. "You know I'd never let this happen to your horse."

"We found this stashed away, sir," says the captain. "He's been hiding this from you."

One of the soldiers kicks aside a bale of hay near the stable and uncovers a pile of broken, empty whiskey bottles.

The captain continues. "He stole these and was getting drunk every night, and now he accuses *us*!"

"No!" says Aaron in shock.

The major stares at Aaron, eyeball to eyeball. "I elevated you from a mere slave, and now my horse which was under your care, must be destroyed. Was my trust misplaced?"

"No, sir. Never." He glances at the broken bottles. "Look at those, sir. They are dusty and dirty. Probably dug out of old trash and placed here."

"But you *have* been drinking, yes?" asks the major.

"The captain ordered me to join them for dinner last night. I felt uncomfortable about it, and when I told the captain I needed to return to the stable, he threatened to kill me. The rest pretended to befriend me, and the captain ordered me to drink their liquor. They set me up, sir, tricked me…and you."

"Listen to the lies of the Jewish swine!" cries the captain.

The major looks again at the bottles, and then at the captain. In the major's growing skepticism of the captain, Aaron glimpses salvation.

"Sir," Aaron adds. "I have done all that you've asked and more. I've been a horseman all my life. Horses were my father's living and my own. You know me enough by now to realize that I would never endanger your steed, sir."

A tense silence ensues as the major looks at the bottles and then again at the captain, whose frustration is visibly growing. Unfortunately, for Aaron, the obvious truth is not enough. Siding with an innocent Jew, and risking disrespect and mutiny from his men, is not a choice the major relishes.

At last, he says to Aaron, "You got drunk and betrayed my trust. You should never have let this happen." He slips his leather gloves off and slaps Aaron across the face with them. Then he turns to the captain, "Handle this any way you see fit."

"Yes, sir," replies the smirking captain, saluting the major exiting crisply out the door.

Aaron just let go—he let go of the struggle, any thoughts of living, all of it. When a gunshot rings out and Chillock collapses in front of him, splattering him with blood, he knows the next shot will bring his own death. Yet he doesn't care.

He feels the barrel of the captain's pistol against his temple, closes his eyes and waits for the gunshot. He feels his pitiful journey on earth, begun in the opening days of World War I, coursing its way through a bucolic childhood in the Carpathian Mountains and then the painful disruption of Hitler's ascendancy, is about to come to an end.

Instead, he hears angry shouts from several officers accusing the captain of cheating. In the noise of heated voices, he hears them grumbling about "the bets." Aaron has to die of exhaustion from carrying the *geppùshka,* not a swift bullet to the head, or most would lose their bets.

The captain replaces the gun with a hard backslap to Aaron's face, ordering him to march—with the *geppùshka,* again.

"We don't break camp for another two days, sir," objects one officer. "You can't have him marching around yet."

"Then what do you want me to do with him?" asks the captain, getting more annoyed.

The officer looks at the dead horse. "It's almost dawn. I'm hungry and so are the men."

The captain sighs, nodding.

"Private Miklos," says the captain. "Give the Jew your knife. Have him butcher the meat. If he gives you any trouble, shoot him."

After believing he'd be shot dead, relieving him from his nightmarish life, Aaron knows that once Miklos puts that knife in his hands, the bleakness of his journey would continue, punctuated by new forms of cruelty that his clever tormentors would invent.

Aaron had come to love Chillock, his last connection to the peaceful world of his past, and he cannot bring himself to butcher his beloved equine comrade. But he comes to realize that the mass of flesh before him is no longer Chillock. He also realizes that vengeance against his mortal enemies one day would be impossible if he follows the fate of Chillock. This realization leads Aaron to mechanically carve up the flesh of the horse he loved and keeps him going when the captain subsequently orders him to cook the horseflesh and serve it to the troops. If he does survive all that they throw at him, he'll find a way to get justice.

CHAPTER 12
"IT'S TIME FOR A KILL!"

HITLER NOW COMMITS ANOTHER grave military blunder. He refuses to heed the advice of his best general, Field Marshal von Manstein, who presses Hitler to allow him to capitalize on his recent brilliant counter-offensive of February and March, 1943, by launching a massive offensive while the Russians are still licking their wounds and re-grouping. Von Manstein intends to surround and destroy the Soviets' exposed salient surrounding Kursk in a pincer movement no later than April.

The Fuhrer, however, wants to wait until July for the assault when his new superior Tiger and Panther tanks will be ready for combat. Von Manstein argues vehemently that the longer the Germans wait to attack, the less chance they have for victory, as the Russians are building up their forces around Kursk with reserves from all over the great Soviet expanse. But Hitler refuses to budge; and von Manstein's fears of waiting too long turn out to be correct, for as the fates of war would have it, the Russians eventually come into possession of the German plan of attack, allowing Soviet Marshal Zhukov to decisively defeat the assault of the Germans, who suffer irreplaceable losses in the greatest tank battle in history.[8]

When Hitler gets word that the Western Allies have landed in Sicily, he finds an excuse to halt the Kursk offensive after a week of furious combat, so that he could transfer much-needed men and supplies to this new front in Southern Europe. The Fuhrer is now repeating the same mistake made in earlier conflicts in history—waging a war on two fronts. With its resources so divided, Germany would never again have the capability to mount a major offensive on the Russian Front.

Following the Axis defeat at Kursk, the beaten Hungarian forces and their slave laborers are dispatched by the Germans to the rear of the Russian front to refit, all the way to the city of Pinsk in the province of Byelorussia by the fall of 1943.

"Another winter," Aaron says as he watches the snowflakes falling from the early morning sky, turning the ground white for the first time since April. "Another Russian winter." He lowers a bucket into a well with a rope.

"Another winter, yes," says Private Miklos. "*Russian* winter, I don't know."

"What don't you know? Has Hitler outlawed Russian winters now?"

Miklos smiles. "After months of retreat, there's only so much of Russia left. Tomorrow, we march south. Toward Hungary and Slovakia. We'll be home by Christmas. We've made it this far, Aaron. Just stay out of danger—which you're so good at. With you nearby, I'll hope to do the same."

Aaron had saved Miklos's life at Kursk when he had motioned the private to join him under the safety of a dry covered streambed during a vicious Russian bombing attack. Miklos would never forget Aaron's act of kindness.

But Aaron is feeling mournful about the loss of his friend Shmiel, who was killed by the Russian shelling at Kursk. Once again, it seems that God, if there *is* a God, has taken away with one hand, what he had given Aaron with the other.

Aaron fills a second pail with water, as Miklos lights a cigarette, then puts it in Aaron's mouth.

"I'd help you with those, but you know I'd get in trouble," says Miklos.

"Of course," says Aaron, as the two start off toward the camp. They haven't gone very far when Miklos abruptly knocks the cigarette out of Aaron's mouth.

"Hurry, Jew!" Miklos shouts. "And don't spill the water!"

Aaron glances at Miklos, confused, and then looks ahead. Aaron had thought he was finally rid of his greatest nemeses — the Hungarian captain and sergeant who had so grotesquely tormented him with the *geppùshka* were killed at Kursk. Unfortunately, he is about to encounter two even greater formidable foes.

Two Nazi SS officers are walking casually along the street, chatting. Several Hungarian soldiers salute in deference to the two. Miklos, likewise, shows them respect by bossing around a Jew, then saluting them as they pass.

As soon as the Germans are out of sight, Miklos breathes a sigh of relief. "Sorry, Aaron, nothing personal. You understand."

"Of course," says Aaron.

"We won't have to put up with this much longer. After the war, I'll come visit; carry water for *you*. And if you still want to help me, well, that will be up to you."

"Not a chance," says Aaron. Miklos grins, slaps Aaron on the back, and moves on. Aaron continues to the field kitchen, where the Hungarian in charge has him pour the water into large pots on the stove.

"Good luck for you, Jew. You might even get a hot meal today." The Hungarian points to the sacks of grain stacked in piles.

"Thank you, sir," says Aaron. "Anything else, sir?"

"Yes. More water."

Aaron heads back to the well with his empty pails, the prospect of a hot meal already making his stomach growl. Aaron wonders if the sun is shining in Bielka; if Helen is surviving, waiting for his return to take her hand, and her plow.

Two shadows are nearing the well, their presence announced by the guttural sound of German voices. Aaron looks up to see the two SS officers approaching, talking and laughing, patting each other on the back.

Hurriedly, he fills one of his pails, and then lowers the second bucket, intent on making a quick getaway. The two men pause to light up cigarettes, their voices now silent. Out of the corner of his eye, he can see that they are staring at him. These are hardened veterans of the most fanatical wing of Hitler's armed forces. The lieutenant appears to be in his mid-thirties, while the taller burly captain seems older, striking an imposing, hulking presence.

At last, the tall one breaks the silence: "That stinking *Juden Schwein* has been hanging around too long. He is fat enough. *Ich denke, es wird Zeit für eine kill.*" —I think it's time for a kill.

Aaron's blood turns colder than the icy water of the well, but he continues to work the bucket, not letting on that he understands what they have just said. Outwardly, he appears calm, but inwardly, all the images he has of home and freedom evaporate in a sudden storm of fear. He furtively touches the handle of the long knife he had stolen from a Russian farmhouse concealed in his rucksack. If the Germans attack him, he will at least put up a fight. Even if he is not assaulted immediately, Aaron knows that within hours or days, the brutish Nazis will reappear, single him out, and kill him for sport.

The two Germans begin to approach him. They speak again, but their words are drowned out by the noise of an approaching wagon. Still, Aaron picks up what sounds like the shorter one asking, *"Jetzt?"* Now? The taller one replies, *"Warum nicht? Etwas besseres zu tun?"*—Why not? Got something better to do?

Aaron quickly drops the bucket into the well. The two Germans watch the horse-drawn wagon roll by. When they resume their short walk to the well, Aaron is gone.

He is, in fact, running through the streets in a panic, his mind focused on escape, his eyes desperately scanning for a hiding place. At last, he slips through a break in the brick wall of a building, allowing him to hide. But if he doesn't get back to camp with the water soon, they'll be searching for him.

Water! thinks Aaron. He realizes that he's left the two buckets behind during his panicked flight. Once the footsteps of soldiers in the street have faded, he returns to the well, finding the buckets still full.

When he arrives back at the kitchen, he immediately dumps the contents into the pots, then hides for the rest of the day. By dusk, he slips into the tent that serves as the slaves' quarters, but he will not allow himself to fall asleep.

Around midnight, when he hears footsteps approaching, he grips the knife, keeping close watch. In the moonlight, he sees a hulking silhouette appear on the wall of the tent.

Aaron withdraws his knife and waits. The tent flap flies open and Aaron lunges, but quickly pulls back when a Jew enters, nicknamed Limpy due to frostbitten feet that had left him crippled.

"What are you trying to do?" asks Limpy, startled. Several other slaves stir.

"What were you doing out there at this hour?" Aaron demands in return.

"Ask the bastard Hungarians. They had me load all their ammunition on the trucks tonight." Limpy hobbles to his blanket and collapses, exhausted.

Limpy's tenacity and will to survive despite his handicap has won Aaron's admiration. Limpy also provides him with valuable information about the Hungarians' movements on nights when he slips out to forage for food.

Aaron crawls over to him. "Limpy," he whispers.

"What now?"

Aaron pulls a hunk of bread from his pocket and holds it out for him.

"Thanks," says Limpy, tearing into it as best he can with a mouth that was missing several teeth. "Have you been out already?"

"No."

"You're in luck," says Limpy, lowering his voice to a whisper. "Miklos will be standing guard. I checked."

"Thank you for the information, my friend," says Aaron. "But I can't go out tonight."

Limpy suddenly stops chewing.

"What's going on, Aaron?"

"Have you seen those two SS men?" whispers Aaron.

"No," says Limpy. "They must be new. What happened?"

"They've been watching me. I overheard them at the well. The big one talked about killing me, apparently because he thinks I look too healthy for a Jewish slave."

"You shouldn't leave camp for a while," says Limpy. "Not until we move out of this place—though I'll miss the food you bring me," Limpy breaks into a lop-sided smile. "Try to get some sleep."

Aaron agrees but is haunted by the Nazi's words: "It's time for a kill." As he hears those words over and over in his mind, he comes to a decision: *It's either him—or me.*

When he hears the sound of truck engines and marching feet in the morning, his spirits rise. He pushes aside the flap to the tent's entrance. Outside, he sees trucks and troops assembling.

"What are you smiling about, Aaron?" asks Limpy, awakened by the noise.

"Looks like we're moving out of here," says Aaron.

He scrambles out of the tent, but immediately spots the two SS men, drinking flasks of alcohol and laughing at the edge of the campsite. Crawling back inside, Aaron waits until they move on. He finally makes his way to the field kitchen, where another slave is already hard at work trying to light the fire, while the Hungarian soldier in charge is feasting on some bread.

"You're here early, Jew-boy."

"We're moving out?" asks Aaron.

"Second battalion is being transferred."

"What about our battalion?"

"We'll be here another month."

"A *month?*" gasps Aaron.

"At least." The Hungarian soldier tosses him the water pails.

"You in a rush, Jew?"

"No, sir," says Aaron, turning to head for the well.

"You had a friend here asking for you, just now."

Aaron pauses. "A friend?"

The Hungarian raises his hand to indicate great height. "Big SS German, and his buddy. Looking for the Jew with the water."

Aaron nods, trying to hide his alarm.

The Hungarian soldier continues. "What business does he have with you?"

"I don't know, sir," says Aaron.

"Hope he doesn't kill you. You're reliable—for a Jew."

"Thank you, sir," says Aaron, setting off for the well. He makes his way carefully, pausing at each street corner and looking ahead to see if his tall nemesis might be standing in his path.

For four days, after delivering the water, Aaron manages to stay out of sight. For four consecutive nights, he follows the big German all over town, but the tall SS man is always in the company of his partner—and both carry revolvers. It seems these two are inseparable. Aaron is more than willing to risk taking on the big Nazi with just his bare hands and his knife—but he is not so foolish as to take on two armed SS men at the same time. Rumors abound that Russian partisans sometimes invade Axis encampments at night to assassinate stray Nazi officers; so the two SS officers never leave each other's company.

On the fifth night of this ordeal, Aaron spots the tall SS man—this time without his partner. His immediate thought is: *Now is my chance! Kill him!*

Aaron sets his buckets down and begins to follow his tormentor, trailing him three blocks, farther away from the campsite. With each block, there are fewer passers-by. Gradually, Aaron draws closer to his mortal enemy.

At last, the German pauses to light a cigarette. From behind, Aaron approaches to within half a block of him and slips the knife out of his rucksack. The SS man shouts out abruptly, and Aaron sees that his partner is emerging from one of the buildings.

Aaron puts the knife away and heads back as quickly as he can. But before he even gets to the end of the block, he hears the big Nazi's screaming voice, *"Raus! Schnell!"*—Get out! Fast!

Aaron turns and sees the younger German herding a family out from the building at gunpoint. They are clearly a Jewish family, identified by the yellow Star of David on their coats. Aaron has been wearing a yellow band on his arm distinguishing him as a Jew for years already, but seeing Jewish stars on civilians' coats is brand new to him.

He crouches in the shadows, virtually frozen in place, and watches as the taller SS man frisks the Jews: father, mother, and two young children—while the younger man keeps them at gunpoint. When the taller German gets to the woman, he turns her around roughly and discovers that she is concealing an infant beneath her coat. The woman screams hysterically as the Nazi rips the child from her arms and tosses it into the air. The big SS man aims and fires, as if this is target practice, shredding the baby in mid-air, its bloody pieces splattering on the icy pavement. The two Nazis laugh uncontrollably, admiring their work.

The mother falls to her knees in shock. Aaron flinches and begins to move forward from the shadows, rage building inside him. But then he checks himself, afraid that the Germans will be able to kill him before he has a chance to take his fury out on them.

He remains riveted, watching from a distance, determined to witness their atrocities so that he can one day repay them in kind. The Germans laugh again and share a drink from a flask before continuing their mission.

As Aaron looks on, the Nazis make the father and children kneel, and watch while the taller one pushes the mother to the ground. He gropes her, then rips her clothes off, unfastens his pants and rapes her. The children whimper, tears streaming down their cheeks. When he is finished, his partner takes his turn with her.

Afterward, they allow the woman to dress, then wave the whole family away. As they run off, the SS officers level their guns and shoot at their legs. The parents are the first to stagger and fall. The children, presenting smaller targets, get farther before they, too, have their legs shot out from under them. They continue to crawl, leaving a trail of blood, their lives slowly ebbing away, between sobs of anguish and screams of pain. When their work is complete, the two SS men share another drink from the younger one's flask. A squad of Nazi soldiers assemble before the two officers, who gesture toward the building from which they have rousted the family. In short order, more families with Jewish stars on their sleeves are rounded up and given the same treatment.

"Juden Schwein! All this just whets my appetite," says the big Nazi to his partner. "Now, I want to put an end to that cocky little Jew-slave, the one who carries the water. Haven't seen him around lately. He seems to be avoiding me."

"I heard he's clever," says the younger German.

"Don't ever say that! No Jew is clever!"

"Word is," says the younger SS man, "He killed an armed Hungarian soldier with his bare hands in a fight to the death."

"That's all the more reason to get him, the sooner, the better, before the morale of the other stinking kikes goes up. They may already think they've got a King David amongst them. They could even start a Jewish revolt! Let's go find him in the slave camps tonight," fumes the big Nazi, with death-heads in his eyes.

Aaron tears himself away. He's overheard enough about his fate and knows that he'll have to finally escape, and soon.

As he slowly retreats, he hears more screams and smells smoke—the peculiar odor he had experienced before, at Davidóvka—the smell of burning human flesh.

That evening, Aaron knows he can't take a chance on being discovered by his Nazi tormentors back in camp. So he finds another abandoned building he feels is safe enough to hide in for a few hours. It is past midnight when the voices outside fall silent. Aaron peers through a cracked opening.

Moving covertly along the moonlit streets, he reaches the area where he has witnessed the day's atrocities, the air thick with the smell of smoke and burnt flesh. Bodies litter the street, their blood frozen and glistening on the pavement. In front of the building, bundles hang from the lampposts. As Aaron approaches, he can see that the bundles are children, hanging from wires.

Horrified, he staggers away and chooses another route. At last he reaches the part of town near the well to get some water for his journey and stops, pressing himself against a wall.

The tall beastly SS officer wanting to kill him is kneeling at the well. Aaron looks around—no partner in sight—no one else at all.

He pauses a moment longer before deciding to balance the scales, however slightly. Approaching the German from behind, he calls out casually: *"Lassen Sie mich Ihnen helfen."*—Let me help you.

"Danke"—Thank you. The German stands up, his back to Aaron, holding out the rope for the bucket.

Instead of taking the rope, Aaron springs forward and grabs the Nazi from behind, slipping his right arm around the big man's throat and yanking with all his might, crushing his windpipe.

Unable to cry out, the SS man begins to wheeze and gasp for air, desperately reaching for his gun. Aaron uses his free hand to grab the man's arm, simultaneously kicking the backs of his knees to force him down, keeping him immobile.

"Es wird Zeit für eine kill?" Aaron hisses into the Nazi's ear over and over—"It's time for a kill? Time for killing me? Remember saying that, captain?"

"No…not about…you," rasps the German in a desperate, barely audible whisper.

"Liar!" says Aaron as he releases his chokehold just slightly. "Who then? Who were you talking about killing?"

"The…the other Jew. The cripple…who walks with a limp," says the brute. "He's no good to anybody, anyway."

Aaron instantly knows who he means: Limpy! In a furious rage, he tightens his chokehold on the beast's windpipe, determined not to let go until he's squeezed the last breath out of him.

The SS officer is large and strong, but he is up against a Jew whose inferno of rage is built by four-and-a-half years of indignity, humiliation, and brutality. Aaron is spurred on further by the unspeakable atrocities to the Jewish families, the women and children, still fresh in his mind. The big Nazi is no match for the smallish farmer from Bielka.

When the German's wheezing becomes labored with guttural grunts and groans as the only sounds coming out of his mouth, his body begins to slump. Aaron frees his left hand to drive his long knife deep into the Nazi's belly, slowly pulling it upward, all the way up to his breastbone, ripping open his flesh. The German begins to writhe uncontrollably as his blood and guts, his intestines and other organs, pour out onto the muddy stones near the well.

At last, Aaron lets go and the body collapses, lifeless. Aaron withdraws the knife from the Nazi's gut and stares at his dead tormentor, watching for any signs of life. He then wipes the knife blade on the SS officer's uniform, slips it back into his rucksack, and then runs for his life back to the slave encampment, never looking backward, desperate not to be discovered.

Aaron spends a sleepless night in his blanket, his knife at the ready. Just before dawn, alarms start blaring all over the campsite. The slaves stir while Aaron grips his knife, preparing to make a final stand, in the event that the dead Nazi's younger SS partner and his troops are coming for him. The tent flap opens, and Miklos appears.

"Wake up, sleeping bastards. Time to get moving"

"What's going on?" asks Aaron.

"There's a big battle brewing," says Miklos. "We're marching back to the front."

The slaves hurriedly pack, then begin marching. Their path takes them past the well, where several German soldiers are gathered around a body, now covered by a thick woolen blanket that fails to conceal the pool of blood on the ground around it.

The marching slaves and Hungarian soldiers turn their heads to gawk as they pass by, while Aaron glances briefly.

"Another Jew?" asks Limpy, struggling to march by Aaron.

"No. A Nazi."

"Your luck changed last night?" smiles Limpy.

"Apparently so—for both of us. More than you know."

---

8 See the map page 296 (Southern Russian Front April – July 1943).

CHAPTER 13

SAX

ON A BITTERLY COLD morning in November 1943, outside the town of Dubno, a horse-drawn wagon emerges from the swirl of thick falling snow and moves slowly into camp.[9]

Aaron, looking gaunt, pauses from gathering water and walks to the roadside to stand next to Limpy to watch.

"What is it? Someone dead?" Aaron asks.

"No, deliverance from death," says Limpy, pointing to the back of the wagon, which holds a shiny metal field kitchen.

The sight is gratifying for the thousand Hungarian troops who would now enjoy a hot meal, and salvation for the hundreds of Jews who could now escape starvation.

The wagon lumbers on to the edge of a field and stops. The driver gets off and unstraps the equipment, which promptly slides off the wagon and falls into the deep snow. Then the driver climbs back onto the wagon and drives off, leaving soldiers and slaves to gather around the object of their mouth-watering hopes.

After a few minutes, the captain comes forward to examine the field kitchen, which is buried so deep in the snow that only the top is visible. He then walks over to the Jews.

"Our friend with the wagon seems to have left us with a little problem," he begins. "We have a nice new kitchen, but as of now it can only cook snow. Who among you Jewish scum will lift it out?"

The fatigued Jews watch with varying expressions of despair, deprivation, and longing, but for a long moment, no one says anything. No one even moves. All are weak and exhausted. Many can barely stand. At last, Aaron begins to step forward, but Limpy stops him.

"You can't move that," he says. "It's a trap. You will fail and then you'll be punished."

"If no one volunteers, we'll all be punished," replies Aaron, as he pushes his way to the front of the group and raises his hand.

The captain nods to him, points to the field kitchen, then gestures to a spot on the road where he wants it moved. As Aaron trudges forward through the deepening snow, the field kitchen seems to grow larger. He dusts off some of the snow and gives it a slight push. It doesn't budge. He stops at one of its corners and tries to lift it. Despite strenuous effort, the kitchen again does not move. Then he digs down into the snow, turns his back to the field kitchen, positioning himself under its overhanging edge. He then takes a breath and pushes with his legs.

The crowd's murmurings grow louder, which only inspire Aaron to push harder. He lets out a groan that swells into a full-throated yell as he pushes. Still, the kitchen fails to budge. He pushes again, yelling even louder, but this time he can hear a lower, grunting voice merging with his own, almost in unison.

He wonders, *am I hearing things? Am I delirious?*

To Aaron's shock, the kitchen moves, slowly at first and then with such speed that Aaron falls over backward. A cheer rises up from the slaves. Aaron turns around to see that the field kitchen is now resting at the side of the road, fully delivered from its snowy berth. Looming over him is a man who appears larger than anyone he has ever seen—well over six and a half feet tall, with a thick neck, massive arms and legs, and a wide red face. This man looks down at Aaron with eyes so deep and black that Aaron recoils. Then the man reaches out with a meaty hand and hoists Aaron to his feet. Aaron continues to stare at him.

"Herskowitz is my name," says Aaron, finally.

"Ignatz Sax," says the brute in a low rumbling tone that quickly explains where the second voice had come from.

They shake hands while Aaron continues to stare, astonished. "Where did you come from?" he asks.

"Béregszasz, in the Carpathians."

"I know Béregszasz well," says Aaron. "I grew up in nearby Bielka, so we were neighbors."

The captain walks over to them. "Well, I'm glad to see you two are useful instead of useless. What kind of work do you know?"

"I was a butcher," Sax says.

The captain looks at Aaron, "I was a farmer."

"You will both work in the kitchen. That is your reward." He points to Sax, saying, "You will be our cook." He then points to Aaron. "You will manage the water, gather the wood, light the fire."

The captain orders them to haul the kitchen to the farmhouse. Needless to say, it takes hours. Sax does much of the heavy lifting, with Aaron helping out as best he can.

"Why haven't I seen you before?" asks Aaron, breathing heavily.

"My group was transferred here last night from near Kiev."

"How long have you been a slave?"

"A year," says Sax.

"How do you—?" Aaron asks, gesturing to Sax's massive arms and shoulders. The man looks like an Olympic weight lifter, with huge muscles bulging everywhere.

"They make all butchers like me into cooks," grunts Sax. "But it gives me access to food. And whenever we're low, I steal from the farmhouses at night when I get the chance."

Aaron smiles. "Me, too. And from stores and warehouses."

"I never thought of stores or warehouses," says Sax.

"You should have," says Aaron, smiling.

A Hungarian soldier supervises when Sax sets up the kitchen while Aaron gathers wood and starts a fire. Sax soon has big pots of soup boiling on the stove for dinner. The Hungarians and Germans are, of course, served before the Jews. Sax, as the chief cook, serves each soldier his portion, pouring soup into each man's bowl with a heavy steel serving spoon. Higher-ranking officers are served privately.

The Jews are given whatever is left over when the Hungarians and Germans have finished eating. The slaves know not to expect too much. Aaron walks single file like all the other slaves in line, passing the table where Sax pours the soup, holding the bowls for those too weak to do it themselves.

After Aaron has eaten his portion, he notices the line has grown shorter but senses the pot still half-full. He decides to slip back in line even though he knows that no Jew is allowed a second helping. He looks around—the only soldiers in sight are sitting off to the side, self-absorbed with eating, drinking, and laughing. He figures they'll be too busy to notice what he is doing.

Back in line, Aaron holds up his bowl to Sax, who promptly picks up the heavy metal ladle. A hard abrupt thump follows, and Aaron realizes that he's been hit on the head, now seeing stars, half-kneeling by the table. Sax has struck him with the big metal spoon.

Sax immediately helps Aaron to his feet, clearly regretting what he has done. Aaron, for his part, is shocked that a fellow Jew would strike him, deserved or not, but later would come to realize that this is very much in Sax's character—reactions of impulsiveness and violence that would later prove both a boon and a danger to both of them.

The next morning, Aaron's head is still sore from his encounter with Sax's ladle. With his stomach howling and empty, he delivers a load of wood to the field kitchen. Sax is already stirring two large pots when Aaron notices several sacks of potatoes lying by the stove. Deciding to take a different approach to securing extra morsels of food, he begins peeling the potatoes.

"What are you doing?" asks Sax.

"Lending a hand," replies Aaron.

"Suit yourself," grumbles Sax.

The two men work side by side in silence.

"How many are you feeding this morning?" asks Aaron.

"The usual; a few hundred. Hungarian scum first."

"How do you know it's any good?"

"What does *that* mean?" asks Sax angrily.

"If they don't like your soup, they'll take it out on you, and maybe on me, too."

"I've never had any complaints," says Sax.

"I think I should taste it to be sure."

Sax glares at him. Aaron taps the lump on his head. "You owe me," he says.

Sax glances around. The nearest Hungarian is leaning against a farmhouse wall, smoking. Sax half-fills the ladle and lets Aaron take a sip.

"Not bad," says Aaron. "I think you should taste it too, just to be sure. A whole ladleful."

Sax finally catches Aaron's drift. He nods and drinks himself.

"I think it needs onions," Aaron says. Sax agrees and cuts some up for him. The two spend the morning helping each other by tasting the soup and adding ingredients in order to perfect the recipe.

After Aaron has his fill, he goes out to gather more wood and manages to scrounge up a live chicken from an abandoned barn. He brings it to Sax, who promptly tears off the feathers while the animal screeches and protests violently, and then wraps the chicken's neck tightly around his big forefinger and rips its head off. As Aaron watches, Sax sucks the blood out of each end of the chicken's neck he's just ripped apart, slurping loudly. Then Sax eats the chicken while it is still alive.

"Most butchers I've known use a knife for that—to slice necks," says Aaron.

"I'm practicing," says Sax.

"Practicing? For what?"

Sax lowers his voice. "For when I finally get my hands on some of these German and Hungarian bastards."

Aaron nods. "For that, I still prefer a knife."

"I'd give up one of my balls to get my hands on a gun," says Sax.

"You know how to use one?" asks Aaron.

"I served in the Czech Army."

"Me too," says Aaron. "Till our 'allies' sold us out."

"I still can't believe what I've seen here," Aaron continues. "Nazis rounding up Jewish families and killing them in the streets, throwing babies up in the air for target practice, raping the women."

"I've seen it all over the Russian front," says Ignatz.

Aaron shakes his head in disbelief, teeming with pent-up revenge.

Sax stops working and looks directly at Aaron. "Listen, Aaron, I owe you an apology."

"For what?"

"For smashing you on the head last night. I want you to know—that wasn't me."

"Then who was it?" Aaron inquires.

"When I lose my temper, something comes over me. But it'll never happen again—I mean, with you."

"You mean, I get a second helping now?" asks Aaron.

"No. I mean because we're friends now. We're alike, you and me. I haven't found any other Jews who've survived like us. Most of them just give up and die—if the Germans or Hungarians don't shoot them first. But you, like me—want revenge."

"For me, survival is first," says Aaron. "Then what I want is to escape, to be free again. But most of all, I want justice against all these bastards—the Hungarians, the Germans, all of them."

"Count me in," says Sax. "We'll make a good team. And besides, you speak Russian. That'll help because I don't."

Aaron spoons soup into two cups and hands one to Sax, gesturing a toast. "To freedom!"

"And vengeance," Sax adds, as they clink their cups, smiling wryly.

Thus, the two men become the best of friends, forming a strange yet inseparable partnership, an odd couple indeed—Sax, the giant of a man with a violent and unpredictable temper—Aaron, the short man, equally as tough but pragmatic. Sax fosters respect for Aaron, especially upon learning of Aaron's courageous "Retreat!" order at the Vóronezh battlefront and his fights to the death against Nazi and Hungarian assassins who were out to kill him.

The two men share humor between military campaigns, playing practical jokes on one another, with Sax often serving as a willing foil to Aaron's antics. He settles into his new role as Aaron's sidekick with relative ease. With Sax, Aaron has certainly met his match. This hulk of a man meets every one of Aaron's challenges. Their actions lift the spirits of the slaves. Sax feels a need to display his bravado, eating animals while they are still alive. He grabs huge, wild jumping bullfrogs, spreading their legs apart, then biting into their torsos and chewing them alive. Some of the men can't watch. He is the most bizarre man Aaron has ever encountered.

Separate from Sax's unsettling eating habits, it has been a long time since Aaron has shared in such comradery. All of Aaron's friends on the God-forsaken Russian front have been lost or perished, leaving an atmosphere of gloom in their wake. But his new friendship with Sax and getting jobs in the kitchen for Limpy and Lederer, another friend and cook, portend a lifeline to hope. He also realizes that he no longer needs to take the risk of scavenging for extra food at night.

Aaron understands that Sax is not the type of man that he would normally befriend back home. But the forces of war create strange bedfellows, and Aaron senses that if he is to ever escape and exact vengeance, he could use a man like Ignatz Sax by his side.

The two men do their best to see that the other slaves are fed, spooning out the stew from the top of the pot for the Hungarians, while scooping from the bottom with its richer content of meat, flour and beans—for the Jews.

Meanwhile, German Field Marshal von Manstein has pulled off another brilliant defensive maneuver as 1943 draws to a close, and 1944 begins. His entire army is trapped and surrounded along the Dnieper River, because Hitler has issued another "No retreat!" order, commanding that "All soldiers will fight to the last man."

Von Manstein correctly calculates that this order will spell the destruction of his entire army group. In defiance of the Fuhrer's orders, Von Manstein shifts the bulk of his forces to the weakest corridor of the Russian encirclement and brilliantly escapes with virtually all his men, allowing them to fight another day, prolonging the war and further buoying the Germans' hopes.

---

9 See the map page 297 (Southern Russian Front July – December 1943).

CHAPTER 14

ESCAPE FROM THE NAZIS AND HUNGARIANS

DURING THE FIRST HALF of 1944, as the Russians resume their relentless assault, Hitler commits another crucial error. He fires one of his finest generals on the Eastern Front, Field Marshal von Manstein. The Field Marshal and Hitler's top generals recommend an orderly retreat against overwhelming odds. Hitler becomes enraged at their "defeatist" attitude, and instead issues another one of his preposterous "no retreat" commands. Von Manstein, who realizes this order could complete the destruction of the German army, can no longer contain himself. According to eyewitnesses at "Wolf's Lair," Hitler's secret headquarters, Von Manstein, in an act of involuntary defiance, mocks Hitler and repeats the Fuhrer's orders while mimicking Hitler's unique, crazed mannerisms. Hitler does not appreciate the impersonation and begins screaming abusive and profane threats at the Field Marshal before declaring that von Manstein would never serve in the German armed forces again.

On a cool March in the late afternoon, Aaron is stirring a pot of soup on the field kitchen stove, as he and Sax prepare to feed the soldiers and slaves near an expanse of rolling hills in the Ukraine.

Miklos, now promoted to corporal, comes running over to them.

"How about an early dinner?" he asks.

"Why?" replies Aaron.

"I'm going on furlough—truck is leaving."

"You'll have to wait," says Aaron.

"Don't be an ass, Aaron."

"What can you give me for risking punishment for your sake?" asks Aaron.

"A letter—from home."

Miklos smiles and holds out an envelope. Aaron seizes it and rips it open.

"Help yourself," says Miklos, scooping up a bowl of soup while Aaron reads rapaciously, his face growing increasingly troubled. He hasn't received any word from his family or from Helen since being shipped to the Russian front, although he has written to them at every opportunity.

Sax comes over to him. "What is it?"

"I don't understand. It's a letter from my mother and sisters." Aaron reads aloud: "We have written many letters to you, but we never hear back. Avrum is very bad to us, and we are scared of what he will do." Aaron looks up. "But I don't know any 'Avrum.'"

"It's been a while since you've been home," says Miklos between mouthfuls. "Surely you don't know everyone in Slovakia."

Aaron nods, then says abruptly: "Adolf."

Sax and Miklos look at Aaron quizzically.

"'Avrum' must be her code for Adolf,'" says Aaron. "She must be worried about censors."

Aaron continues reading the letter aloud, "We have not had chicken for many Sabbaths now." He looks up. "Food is scarce."

Aaron reads more: "We have sewn bright yellow stars on our clothes." Aaron shudders as he recalls the yellow Star of David on the sleeves of the Jewish families he witnessed being raped and murdered by the Nazis in Pinsk and elsewhere.

Aaron continues. "The cut on Leah's head is healing well." He stands up and looks at Sax. "They've been victims of violence."

Sax nods. "At least they are still alive, Aaron. I haven't heard from my family at all, and I have a wife and two children."

Aaron quickly skims the rest of the letter, then looks over at Miklos, who is finishing his soup. "Miklos," he says, digging into his pockets and pulling out a stash of cigarettes. "On your way back home, could you stop in my town? Bielka?"

Miklos shrugs. "Hmmm, I guess so. It's not too far."

"Here. Do me a favor. Find my uncle, Joseph Klein. It'll be easy. He has a grocery store in the center of town. Give him some of these cigarettes and ask him about my mother and sisters."

"I'll see what I can do, Aaron."

"And as long as you're there," he continues, digging up more cigarettes out of his pocket, "There is a farm just outside of town. The name is Lazárovic."

"Yes?" says Miklos, inquisitively.

"Ask about Helen." He holds out more cigarettes to Miklos.

"It will take more cigarettes than that, Aaron," says Miklos.

"Please. That's all I have," says Aaron.

Miklos shakes his head, then smiles. "Put them away. I will try to find her, and if I do, I'll tell her you'll be back to her soon."

During the weeks that follow, Aaron waits anxiously for news from Miklos. However, the Germans and Hungarians are retreating so rapidly now, that at times he thinks he could reach Bielka before Miklos returns.

Later that spring, as Aaron is again stirring a pot of soup, this time outside a barn on a small farm in the Western Ukraine, a jovial middle-aged farmer named Sergei emerges from the farmhouse carrying a warm sweet cake.

"What's this?" asks Aaron.

"An exchange for that sugar you gave me. You see, it's the miracle of the oven. Sugar and flour become cake, especially if my wife has anything to do with it."

Aaron takes a piece as does Sax.

"She put that sugar to good use," says Aaron.

Sergei sets the cake down. "There'll be more soon. My daughter's baking one. She's even better than my wife." Sergei had mentioned that he was seeking a suitor for his daughter.

"She can visit any time," smiles Aaron.

"Aaron, I think your friend is back," says Lederer, pointing at a truck just arriving at the campsite.

Aaron sets down his ladle and rushes over to the truck from which troops have already begun to disembark. Sure enough, he spots Miklos, who waves to him.

"They are okay," says Miklos.

"Thank God," Aaron sighs with relief.

"But things are very difficult."

"Who did you talk to?"

"I found your uncle. His shop was closed, the windows had big Jewish stars painted on them. But I asked some friendly townspeople where he lived, and I found him. He says your family is coping; it sounds like they're doing okay."

Miklos continues. "But I have bad news about your farm, Aaron. Most of the land no longer belongs to you and your family. The Hungarian government confiscated it, then subdivided it into eighteen different new homesteads. Hungarian families have moved in to occupy them."

Aaron shakes his head in disbelief. Miklos continues on, "Here's some good news for you. Your sister Sarah got married, though she had to do it secretly."

"What do you mean, 'secretly?'" asks Aaron.

"Jews are now forbidden to marry—not even to another Jew," says Miklos. "So Sarah got married in a quiet ceremony in the backyard of your older sister Hannah.

"What?" says Aaron, incredulous. "So *that's* their plan—to wipe out the Jewish race. No more marriages, so no more Jewish children."

Aaron feels anger rising within him. He then asks, "What about Helen?"

"On my way out of town, I finally found her. She was wearing a yellow Jewish star."

Aaron says in anger, "A yellow star? That means the beginning of the end!" Aaron recalls the savage public torture and murders of Russian Jews wearing yellow stars.

Miklos continues, "Helen burst into tears when I told her you were alive and well. She never got your letters. She thought you'd perished long ago, but this news gave her hope, in spite of—"

"In spite of what, Miklos?"

"Her father. He was taking a walk when some Hungarian gendarmes called out to him. He's elderly and hard-of-hearing, so he didn't respond. They beat him up pretty badly, believing he was defying them."

"Bastards," says Aaron.

"You know, Aaron, I'm not one of them—not anymore."

"No. You're one of the good guys now, Miklos."

"I envy you, Aaron."

"You envy me? A slave?"

"She is very beautiful. To have the love of a woman like that—well, I told her not to worry—either God or one of His angels must be watching over you."

"Thank you, Miklos. I won't forget this. You've lifted much darkness from my life with this news."

"I'm glad," says Miklos, now turning away.

Aaron, sensing that he had something more to say, holds out a hand to stop him. "What is it, Miklos? Something wrong?"

"Yes. In every Hungarian-controlled town that I passed through, even my own, things were getting worse for Jews."

"Worse, how?" asks Aaron, anxious all over again.

"So many yellow stars, random beatings increasing. In some towns, the Jews are gone. Disappeared. And—"

He pauses.

"What is it?" says Aaron.

"The Germans are taking over Hungary, occupying everything. And they have plans."

"What plans?" asks Aaron fervently, growing more fearful.

"All the Jews are going to Germany and Poland!" shouts a soldier who overhears Aaron's conversation, getting off a truck.

Aaron turns to him. "What do you mean?"

"I mean all of you people. And your families, too. You are going to concentration camps."

"Not *my* family," says Aaron. "Not the Jews from *my* town. I just got a letter from my family last month."

"I don't know anything about your Jews or your town," the soldier says. "That letter you got is probably six months old, maybe more. It's a miracle you got it at all."

The soldier moves away while another soldier hops off the truck. "They are going to burn you up," he says wryly.

Aaron swings around to face this one. "What do you mean?"

The third soldier shrugs. "I heard the Germans are taking all the Jews to Poland and Germany to exterminate them."

The truck had begun to pull away when a voice cries out: "Halt!" It is a Hungarian sergeant, running from the command post. Fast on his heels is the captain.

"We are moving out tonight! In two hours! Move! Move! Move! Get ready."

Instantly, the scene is a mad scramble of soldiers and officers as a murmur of voices repeat that the Russians have broken through. Aaron stops the last soldier who has spoken to him.

"Where did you hear this? About the burning of the Jews."

"I don't know. Ask the captain."

Aaron makes his way through the chaos and catches up with the captain.

"Sir," he says. "I have heard that all Hungarian Jews here are being sent to concentration camps to be burned. Is this true?"

"You need to get your things together, Aaron."

"Please, sir. Is this *true*?"

The captain stares at Aaron, then says, "We have orders to take you to the German border and turn you over to the Germans. After that, I do not know."

"But the Germans—they'll surely kill us."

"I'm sorry, Aaron. You're a hard worker. But it's beyond my control." The captain disappears inside Sergei's farmhouse.

Aaron watches for a moment as the troops scramble to pack and assemble, then rushes back to the slaves who are quickly gathering their belongings. He repeats what he has heard to Sax, then to Lederer, the slave he has befriended in the kitchen.

"Impossible!" cries Lederer. "The Germans are losing the war. They still need us to do their dirty work now more than ever."

"What if they don't?" asks Aaron. "We need to escape tonight—to join the Russians. I know that the two of you don't speak Russian, but I know the Russian language. The three of us can make it."

"What if we're caught trying to escape? We'll be shot on sight. That's a chance I'm not willing to take, Aaron," says Lederer.

"Well, I'm escaping tonight," Aaron insists. "If you two want to stay with the Hungarians and the Germans, then do so. But I am not."

The Jews assemble and march in groups of fifty, each group guarded by one Hungarian soldier, their pathway lit by the glow of a fuel dump that has been blown up earlier by a Soviet air attack and whose fires now rage uncontrollably. The imagery is not lost on Aaron, especially after what he's heard about the burning of the Jews. He feels he is marching into the inferno. He can feel the heat on his face as each step brings him closer to it.

After marching for miles through open fields and rolling pastures ill-suited for Aaron's escape, the column at last reaches the edge of a tall cornfield. Aaron moves closer to Sax as they march beside the cornfield and fall behind the column in the darkness.

"This is it," he whispers. "This is our chance. We can hide in the cornfield, double back, and wait for the Russians."

Sax nods. The two are about to break away when Miklos rushes over. But instead of scolding them, he whispers, "What are you up to? Are you going to make a run for it?"

"You want to go with us?" Aaron asks.

"Go with you?" Miklos repeats, surprised.

Aaron nods and points, "We'll be safe. I speak Russian, I'll protect you."

Miklos looks around; no Hungarian troops are in sight. "You know? I would. We've protected each other this far, Aaron."

"Yes."

"But I cannot," says Miklos. "But I do think it's wise if you can escape, my friend. Be careful and make it quick. Good luck."

Miklos drops back to his position.

Then Lederer moves over to them as they march, asking, "What were you saying to Miklos?"

"Now is the time to escape," says Aaron. "Either you want to go with us, or you don't. Which is it?"

Lederer stops walking, and Sax and Aaron stop with him. Corporal Miklos exhorts the rest of the company to move past them.

Lederer trembles and rubs his hands together, "God, oh God! What should I do? Should I do it? God, please help me!"

"This is no time to ask God for anything," says Aaron. "It's up to you, not God. And since when did you become so religious? All you sell is *cházar* (pigs) in your store back home."

Lederer remains frozen, looking to the sky for an answer, still rubbing his hands together as if to wear the skin away, cracking his finger joints. The rest of the company has already moved past, and they now hear the tramping of the next company approaching in the darkness. So far, no one seems to notice them.

"Well, Lederer?" asks Aaron. "What are you going to do?"

Lederer only prays, staring down at his feet. Sax nods to Aaron, and the two of them sprint for the safety of the cornfields, leaving Lederer standing in the road, awaiting his signal from God. The signal never does come for Lederer—he and the rest of the slaves will meet their end at the Buchenwald concentration camp.

Aaron and Sax move a considerable distance into the field and crouch down and wait. After a few moments, they can hear someone approaching. They exchange worried glances.

"Lederer?" whispers Aaron.

Sax shrugs. "Or Hungarians. Or Germans"

Aaron nods, slipping the knife out of his rucksack.

Soon enough, the intruder appears, out of breath. It's Limpy. Aaron puts away his knife.

"Limpy! What are you doing here?"

"I'm escaping with you."

"You can't," says Sax. "We're going to be moving fast. You'll never be able to keep up. Go back to the column."

"No," replies Limpy.

"It will be dangerous for you—and for us" says Sax.

"No, Ignatz," says Aaron. "Limpy stays with us." How could Aaron deny Limpy, a fellow Jew and a trusted friend?

The three wait in silence, listening for the marching of the Hungarian troops. At last there is silence, and they move to the edge of the cornfield. They begin their slow trek backward toward the Russians, staying as far to the side of the road as possible.

They arrive back at Sergei's farm just before dawn and slip into the barn, startling the farmer who is milking his cows.

The farmer soon recognizes Aaron. "What are you doing here, Aaron?"

"Sergei, are there any German or Hungarian troops nearby?" whispers Aaron.

Sergei lowers his voice. "No. Everyone left last night. What's going on?"

"Didn't they tell you?" asks Aaron.

"I haven't been told anything."

"The Russian army is on its way. They should be here in the next few hours."

Sergei drops his milk pail and stands up, clearly upset.

"Oh my God," he says. "What will they do? I've let both the Hungarians and German soldiers stay in my house. They'll call me a traitor. You know what the Russians do to people who help the Germans? They'll kill me and rape my wife and daughter."

"But now you are helping *us*," says Aaron. "I speak their language. I can protect you."

"You? A Jew can protect me?" Sergei questions.

"Yes—but we need a place to hide until they get here."

Sergei hesitates.

Aaron explains further, "Sergei, I'll marry your daughter. That way, she'll be safer from the Russians."

"You'll marry her?"

"Of course. It would be my honor, Sergei."

"Good. You must meet her," says Sergei, smiling.

"That's okay," says Aaron. "I can meet her another time."

Sergei waves him off and quickly goes to the farmhouse.

Of course, Aaron has other plans with respect to marriage, those involving one Helen Lazárovic of Bielka. But survival and expedience of the day forces his response to Sergei and forces it quickly.

In a corner of the barn, Sax, who is munching on a hunk of freshly baked bread, looks at Aaron and shakes his head. "Why do *you* get the girl?"

Aaron shrugs. "I know Russian."

"You'll have to teach me."

Sergei quickly returns with his wife, both of them carrying blankets and food.

"Up there," he says, pointing to the loft. After Aaron and Sax climb up, Sergei and his wife hand them supplies. Limpy then tries to get up to the loft but can't.

"He can stay with us in the cellar," says Sergei. Aaron nods.

The farmer and his wife escort Limpy out of the barn.

After a short while, Sergei reappears, accompanied by a young woman with long auburn hair, which complements her red dress. Aaron jumps down from the loft and smiles, then recoils slightly. He has been around horses all his life, and in that instant, he realizes he's cared for many horses who had more sex appeal than the farmer's daughter. He smiles as best he can. Sax grins from his perch on the loft.

"Aaron, this is Natasha," says Sergei.

"I'm honored to meet you, Natasha. I wish I had flowers for you," flirts Aaron, almost convincingly, as he takes her hand.

"Quite all right," she replies shyly. "I understand."

"That's a beautiful dress. Did you make it yourself?"

"Thank you, yes. My mother helped stitch the buttonholes, but I did the rest."

"The buttonholes are very fine," says Aaron. "But I like the rest of the dress even better."

"Thank you," she blushes.

"Well, I shouldn't keep you, Natasha."

"You're not keeping her at all," says Sergei. "Take your time. Take all day."

"I need to hide—it's still quite dangerous," says Aaron.

"You're right," Sergei agrees. "Maybe she can visit tonight and bring you a meal."

"I would like that very much," smiles Aaron. "Nice meeting you, Natasha."

"Likewise," she replies.

Sergei takes Natasha by the arm and escorts her out of the barn as Aaron climbs back up to the loft and sighs.

"You still want to learn Russian, Ignatz?"

"Teach me at the wedding," he laughs.

That evening, as the two men eat the meal that Natasha has brought them, Aaron suddenly stops to listen intently. Sax hears it, too—the distant clomping of horses, the squeaking of wagon wheels, the marching of soldiers.

"This is it!" says Sax.

Aaron nods. "The Russians. We'll wait for them to get to the barn, and then I'll call out to them."

Aaron and Sax wait perfectly still in the darkness, listening to the sounds drawing closer. There is a knock on the door to the barn, and Aaron can hear voices, though he can't make out what is being said.

At last, they hear a contingent of boot steps approaching the barn. The steps pause near the entrance. There is hearty laughter. Then at last, words: *"Du bist ein Idiot. Dafür schuldest du mir ein Bier"*—You are an idiot. You owe me a beer. A second voice replies, *"Klar doch, aber erst wenn du mir die Zigaretten gibst, die du mir noch schuldest."*—Sure, but you owe me a cigarette.

Aaron's eyes widen, then he slumps in dismay. "Germans!" he whispers to Sax. "What are *they* doing here?"

Although the Hungarians are the first to retreat from battle, their German allies are the last to give up ground to the advancing Russians. Unbelievably, the two Jews are now hiding out in a barn in the middle of a German encampment outside.

"Quickly—the bread—the smell!" says Aaron.

Sax looks at the bread, then breaks the loaf in two and hands half to Aaron. The two wolf it down quietly and continue to listen.

Well into the night, they hear shouting, coarse drunken laughter accompanied by reckless gunfire, and the smell of cigarette smoke. Sporadic fights break out among the drunken Germans. At last, the door to the barn opens and two Nazi officers enter with a lantern. Aaron holds his knife at the ready, while the two poke around. He glances over at Sax for reassurance—and finds him fast asleep. *Incredible*, thinks Aaron, at the very time when he could have used

Sax's strength and fearlessness to fight back and help make a stand. The last thing he wants is to be caught alive by the Germans.

Aaron glares at his sleeping comrade, while the German officers, still conversing loudly, gather piles of hay to use for bedding. He is thankful when they fall asleep.

All that night, while Sax sleeps, Aaron keeps a silent, fearful vigil. When the lantern runs out of fuel, Aaron is left in the darkness with the smell of alcohol and heavy breathing as the only evidence of the Germans lying not more than a dozen feet away.

Before dawn, there is much activity and shouting outside. The two German officers beneath the loft groan loudly as they pull themselves to their feet and grab their firearms and leave. Aaron can hear the distinct sound of marching men, followed by a period of quiet, before the barn door swings open again.

"Aaron—are you here?" comes Natasha's sweet voice as she enters the barn holding a breakfast tray with porridge and bread. "They've gone."

At last Aaron stirs.

"You're sure?" he calls out.

"Yes. All of them. And we're lucky—my father says there are Germans asking farmers to hide them. Two of them wanted to stay here but Father convinced them it wouldn't be safe yet."

Rapid footsteps are heard outside, and then Sergei appears at the door, out of breath.

"They're coming! The Russians this time. I'm sure of it."

"Go back to the house. Don't say anything," orders Aaron.

"No, no," pleads Sergei. "I need you to talk to them, Aaron. You need to help me now. My family. Please!"

"I promise you that I will, Sergei, but you can't give us away until we are sure it is safe for all of us."

Sergei nods and leads his daughter out of the barn, only to return a moment later.

"Aaron—they are headed right for the barn!"

The two Jews shrink deep into the loft and wait. Again, Aaron can hear voices. Sax looks to Aaron.

"Russians," Aaron whispers.

They wait until they can clearly hear footsteps entering the barn. Aaron calls out in as cheerful a voice as he can muster, *"Tovarich! Tovarich!"* Greetings! Greetings!

The soldiers beneath them immediately draw their weapons while a Russian major shouts, "Come down!"

Aaron and Sax leap from the loft, hands raised, hoping their endless nightmare of slavery is finally over.

"We've been held as prisoners of the Hungarian and German armies, but we escaped in order to join you," says Aaron in Russian. "We wish to fight the enemy alongside the Russian army."

The Russian major, a strong burly man with piercing blue eyes, looks them over from head to toe, pointing his revolver at them. "Prisoners, eh? Are you *Yevrai*?"—the Russian idiom for Jews.

"Yes," says Aaron. "We've been toiling as slave laborers of the Germans and Hungarians for many years. There are three of us—one more in the farmhouse, who's injured."

Aaron turns to Sergei, "Please bring Limpy here."

The major assigns one of his soldiers to accompany Sergei, then turns back to Aaron and Sax, his revolver still cocked. "You are Nazi spies."

"No!" says Aaron. "See? They made us wear these." He gestures to the yellow band on his jacket and points to Sax's.

"Yes, you got them from dead Jews somewhere in order to spy on us. Your ruse does not work, *Yevrai*. Sergeant!"

A sergeant steps forward and Aaron, seeing his long-sought freedom evaporating before his eyes, rambles on, grasping at straws. The sergeant stands by, waiting for his next command.

Aaron quickly says, "I come from the Carpathian Mountains, sir. We grew up speaking Russian there. I also speak German, Czech, Polish, and Hungarian."

"We could be very useful to you. I can translate well," says Aaron. "I know we can be of value to the Red Army. We can help interrogate prisoners. We'll do anything you ask. *Anything*."

The major glares at the two Jews for a while, rubbing his chin. Soon enough, Sergei brings Limpy into the barn.

The officer circles around the three Jews, spending extra time assessing Sax's huge stature.

"You want to interrogate prisoners?"

"Yes sir, we can do that," says Aaron. "Anything you need."

"In order to interrogate prisoners, we need prisoners."

"Yes, sir."

Then, almost as a lark, the major says to Aaron, "Then go bring me a prisoner—German or Hungarian. You have six hours."

"Six hours, sir?" Aaron repeats, incredulous.

Sax and Limpy look on, not understanding the conversation, but well aware of Aaron's troubled expression.

"You must prove to us that you are not spies. If you bring us a prisoner, we will know you are telling the truth."

As the major starts to turn away, Aaron speaks up again, "Sir, we cannot capture an armed soldier with our bare hands."

The major stares at Aaron, then Sax and Limpy, for a long while, then commands, "Sergeant? Your gun, please."

The sergeant hands his firearm to the major who promptly empties it of bullets, then hands it to Aaron.

"After you've proven yourself, you get bullets. Good luck."

Aaron, resigned, accepts the empty gun. "Limpy can't come with us," he says. "Can you please look after him here?"

"If you are not back with a prisoner by sunset, he goes to Siberia this evening."

Aaron nods and salutes the major, who spins on his heels and leaves with his men, escorting a very anxious Limpy.

Once the others have gone, Sax walks over to Aaron. "What's going on with the unloaded gun?"

"I think we're in trouble," says Aaron, quickly explaining their predicament.

"Our course of action is simple," Sax says at last. "We have six hours to find a place to hide. Then maybe we can surrender to another Russian unit."

"Then Limpy goes off to Siberia, for sure."

Sax asks to see the gun. "I suppose we could throw it at a German or Hungarian," he says wryly. "It might do some damage."

Aaron, deep in thought, doesn't respond. At that moment, Sergei rushes into the barn, looking agitated. "Have you spoken to them about me?" he asks Aaron. "Have you told them not to harm me or my family?"

Aaron doesn't respond, asking instead, "We need your help."

"With what?" says Sergei.

"The Russians won't listen to anything I say until we bring them an enemy prisoner. I can't save you until you help me do that."

"How can I help?" asks a fearful Sergei.

"You said some farmers around here are hiding German and Hungarian soldiers."

"Did I?" asks Sergei.

"Well, your daughter told us. Sergei, you must take us to a farm where soldiers are being hidden. It's the only chance we have."

Sergei shakes his head from side to side saying 'no' fearfully.

"If you don't, I cannot help you or your family."

Reluctantly, Sergei leads Sax and Aaron down a back road, then pauses. "Over there," he points. "I know they are hiding a German soldier on that farm. In the cellar or stable."

Aaron and Sax nod, then stand, waiting.

Sergei sighs. "I will take you."

He leads them down the dirt road to the farmhouse and knocks on the door. Soon, an elderly farmer appears.

"Dmitri," says Sergei to his neighbor, but before the farmer can respond, Aaron pushes his way inside and points the pistol at the old man's head.

"We know you are hiding a German soldier here," says Aaron. "Turn him over or I'll kill you. Where is he?" asks Aaron, as he cocks the hammer of the empty pistol.

"I've got two," the trembling farmer says. "In the cellar."

"We will put in a good word for you with the Russians," says Aaron. "And these Germans won't be executed if they give themselves up."

"I don't care what you do with them," says the farmer. "But yes, please put in a good word for me." By then, Sergei has disappeared, apparently fleeing Aaron's unexpected violence.

Sax kicks open the cellar door, and Aaron points his gun down the stairs, shouting, *"Sie sind festgenommen!"*—You are under arrest! "Come out with your hands up."

There are footsteps on the cellar stairs when two frightened looking Germans in civilian clothes appear downstairs, their hands raised. Aaron quickly frisks them while Sax holds them at gunpoint.

"Wo sind Ihre Waffen?"—Where are your weapons? Aaron asks.

The taller one gestures to the opposite end of the cellar. Sax rumbles down the stairs and after a few moments, reappears carrying two submachine guns and ammunition.

"Look," Sax says, pointing to the ammunition clips. "Bullets." He tosses one of the guns to Aaron, then smiling, cocks the other and aims it at the Germans.

Aaron puts the Russian sergeant's pistol away and aims the machine gun at the Germans, who look on quizzically. Aaron wonders why they haven't opened fire since possessing such weaponry, but when he looks over their camera, maps, and reconnaissance material, he realizes he's stumbled upon Nazi spies.

Aaron yells, *"Draussen!"*—Outside!

Aaron and Sax push them out into the yard at gunpoint.

"Wo sind Ihre Uniformen?"—Where are your uniforms?

The taller German shrugs his shoulders.

Aaron shouts, *"Also, Sie sind Spione!"*—So, you are spies!

"In the yard," says the shorter soldier, gesturing to a patch of recently disturbed earth.

"Dig!" Aaron commands.

The two bend down on their knees and frantically dig the ground with their hands, quickly uncovering their uniforms.

"Put them on," orders Aaron.

The Germans tremble as they peel off their civilian clothes and put on their filthy uniforms. The farmer returns with rope from the stable, which Aaron uses to tie their hands behind their backs. He then runs his fingers along their shoulder patches and arms, from which Aaron recognizes the uniforms of Nazi officers.

"As officers, you must be very smart," says Aaron. "Smart enough to know that you are now prisoners of war and that no harm will come to you."

"Yes, sir," says the taller German.

Aaron smiles to Sax upon hearing the word "sir" in deference to him, spoken by a high-ranking Nazi officer to a Jewish slave.

"Let's take them back," says Sax.

"Not quite yet," says Aaron, turning his attention back to the prisoners. "Since you are smart men, you will realize that if you help us, we will put in a good word for you with the Russians. That is who we serve."

Both prisoners nod.

"If you help us find where other soldiers are hiding," Aaron says. "I will see that you are treated well."

"If they won't, I will," says the farmer. "I know where more are hiding. I'll get some rope to help you tie them up."

"Good. Then let's get started."

"But please," says the farmer. "Do put in a good word for me with the Russians. I've heard about what they do to families who allow Nazis to stay in their homes, and I have a wife and two daughters."

"You are not to worry, Dmitri," says Aaron. "I'll tell the Russians that you supplied the rope to tie up these Nazi bastards!"

As evening falls, the Russian major is busy doing paperwork in the new command post he's set up in the living room of an elegantly appointed home. Limpy sits nearby, looking apprehensive. The major looks at his watch.

"Your friends are late."

"Major!" calls a soldier standing guard outside. "Come look, sir."

"What is it?" asks the major, walking toward the commotion.

"The Jews!"

Aaron and Sax, weighed down with guns, ammunition, and sacks of booty, are prodding thirteen shackled prisoners by gunpoint: ten Hungarians and three Germans—toward the house.

The major, along with the sergeant and a group of Soviet soldiers, gather 'round and stare as the Jews lead their prisoners to the front of the command post, where Aaron orders them to halt.

Aaron barks to his captives, *"Stillgestanden!"*—Stand at attention!

Aaron goes down the line. "Sir," he says to the Soviet major, "These three are from the Hungarian 32nd Artillery Battery, Third Regiment. These four are from infantry companies attached to the Hungarian 33rd Battalion, also from the Third Regiment. These three are from a Hungarian security detachment. The Nazi officers are part of a reconnaissance platoon left behind to report Russian troop movements."

Aaron and Sax set their bags of booty before the major. "Six submachine guns, seven rifles, twelve hand grenades, eight side arms, and—bullets."

"And one more thing, sir." Aaron slips the sergeant's pistol out of his rucksack and hands it back to him.

"Thank you for letting us borrow this, sir."

The major is smiling from ear to ear, glancing at the sergeant in disbelief.

He bellows at Aaron, *"Khoroshi Molidets!"*—Good man! "How did the two of you capture so many prisoners? And spies— you brought me Nazi spies!"

He then does the unthinkable—he kisses Aaron and Sax on both cheeks, and the Russian troops cheer.

What follows Aaron's and Sax's astonishing capture of the thirteen prisoners remains a swirling blur to Aaron. A celebration quickly ensues where Sax and Aaron are treated to the finest food that the Russians could seize from houses in the vicinity: caviar, small blinis [pancakes] with sour cream—served on fine china. Mahórka [tobacco] is given to them to smoke. They are toasted as heroes, repeatedly— "Na Zdróvia—to our friends, the Jews!" Their glasses are refilled with vodka so many times that they lose track, as their Russian comrades play music on balalaikas and an old accordion, singing and dancing the traditional Kazáchki, kicking their legs out.

When they are so lost in drink and exhaustion that they could barely keep their eyes open, the major sent Limpy to the infirmary for medical attention to his injured foot. He then brings Sax and Aaron to the finest bedroom that Aaron has ever seen. "Take anything you want from this house," the major says. He closes the door, and for the first time in five years, Sax and Aaron have sanctuary—the kind of peace and relief that comes with not worrying if they would be allowed to live through the night, the next day, or even the next hour. It is as if the war was over for them. They run their hands along the silken bedcovers, then leap into two twin beds. They quickly discover that they could not get comfortable. After five years of sleeping on floors and hard ground, the beds are too soft. After struggling for several hours, they both end up sleeping on the floor.

In the morning, Aaron and Sax are awakened to a sumptuous breakfast and invited to accompany the major to the Komandatúra—the divisional headquarters for Western Ukraine. Here, they are introduced to the commander, Colonel Metz (who, because of his carriage, speech and mannerisms, appears to be Jewish) and other high-ranking officers, and presented with papers that granted Aaron and Sax official status as special agents of the Soviet army. Their days as slaves are officially over.

Upon their return from the Komandatúra, Aaron checks in with Sergei and thanks him one more time. He assures Sergei that he has spoken to the major to ensure that Sergei and his family would not be harmed. Sergei thanks Aaron profusely but does not mention his daughter again—apparently Aaron's ferocity with the gun had caused him to change his mind about Aaron's suitability as a son-in-law.

Aaron also checks on Limpy and finds out that he will be transferred farther to the rear for medical care. Again, Aaron receives assurances from the major that Limpy would be well treated.

The sensation of being free at last, alive and safe, is almost enough to heal the scars from the last five years of brutal torment. This feeling is transcended only by the euphoria that Aaron has experienced upon arresting and capturing the enemy prisoners. This sensation he wishes to exploit again, and soon.

But first, the Russians need Aaron to serve as an interpreter. Ever greater numbers of German and Hungarian soldiers are being captured in the wake of the Soviet advance, and the Russians want information and intelligence from their captives. Few Russians could speak German or Hungarian, so Aaron serves them well in this regard. Since Sax hasn't yet mastered the German or Russian languages, Aaron directs Hungarian prisoners to Sax, while Aaron takes on the Germans and reports back their findings to the Russians. And Aaron and Sax observe with great interest, the force and brutality used by the Russians when their prisoners refused to talk.

Sax and Aaron volunteer to make forays into enemy territory to capture prisoners and booty—as bounty hunters. To this end, they decline rank and uniform in the Soviet army so that they could easily infiltrate the local population and terrain incognito. The major obliges by giving them more than guns with bullets—he also gives them a squad of Russian soldiers for Aaron to command and a wagon in which to place their prisoners and captured equipment.

The major now gives Aaron and Sax the authority to interrogate their own captives independently. Their superiors are very pleased with the valuable intelligence they obtain regarding the enemy's military plans and positions.

Naturally, Aaron wants the war to be over and to be reunited with Helen and his family as soon as possible. Yet at the same time, he cannot suppress his all-consuming passion for vengeance. He is thankful his army unit is to help spearhead the invasion of Hungary, as the war continues.

As Aaron stands on a rise with his Soviet-issue automatic weapon and looks at nearby enemy territory, he thinks of the atrocities he has seen and endured at the hands of his mortal enemies. He is grateful that he would now have a chance to repay them in kind.

CHAPTER 15
FROM SLAVE TO MASTER

JUST AS AARON IS achieving astounding success as a special agent for the Russian army, on the first night of Passover, 1944, back in his hometown of Bielka, Helen and her family are gathered around the dining room table in their home, celebrating the holy night with the traditional *seder* hymns, prayers, and wine, along with the special Passover dinner. They are interrupted by a knock on the door. As Helen gets up to see who's there, she welcomes in their kindly Ukrainian Christian neighbor, Mihai Barzoún, a farmer who lives in the hills, and who appears very agitated. Helen invites Mihai into the family dining room.

"What's wrong, Mihai?" asks Helen's father.

"I have bad news for you, Herman," says Mihai, addressing Helen's father in his native Ukrainian name. "I just came back from a special service at church, and the priest and town elders learned that the Hungarian gendarmes will be rounding up all the Jewish people in our town during your holy Passover dinner services. The reason they are timing this for tomorrow night is because they know all members of the Jewish families will be home praying and celebrating the second night of your Passover dinner."

As Helen's family reacts in shock upon hearing this news, Helen's father asks Mihai, "Where will they be taking us?"

"For sure, I don't know. But the rumors suggest 'work camps' in Poland or Germany. It sounds like your lives are in danger, and I came here to warn you to go into hiding. My wife Ana and I want to take your teenage children still living with you: Helen, Gitu, and Ludwig, and hide them in the middle of the high haystack near the roof of my barn. We will feed them and keep them as comfortable as we can until the war is over and when the danger to the Jewish people is gone. Since my home is way up in the hills, it would be very seldom that Hungarian patrols would even ride by, and if they do, and they ask about the barn, I will simply tell them that I keep all the horses, cows, and pigs there."

Mihai continues, "But I'm so sorry that I cannot take you and your wife, Herman. I worry that you are too frail and elderly to survive up there in my barn. Perhaps the two of you can find a hiding place elsewhere."

After Helen's family initially reacts in shock upon hearing the news, Helen says, "Thank you for your kindness, Mihai. I agree with you that it would be wise for my younger brother and sister and me to take refuge in your barn. Who knows what the Hungarians and Germans really have planned for us in these 'work camps'?"

Helen's mother, Ruth, breaks out into tears. "I'm sorry, I can't help it, but we've never been split apart from our children like this ever before."

Helen, upon seeing her mother's grief, feels sorry for her and tells Mihai, "Thank you for your kindness and goodwill gesture, Mihai, but my brother and sister and I cannot accept your offer to hide us. We will stay together as a family and hope that God keeps us out of harm's way."

"Please, Hersh-Behr," says Mihai, addressing Herman in his Hebrew/Yiddish name. "I beg of you; I know you are all afraid and upset, but you and Ruth will at least be at peace knowing that nothing bad will happen to your children. Ana and I have always regarded you and your family among our best friends."

Hersh-Behr's face is looking down in despair at Ruth as she sobs uncontrollably.

At last Helen says, "No, Mihai, we will never forget your kindness and goodwill, but I think it will make our family stronger if we stick together, no matter what they throw at us."

"I understand, Helen. But at least let me take care of your family's livestock so that you can take them back when you return."

"Thank you, Mihai," says Hersh-Behr. "We will be forever grateful to you for offering to save our children."

On the second night of Passover, Helen and her family are again gathered around the dining room table for the seder. Suddenly, there is a loud banging on the door during the middle of prayers. As

Helen's father answers the door, about a half-dozen Hungarian Nazi policemen ferociously push Helen's father aside and make their way into the house and point their guns at Helen and her family members.

The Hungarian sergeant barks, "You are all under arrest! You have ten minutes to get your belongings and follow my men out the door!"

"Why?" asks Helen's father. "We've done no wrong."

"Yes you have!" screams the sergeant. "You are Jews! We looked you up and you are the Lazárovics!" The Hungarians had long known which residences are Jewish, and they learned that all members of Jewish families will be at their homes around the dinner table during their religious holy night, saving the Hungarians the time and effort to track down any Jews of Bielka outside of their homes.

All members of Helen's family are shocked and frightened by the guns pointed at them as they quickly grab essential items to bring for this uncertain future in addition to the items they packed after Mihai's warning the night before. They wonder what the Hungarians have in store for them.

The sergeant and his policemen prod Helen's family members with guns pushed at their backs into a truck, carrying other Jews from their homes down the street.

On the other side of town, Aaron's mother and his two youngest sisters living at home are forced into a different truck. While the Jewish men under age fifty are serving in slave labor camps in Russia and elsewhere, there are still many hundreds of elderly Jews, women and children in Bilke. They are all driven in different trucks to a ghetto in Béregszasz (Sax's hometown) that has railway connections to Germany and Poland.

The experience in the ghetto lasts for three weeks but feels like three months. There is little food to eat and very little water to drink. Helen's family and all the other Jews in the ghetto begin to starve, while the Hungarians treat them like vermin and call them out as swine.

The Hungarian commander of the ghetto warns, "Any of you Jew-bastards who tries to escape from this ghetto will be hung!"

Then, a few days after the deportation to the ghetto from Bielka arrives an angel of mercy in the form of none other than Mihai Barzoún, the Lazárovics' kindly Christian neighbor who tried in vain to save the Lazárovic children in his barn. He arrives on a horse-drawn wagon stocked with plenty of food to eat and fresh, clean water. Of course the Lazárovics share some of the food and water brought by Mihai with other family members and close friends.

Mihai makes the journey from Bielka to the ghetto two to three times a week with food and other provisions to make sure Helen's family is as healthy as possible to withstand an uncertain future.

It is with deep gratitude that Helen's father, Hersh-Behr, and the rest of the family thank Mihai for all his efforts and good will to help keep their family healthy and alive.

At last the Hungarian commander orders all Jews in the ghetto to get their belongings together for transportation in cattle cars that will deport them to Poland where they will hand off the Jews to the Germans. Although the Jews in the ghetto don't know it at the time, they will be taken by the Nazi SS to Auschwitz in Poland.

"Now get on the cattle cars, you dirty Jews!" barks the Hungarian SS officer. There is no food or water provided in the cattle cars by the Nazis—and only one bucket for the Jews' excrement to be passed around to those who need to use it. The stench is gruesome. There are several elderly Jews and young babies who cannot take it and die from these grisly conditions before they reach their destination.

Upon arrival at the Auschwitz concentration camp, the incoming Jews from all over Europe are forcibly separated into two lines: one line is comprised of young and middle-aged Jews capable of working, so long as they look healthy.

In the event that a Jew breaks ranks from the line for any reason, such as Helen's older sister running after her frightened wayward child, she is met by a Nazi soldier screaming, "Get back in line, *Juden-schwein*! – (Jew-pig)". The Nazi SS man beats Helen's sister trying to retrieve the child with a club and cracks his whip against her skin until enough blood spurts out to the satisfaction of the SS soldier, who laughs uncontrollably, together with cries of pain from

Helen's sister, as she brings her wayward child back into line, while the other onlooking Jews watch, incredulously, filled with fear.

The arbiter to make the decision as to which Jews who appear healthy enough to work or not is none other than the infamous Dr. Joseph Mengele. Those Jews deemed able to work are directed by Dr. Mengele to be marched in a direction to have their heads shaved and their arms permanently tattooed with numbers instead of their names for their identification. Henceforth, these Jews are referred to by the Nazi SS men and women by the numbers on their arms, not by name. Their names are either stored away or simply discarded.

Although Helen doesn't know it at the time, the other line consisting of the elderly and women with young children are pointed out by Dr. Mengele to march in a different direction where the gas chambers are waiting to murder them. That is the direction where Helen's parents go, as well as Aaron's mother and his older sisters along with their young children.

Nicknamed the "The Angel of Death," the notorious Dr. Mengele performs deadly perverted experiments on Jewish prisoners at Auschwitz, and he is also often seen by the other Nazi doctors and SS men on his team to administer the gas to murder the Jews. Although Helen doesn't know it at the time, Dr. Mengele will become one of the most sought-after war criminals in history. He manages to evade justice and is never caught..

Back at Auschwitz, the Nazis' rules mandate that for those Jews whose lives are spared, no Jewish family members are allowed to stay in the same barracks together in order to further demoralize and isolate the Jews. The male and female prisoners are housed in separate barracks. However, the Nazis have made a mistake when Helen realizes that her younger teenage sister, Gitu, is assigned to Helen's barrack. After disregarding the prisoners' names, the Nazis cannot discern that Helen and Gitu are sisters. With the two sisters having each other to lean upon, they know that their closeness will boost their morale and their chances of survival. They swear to each other that they must keep the fact that they are sisters a secret—from everyone. Gitu and Helen share the same bunk. There are no mattresses, just wooden boards to sleep on. They hold each other tightly and manage to keep each other as warm as possible.

The next morning following their arrival at Auschwitz, the burly female commandant of the barracks arrives and barks at her prisoners, "You Jew-bitches are going to march to the other side of the camp where you will be given prisoners' uniforms. Now, strip off your clothes and lay them on your bunks!" Many of the Jewish women are so incredulous and dumbfounded by the seeming absurdity of the order that they are too stunned to move. The commandant calls for her guards to enter the barracks, who beat the prisoners with clubs and strike them with their whips amid bloody cries and shrieks of pain, as the guards constantly yell, "Dirty Jew! Dirty Jew! Dirty Jew!"

Helen tries to cover Gitu with her body, while she raises her arms to protect her head. The guards approach Helen, as they scream, "Jew-whore! Jew-scum!" They beat and whip Helen into a pulp.

Helen's mind goes into a dream-like state, seeing Aaron approaching her with his horse, trying to rescue her. The momentary image lasts long enough for Helen to briefly escape from the beatings to compose herself and Gitu into her arms.

The guards harshly push the naked Jewish women into line, and they begin their march to get the prisoners their uniforms as they try to cover their genitals with their hands. The commandant constantly yells, "*Macht! Schnell!*" (Do it! Fast!). Along the way, they pass lines of other naked Jewish prisoners, men and women, everyone trying to cover their genitals out of utter shame and embarrassment, which are the precise reactions the Nazis are trying to extract out of the Jews.

The only other crime against humanity that most of the Jewish women evade is rape. Since Jews are considered by the Nazis to be subhuman, it is *verboten* for a German to have intimate relations with a Jewish female.

In June 1944, after a short operational pause to regroup and refit its forces, the Red Army begins its massive summer offensive, striking westward into the Soviet province of Belorussia. By then, the Western Allies have landed in France on D-Day and have established a bridgehead in France, draining the already depleted German reserves from the Eastern Front. Hitler is now fighting a three-front war: In Western Europe, Italy, and Russia. Under these circumstances, the German forces are now inadequate to stop the Russian advance.

By August, while the Red Army is marching toward the Carpathian Mountains to the south, Aaron is situated in the vanguard of advancing Russian forces then fighting across the Hungarian border. His primary assignment here is to requisition food from Hungarian farms and warehouses to be loaded onto trains and sent back east to feed the starving Russian people. The goods include everything from cows and pigs to wheat and grain. At the *Komandatúra*— [Command post], he would load up his wagon with dozens of sacks of brand new rubles to be used to pay for the goods. If Aaron is surprised by the trust the Russians place in giving him such astonishing amounts of money, he is even more surprised that they are willing to have him pay the Hungarians for their goods instead of just seizing them. But Aaron had convinced his superiors that he and Sax could obtain more intelligence on the activities of enemy units from the Hungarian locals by currying their favor in this fashion, and ingratiating themselves in their native tongue, offering "friendship and protection" as civilian agents.

After one of their forays in the late summer of 1944, Aaron's wagon, loaded with grain, guns, ammunition, and blankets, is rumbling up a dirt road leading to a cottage on the edge of a small Hungarian town near the border. A Russian soldier is driving the cart. A gaggle of Hungarian and German prisoners, hands bound, walk behind the wagon guarded by a second Soviet soldier. The wagon is flanked by four more Russian troops.

As they reach the house, Aaron leaps off the wagon, grabs the lead prisoner—who wears a German uniform—and with Sax and two Soviet soldiers, cautiously approaches the house.

"Is this the one?" Aaron asks the prisoner.

"Yes," he says glumly.

Aaron knocks hard on the door, then steps back while Sax and the soldiers hold their guns at the ready. A middle-aged homeowner appears, and immediately gasps in fear. "You have German troops hiding here," Aaron states bluntly.

The homeowner hesitates. Aaron cocks his submachine gun and points it at him.

"Six," he says. "In the cellar."

"Show us."

The homeowner leads the way as Aaron prods the German prisoner in front of him. The homeowner points to a door. "Through there and—" he says, before his words are interrupted by a burst of rifle and submachine gun fire erupting through the wooden floor. The German prisoner is immediately hit and falls. The wife screams. Sax and the others step back and return fire through the floor. Aaron then levels his submachine gun at the cellar door and fires until it wheezes off its hinges, at which point he tosses a hand grenade down the stairs.

The blast silences the guns from below. The Russian soldiers quickly toss down two more grenades, after which Aaron rushes down the stairs, gun ready. There is a quick burst of fire before he yells out that it's safe.

The homeowner's wife sobs uncontrollably in the arms of her husband, while one of the Soviet soldiers tends to a wounded German as the others proceed to ransack the house and barn, seizing sacks of grain and other goods, then carting their haul to the wagon while Aaron makes notes on a piece of paper.

"What are they doing?" asks the homeowner in trepidation.

"These items are being seized by the Red Army in order to help with the war effort. You will be compensated."

When the troops are finished, Aaron counts out, then hands the homeowner a wad of freshly printed rubles. "These should cover the cost of the goods, and the damage to the house."

The homeowner looks at the money, astonished. "I have six dead bodies in the cellar. Can anyone help me?"

Aaron counts out a few more rubles. "For the undertaker," he says.

Aaron then moves quickly down to the basement where he finds, aside the six bodies, stacks of documents. He brings these upstairs and examines them quickly.

"What is it?" asks Sax.

With the big man at his heels, Aaron rushes out to the wagon, where the wounded prisoner is being patched up.

"Was this a command post?" he asks harshly of the prisoner.

"Yes."

"For what?"

"A reconnaissance battalion."

"Nazi spies, eh? How many?"

"A few dozen is all that were left."

"When do they come back?"

"I don't know," the prisoner says wearily.

Aaron looks again at the documents, then heads back to the house with Sax.

"These weren't deserters. They were trying to set up a command post. There are German combat patrols in the area—we must have slipped past them."

"Can we slip past them again? With that?" Sax points to the overloaded wagon.

"They'll be coming back here eventually. Let's wait."

Sax nods. Aaron quickly orders the wagon and prisoners to be moved to a nearby stable, leaving one soldier to watch them. Then he, Sax, and the five remaining Soviet troops stock up on grenades taken from the Germans, taking positions in the house and a few other houses down the street.

Aaron and Sax go to the upstairs bedroom and scan the horizon with binoculars.

"Where are the Jews?" asks Sax abruptly.

"What do you mean? We're here."

"We have been advancing with the Russians for months now. We've been through Ukraine and a dozen Hungarian towns, and I have not seen any Jews. No women. No children. The Hungarian men were sent to the labor camps, but where are the women and children?"

Aaron shakes his head.

"Did these Hungarians turn them over to the Nazis? Put them on trains to concentration camps? Nice little Hungarian grandmas and grandpas like the ones downstairs?" Sax spits on the floor, disgusted.

"We need to get home," says Aaron. "To Bielka and to Béregszasz. And soon."

"What do you think we'll find there, Aaron? Do you think it will be any different from here? What do you think *Avrum* had planned for your family? And mine?"

"You don't think I worry about Helen and my family every day, every hour, every minute, Ignatz?"

The two watch in silence for several hours, fear eating into their souls, before Aaron abruptly whispers: *"There!"*

A German patrol is making its way casually up the road toward the house.

"How many?" asks Aaron.

"I think we can handle a dozen." Aaron signals to the Russian soldiers across the street, then turns to Sax. "You go down to our men. Grenades front and back of the column; cut down everyone left standing."

Sax stands up. "Of course."

As Sax prepares to leave, Aaron looks back out the window. His jaw drops. "*Ignatz!*" he whispers. "Can we take on *two* dozen?"

Sax quickly turns around and levels his own binoculars at the scene below. Another German patrol with a wagon pulled by two horses is heading their way from the opposite direction.

"I don't think so," says Sax.

Aaron takes another look at the second approaching column.

"Enfilade," he says abruptly. Aaron wants to hit the Germans while they are exposed single file. "We know where they're going. I'll take them on."

"You? Alone?"

"Ignatz, you and the others take out the first group, and then come help me. I'll try not to shoot until I hear from you. But I can't promise anything."

Sax nods and the two men scramble downstairs. Sax and two Soviet soldiers take up positions on the first floor facing the first column. Aaron drags the homeowner out to the back garden and orders the old man to show him a spot where he can position himself to watch the street from which the second column will be approaching. Once he is in position, he tells the homeowner to get back inside and keep quiet, or else he'll be killed.

After a while, the point man of the Nazi patrol appears. He is moving cautiously up the street, directly toward Aaron. A few moments later, more of the patrol appear, moving more casually. Aaron remains absolutely still, sighting down the short barrel of his machine gun, finger on the trigger.

The twelfth man now swings into view as the entire patrol moves in single file, straight toward Aaron's position. Finally, from the next block, he hears the sharp snap of two hand grenades exploding in quick succession, followed by screams and gunfire.

Aaron pulls the trigger, his bullets striking the point man and several others. Six men go down in quick succession before those remaining have a chance to find cover and start returning fire.

Aaron pulls back as bullets pummel his position. *"Damn!"* he shouts to himself as he climbs a vine-covered wall and crosses into a neighbor's back yard. From there, he'll be able to cut off the Germans' chance of retreating down the next block. Once in position, he waits for the gunfire a few blocks over to stop.

One of the German troops sticks his head around a building down the block. Aaron fires but misses. The soldier disappears.

Aaron waits in silence, breathing hard, his heart pounding. Finally, he hears the distinctive pop of standard-issue Soviet automatic guns, which tells him the first battle is over and Sax and the Soviet soldiers are moving in on the second patrol.

There are more grenade blasts and gunfire. Soon, a few more German troops try to exit the house in which they've taken cover, only to be forced back inside by Aaron's gunfire.

After more tense moments, a Nazi soldier holds out a white rag stuck on a rifle barrel, shouting in broken Russian: *Ne strilayte! Ya pidayusia!"* Don't shoot! We surrender!

Aaron replies in German: *"Kommen Sie mit erhobenen händen raus!"* Come out with your hands up!

The remaining German troops—three in all—ease carefully out and onto the street, their hands raised. Sax and some Soviet troops appear at the end of the block, at which point Aaron walks out and directs the Russian soldiers to line up the Germans against a wall and frisk them, before he orders the Nazis to spill the intelligence information regarding the German military locations and their plans for defense against the Russians. Aaron then orders the Nazis to bury their dead.

As the sun sinks lower in the western sky, Aaron's horse-drawn wagon trundles into Russian headquarters, piled almost to the breaking point with captured booty, a wounded Soviet soldier, and the wounded German prisoner. The remaining German and Hungarian prisoners struggle behind them.

The major emerges from his command post and greets Sax and Aaron with a big smile.

"Arón," says the major, using the Russian variant of his name. "You are creating a problem for us. You are taking too many prisoners. We're running out of room to detain them. You're getting too good at this."

"We decided to take a few less this time than we could have, sir," Aaron smiles wearily. "But from those left alive, we obtained some valuable intelligence."

"Your intelligence is no doubt helping us win the war. But still, we need the trains to carry supplies back to our starving people in Mother Russia, before we send them Nazi pigs," says the major.

"Sax and I can arrange for you to have *no* more prisoners from us, if that's what you wish, sir."

Still smiling, the major invites the two returning warriors into his headquarters where he pours them each a hefty vodka. "No, that would be a waste of manpower, especially since there is so much work to be done around here. There are train tracks and roads to be repaired and supplies that need to be hauled. We need your prisoners to do those jobs. Our own soldiers are very busy these days."

As Aaron and Sax drain their vodkas, the major pours them two more and continues with his train of thought. "I think what we need here is a labor camp, don't you?"

"Yes," Aaron agrees.

"I have no experience running a labor camp, and none of my officers do, either. But I understand you and Sax have spent much time in labor camps—*slave* labor camps."

Aaron nods.

"Then I think you two would be the best men to run such a camp, don't you?"

Aaron smiles. "Yes, sir. I agree."

Sax, whose understanding of Russian has been rapidly improving, likewise smiles at the major.

As a brisk October wind sweeps through the Hungarian town of Mohács, an army of tired, hungry, ragged German and Hungarian soldiers, more than five hundred in all, are hard at work in the rail yards, hauling sacks of grain, corn, and beans from what seems like an endless line of horse-drawn wagons to what seems like an endless number of freight trains heading east. The men are inadequately dressed for the cold, harsh winds blowing through the labor camp. Several are sick; all are on the edge of exhaustion. Most have not seen home in many months or even years. A handful of Soviet soldiers stands guard over the untidy lot in support of the two labor camp commanders—Aaron and Sax.

At dusk, one of the German soldiers limps through the camp pushing a wheelbarrow and handing out pieces of bread to the laborers. As two exhausted Hungarian soldiers put down their burdens to eat, Aaron prods them with his now familiar automatic weapon, shouting— "On your feet! Keep working!"

The role reversal is not lost on Aaron—that he, the former slave, is now taskmaster of his erstwhile persecutors.

Nearby, sitting atop a pile of tires, Sax, with his gun propped next to him, consumes a steaming hot meal of soup, bread, meat and potatoes.

An automobile with Hungarian license plates and a red star painted on its side approaches the camp. Sax sets his meal aside, picks up his gun, and scrambles down from his perch. The vehicle draws to a stop, the door swings open, and the major gets out. Aaron and Sax salute. The major looks around and smiles.

"You're not having them quit for the night?"

"It's still a few hours before midnight, sir, and the train is only three-quarters full."

"These men will drop from exhaustion."

Aaron gives a wry smile, "I hope so, sir."

The major laughs heartily. "You've set a record for food shipments to Russia. You're helping to ensure the people back home do not starve this winter. The people of Russia thank you."

"What about *my* home, sir?" asks Aaron. "Our families. How is the progress toward Bielka, toward Béregszasz going?"

"Slow, I'm afraid. The Carpathian Mountains provide the Germans a natural defense that we haven't been able to break through."

"Major, do you think we can assemble a group of special agents to infiltrate the Carpathians to rescue and smuggle my betrothed Helen and my family—and Sax's family, too?"

"I wish I could say yes, Aaron. But unfortunately, I could never get approval for that type of operation. Our high command has put the highest emphasis on destroying the Germans and their allies on the battlefields. I'm sorry, Aaron."

"I understand sir. But I think we could help the war effort more if we were returned to active duty. We might be able to gather some intelligence that would speed a Russian victory."

The major considers this for a moment then says, "You know, this war is very expensive for Russia. It's not just the food our people need." He gestures to the town of Päks on the horizon, its lights twinkling in the dark. "In every one of these quaint Hungarian towns, there are villas and castles belonging to people who have made a fortune on this war; wealthy Hungarians who hate the Jews and support the government's policies that made war on my people—and yours. What do you think should happen to this wealth,

Aaron? And what do you think should happen to these people who have benefited so well from so much misery?"

The major takes a deep breath and exhales slowly. "Maybe now is the time for them to pay it back. You and Sax speak their language. And I trust you, not only with their property, but with their money. You could be our point men."

At nine the next morning, in a villa on a hill above Päks, Jeno Katonah and his wife Klara are being served breakfast by an unobtrusive servant. A fire warms the dining room, which is lit by a crystal chandelier and filled with fine furniture, oil paintings, and intricate woodcarvings. Gold-framed photos of the Katonahs' extensive family adorn the mantle. Jeno reads through the abbreviated newspaper—the first issue to come out since the Soviet occupation began. The news is fragmentary, and none of it good.

Still, Jeno and Klara can take comfort in the knowledge that two of their grown sons are safe—and at the moment, are sleeping upstairs because they happened to be visiting when the Russian spearhead swept through town and drove out the Axis forces.

Their breakfast, however, is suddenly interrupted by a loud banging at the stout wooden door. As soon as the servant responds to the knocking, Aaron pushes his way into the room, machine gun ready.

"Yes? What is it you want?" asks the servant.

A moment later Sax, his huge hulk taking up most of the doorway, pushes himself inside, followed by Aaron's major and five soldiers.

"Who is it?" asks Jeno, coming from the dining room.

"How can I help you?" he asks nervously, as Klara hovers behind him.

"Money," says Aaron. "In the bag. All of it." He points to a sack held out by one of the soldiers.

Jeno nods. "This way, please."

The major turns to the soldiers. "Search the house and take whatever you think will be of value to Russia."

Sax and the soldiers immediately fan out, ransacking cabinets, drawers, bookshelves, and overturn furniture, while Jeno leads

Aaron and the soldier with the sack to a wall safe in the hallway. He quickly opens it and pours paper money and coins into the sack while Klara looks on.

"What else do you have?"

"That's all," says Jeno.

"What about jewelry?" Aaron demands.

"We have none."

Aaron pushes the barrel of his gun against Jeno's head. "Don't you ever buy your wife jewelry? Or for your mistress?"

Jeno promptly leads them upstairs to the master bedroom, whose contents have already been pillaged by the Russian soldiers and opens another wall safe. Aaron reaches in and tosses one piece of jewelry after another into the sack, and then marches Jeno back down the stairs. Soon afterward, a soldier shoves the Katonahs' two sons into the living room at gunpoint, and another prods three more servants into the room. The soldiers reappear carrying sacks bulging with booty, which they haul outside to the wagon.

The major then has Aaron instruct Jeno, Klara, their two sons, and the servants to stand in a row at attention, while Sax and the soldiers bayonet paintings, smash chandeliers, and destroy furniture and fine china.

When the demolition is complete, the major orders his men out of the house. Aaron and Sax are about to follow when the major stops them. "You did well, Aaron. You too, Sax. Take whatever valuables you want for yourselves."

"Thank you, sir," says Aaron.

"One more thing."

"Yes sir?" says Aaron.

"Burn the house down. Spare nothing."

The major then exits, leaving the Katonahs looking quizzically at Aaron, as they do not speak Russian. In disbelief, Aaron repeats the order in Hungarian so that Sax could understand more fully. The Katonahs gasp. Sax smiles and cocks his automatic weapon, while Aaron orders everyone out of the house.

Sax then takes flaming logs from the fireplace and approaches Aaron, who has paused with a pensive look on his face.

"What the hell are you waiting for, Aaron? The Hungarian bastards who own this place are the biggest Jew-haters in Europe. The least we can do is take the house down like the Russians want us to."

"Yes…yes, of course. Let's go."

And with that the two men ignite whatever flammable material they can find before they, too, go outside, where the major and his men have just finished loading up the wagon. Several high-ranking Soviet officers, including a few generals, are sitting in their own motor vehicles, inspecting the finer valuables brought to them.

As the convoy takes off, heat from the fire is shattering the windows, flames are spreading up to the second floor, and a column of smoke is rising into the otherwise clear autumn sky, all while the family watches in disbelief and shock. At the end of the night, six columns of smoke from other villas and castles rise above the countryside, smearing the air with the snuffed-out superiority of Hungarian aristocracy; those who have thought they would survive the long war unscathed. As the weeks wear on, the number of smoking columns in other towns would be in the dozens as the vengeful Russians, along with their two Jewish former slaves, continue their desperate, wayward quest to right the unimaginable wrongs that had been done to them and their people.

Aaron peeks into his sacks at the riches he has plundered from the hated Hungarians for the cruelty which they and their Nazi cohorts had mercilessly inflicted upon him and the Jewish people. Practically overnight, he had become a wealthy man. What would Aaron do with all these riches? If Helen and his family survived, they could start a new life with these treasures. And yet, Aaron knows in his heart that there could never be just redress for the atrocities committed by his mortal enemies.

Likewise, the Russians are angry about what the Germans and Hungarians had done to them and express it vengefully. Sax and Aaron are happy to help them express it. Whenever the Red Army advances, Aaron, Sax, and their band of troops are never far behind, interrogating and rooting out deserters and spies, and seizing whatever valuables they wish from the wealthy Jew-hating Hungarian aristocrats, and appropriating whatever they thought would be of use to Mother Russia.

Aaron observed that although the German soldiers may have been better trained, the Russian soldiers had greater staying power and could outlast their enemy on fewer rations and supplies. The boundless enthusiasm of Aaron's Russian comrades was contagious. They showed a passion and joy for music, singing patriotic songs, and beautiful Ukrainian folk tunes that were perfectly suited for marching. Aaron couldn't help joining in, as he had grown up singing many of these tunes in his youth. They all bonded together, and Aaron was treated as a brother, especially by the Ukrainians, since he had grown up with them back home.

After an exhausting advance to the Danube River, their unit stopped in the town of Gérjen —pronounced "Géryen" and the Red Army paused to consolidate its gains. Aaron feels at home in this town, which reminds him of his hometown of Bielka.[10]

---

[10] See the map page 298 (Russian Front June – October 1944).

CHAPTER 16
BLOOD RAGE

MANY MILES AWAY FROM Aaron's station with the Soviet army, Helen and her little sister Gitu are somehow able to continue surviving in Auschwitz, despite being ordered to perform harsh slave labor with very little food. If they work too slowly, they are beaten or shot by female Nazi and Hungarian guards.

Helen often wonders about the fate of Aaron. Is he still alive? Will she ever see him again? The rumors coming out of Russia are not very encouraging. Most of the Jewish slave laborers from the Carpathians sent to Russia are presumed to be dead.

Helen's little sister Gitu is not only the younger sister, but the weaker sister of the two. She grows ever wearier from the excessive beatings from the female guards who rule the Jewish women's barracks in addition to enforcing the horrendous conditions of the camp.

Many Jews who can no longer take it, run to the electrified fence surrounding the camp, immediately electrocuting themselves. The Nazis laugh throughout the camp and revel at news of a Jew who commits suicide this way, leaving one less Jew for them to beat up and eventually march them to the gas chambers.

One night, Gitu tells Helen that she is so demoralized and ill from conditions at the concentration camp that she wants to end her life. She gets up and runs toward the electrified fence. Helen immediately runs after her and tackles her little sister to the ground, telling her, "You are not going to die! Because, if *you* die, *I'll* die!"

Then, one day, months after the Lazárovic family arrived in Auschwitz, the Jewish women who have survived in Helen's and Gitu's barracks are ordered by the Nazi commandant to come outside and stand at attention, when he declares, "You Jewish swine are lucky you have survived Auschwitz this long. You are being taken by cattle car to another concentration camp in Germany where you will work. Now march behind me to the train station." The female German and Hungarian guards accompany the Nazi commander, and the Jewish women march onward toward another uncertain fate.

At last, they arrive at a concentration camp named Bergen-Belsen where the stark conditions are no better than those of Auschwitz, but Helen and Gitu manage to hang on, keeping each other warm. They are put to work at hard manual labor and are again beaten by female guards if they work too slowly. The food and water are again scarce, and women in the barracks continue to die, whether working outside or inside the barracks.

Within a few months, Helen, Gitu, and several other female Bergen-Belsen survivors are again told to go outside and stand at attention. This time, they are told by the commandant, "You Jew-pigs think you are the ultimate survivors? You Jew-bitches will get in line to prove yourselves for a march on foot from Belsen all the way to a factory in Germany where you will be put to work as slave laborers to make uniforms for German soldiers. Let's see how many of you Jew-whores survive this march!"

Many of the women are not strong or healthy enough to survive the march, and the Nazis refuse to treat or care for them. Instead, any Jewish women who couldn't sustain the march and fall to the ground are shot and left for dead.

Dozens of times along the march, Gitu falls down, telling Helen, "I can't get up! I just can't walk any more. Please just leave me here!"

Helen replies, "I'm going to pull you up, Gitu, because you'll be shot and die out here! And I won't be able to make it without you!"

Helen props Gitu up and pulls and carries her little sister until the end of this miserable journey. The two sisters and the other women end up in a grisly factory in Leipzig, Germany, where they will sew uniforms for the German army. Would the two be able to survive yet another prison environment with very little food?

Helen comes up with an ingenious plan to thwart the Nazis' mantra to eventually kill all the Jews. She notices a non-descript location of the camp. She also notes that the guards at Leipzig are not sticklers for detail compared with those of the concentration camps. The survivors at the Leipzig factory are fed very small servings that sometimes include potatoes. Helen and Gitu plant the seedlings of the potatoes late at night at the location outside that Helen had noticed located near the barrack. The two sisters' background in farming makes a big difference in their survival, though they realize they are taking a fatal risk if they are caught, for the Nazis would surely hang them. But when the potatoes sprout, Helen and Gitu survive by getting access to this extra nourishment, eating their own potatoes raw. The two sisters swear to each other that if they survive, for the rest of their lives, they will each cook a baked potato every night for supper to commemorate this life-saving action.

Helen continues to think about the plight of Aaron nearly every day. She prays for him. Is he still alive? Or has he used his cunning and guile to evade death, whether from the bombs along the Russian front, or from the Nazi or Hungarian soldiers who want to eliminate Jewish slave laborers who can no longer serve them?

Hundreds of miles away from the plight of Helen and Gitu, Aaron and Sax are sitting with their Russian major, now promoted to colonel, and several other officers at a table in a small restaurant in Gérjen. The owner and waiters hover in the background, refilling plates and glasses.

"What do you think of this town, Aaron?" asks the colonel.

"I like it so far, sir. In this town, the main course is even better than the appetizer."

The colonel and other officers smile. "Which main course, Aaron? You've had at least three, and you, Ignatz—four, I think."

Sax stops eating for a moment and smiles. "The first main course was so many vodkas ago," says Sax. "I've lost track."

The colonel laughs, and the other officers laugh with him. "This is all just an appetizer, unless you two are willing to settle down for a while."

Now Aaron stops eating. The table falls silent. The colonel leans back and lights up a cigarette before speaking. "I have lost many good officers over the last few months," he says.

"It has been a difficult fight," Aaron agrees.

"It has, but I'm not speaking of combat. As you know, every town we liberate comes under the protection of the Soviet government, and I am forced to leave behind at least one officer to see that order is restored. I can't spare any more. And there is no one left who speaks Hungarian—or German. I can't really spare you, either, Aaron, but how would you like to be the overlord of this town? Sax can be your second-in-command."

Aaron and Sax are astounded. "It would not be so bad for you," continues the colonel. "You can choose whichever house or villa you want to be your headquarters, Arón," using the Russian idiom of Aaron's name. "You would be judge, jury, and executioner. You can get whatever you want. If the townspeople have it and you want it, you just take it. I could spare you a few soldiers. You and Sax would be allowed to do whatever you want with this town. I would just ask that you continue to send food and supplies back to Russia; and of course, continue to root out Hungarian and German soldiers and spies. But I'll be honest with you, I have very little space for any more of your prisoners—so from now on, after you interrogate them and send us the intelligence, just do with them whatever you want."

Aaron and Sax glance at each other, speechless.

"Unless, of course, you capture a big general," says the colonel. "In that case, you'll bring him directly to me, and you will be richly rewarded—as will I!" The colonel breaks into a hearty belly laugh at his own joke and everyone at the table joins in.

"How would I run things?" asks Aaron politely. "We are irregulars. We have no rank in the Red Army."

"True," continues the colonel. "Since you are partisan fighters of the Soviet Army without rank, the official title of 'ruler' must be given to one of our uniformed officers. But it would be rare for him to ever be here. It will be you who runs the town. If you need money, new rubles will be waiting for you at headquarters in Päks. We can even spare you a motorcar…well, occasionally. And you'd have a small squad of Red Army soldiers under your command."

Aaron and Sax exchange astonished looks.

"You two have done more than we have asked of you, and we trust you. Your intelligence has been invaluable in helping us kick the Nazi and Hungarian invaders out of Russia, and now you've helped us in our invasion of Hungary," says the colonel. "My soldiers and I think of you as comrades; as brothers."

"We feel the same way about you and the men, sir," says Aaron, as Sax nods.

Aaron then adds, "Sir, can you locate our comrade, Limpy?"

"Limpy?" asks the colonel.

"His native tongue is Hungarian, and he could be very useful to us in running this town, getting the maximum supplies shipped back to the homeland, while Sax and I enforce security and intelligence, concentrating on larger concerns. He has been getting treatment at a Soviet infirmary for frostbite on his foot. He is loyal to me, and I know he will serve Mother Russia with gratitude and honor."

"You continue to surprise me with your wisdom, Aaron. I understand your plan." The colonel smiles, "You are not yet ready to give up your jobs as bounty hunters. I will try to find your Limpy and deliver him to you. But remember, I hold you responsible for the actions of all subordinates under your command."

"Of course, sir," Aaron nods in agreement.

"Well?" says the colonel. "You don't have to decide tonight. Tell me in the morning."

"Sir, you don't have to wait until morning," says Aaron, as he stands up and raises his glass of vodka, blue eyes sparkling. *"Na Zdróvia"*— "A toast," he says. The colonel, his officers, and Sax likewise stand and clink their glasses in camaraderie and celebration.

Long after the Russian officers retire for the evening, Sax and Aaron salute each other.

"To you, fellow ruler," Aaron toasts, as he raises his glass to Sax.

"To me," Sax teases back, slamming down another vodka.

"To Jewish kings," they say together, and laugh as they drink.

"Aaron," says Sax with a wide grin. "Did you hear what the colonel said? We can do with the prisoners whatever we want!" Sax's eyes light up and Aaron can see his comrade's soul filling up with a thirst for vengeance. It is a feeling Aaron shares as well.

Even in the midst of their drunken haze, the irony of Aaron's reversal of fortune is not lost on him. The last few years of his life flash before him, as he ascends from lowly slave to ruler of an enemy town, ruler over those who have brutally tormented him and his people. What would Aaron do with all this power?

The next morning, Aaron and Sax, looking none the worse after a long night of drinking and celebration, stride down the main street of Gérjen trailed by four Soviet riflemen. They pause by an open-air vegetable market where the proprietor, a sinewy, bald man in his fifties, approaches them with a smile.

"Lower price today for you gentlemen, you're welcome to it," he says. "Freshest in the district."

Sax picks up an apple and takes a large bite.

"Or it's free for you today; that's my special for you."

Aaron and the Russian soldiers help themselves to as much fresh fruit as they can carry, and then proceed farther up the street as the owner calls after them. "Come back any time, sirs, you are welcome!"

A baker emerges with a tray loaded full of pastries and offers freshly baked items to the new conquerors.

"We hear you are the new commanders of this town. Thank heavens, we needed it. Welcome."

As they load up on bread and sweet rolls, Sax notices two women peeking out from the bakery shop, when the baker notices him looking at them.

"Christina and Theresa—come out! Meet the new leaders!" calls the baker.

Two attractive young women—neither older than twenty—emerge from the bakery, wiping their hands on their aprons, smiling shyly.

"We live right above the bakery. Come visit any time you like," says the baker.

As Aaron, Sax, and their squad proceed up the street, more townspeople gather to greet them.

"You don't wear Russian uniforms and you speak Hungarian so well," the baker continues, following closely behind. "So it feels like you are one of us. Anything else you might need that we can get you?"

"A place to call home, quarter the troops," says Aaron.

"I'd offer mine but it's very small, two rooms, four adults," the baker replies. "However, there are plenty of other homes. I'm sure you'll find something good. But baked goods, you know where…"

The baker suddenly realizes that Aaron and Sax are staring at a kosher food store that appears abandoned, its windows broken and gaping darkly. The crowd grows silent.

"There were Jews in this town," Aaron mutters.

"Yes," says the baker.

"Where is the rabbi? Can you take us to see him?"

"No," says the baker. "He is not here. No Jews here. Not anymore."

"Why not?" asks Sax.

"They went away."

"Went?" asks Aaron.

"Police took them," says the baker. "Came right in and took them away. Gave them to the Germans. Took them on a train to Poland, is what people say. We didn't know. What could we do? We didn't approve." He turns to the other townspeople who have gathered. They are all nodding in agreement.

Sax's face reddens. A blood vessel on his temple pulsates. "You tried to help them, of course."

"Yes, but what could we do?"

Sax grunts.

Aaron takes the baker aside. "Where are the police? Can you point them out?"

The baker backs away fearfully. "No sir, I cannot."

"Why not?" growls Aaron.

"They have gone, sir. They are not here anymore."

Aaron nods, then looks farther up the street and points to a villa near the highest point of the downtown area. Sax nods, and the two set off, followed by the soldiers. Some of the crowd begins to disperse; some follow at a distance.

When they reach the villa, Sax pounds on the door and a portly woman of mature years appears. Sax pushes his way inside. It appears that the woman and her elderly husband have just sat down to dinner. As the soldiers fan out to inspect the place, Aaron walks to the window.

"Good, Ignatz, look at this," he says. "Good view. The whole domain."

Sax nods.

"What do you want?" asks the woman.

Aaron and the others ignore her.

"Kitchen not bad, plenty big enough," says Sax.

"I'm glad you like it," the woman says. "Now please leave."

"Catharine!" The old man remonstrates.

"We were about to have dinner," she persists.

"We just want the house," says Sax. "You can keep the dinner."

"What do you mean, you want the house?"

"Catharine!" the old man says again.

But she persists. "This house has been in our family for three hundred years!" she says, pointing to a portrait of a distinguished looking eighteenth century nobleman hanging in the adjoining room.

Sax replies by shredding the portrait with submachine gun fire. The woman almost collapses in shock. The man takes hold of her and the two run out of the house. Aaron looks at the table, still laden with steaming food.

"I guess they weren't hungry after all. Everyone eat," Aaron says.

As the sun sets and the dinner is picked over, Aaron and Sax sit by the window, smoking cigars and drinking as they look out at Gérjen and the hills in the distance. The soldiers lounge nearby, one smoking a pipe taken from a display on a bookshelf with tobacco liberated from the old man's stash while the others play cards, using the woman's jewelry for wagering. Radio equipment and supplies for a command post are now stacked against the walls.

"Bé regszasz," says Sax quietly, thinking about his hometown. "It's *that* way." He points out the open window. "I can almost see it. I want our families to see us; see that we're kings now, ruling over the bastards who were giving us hell, and that we can do to them what they did to us."

"Me too," says Aaron. "I want our families to see that we're going to make it, we'll be alright; give them strength to hang on. I want them to be here, so we can protect them, instead of hiding in Bielka or Bé regszasz."

"Bé regszasz?" asks one of the soldiers.

"Yes. It's up at the edge of the Carpathian mountains," says Sax.

"Gyorgi has seen Bé regszasz," says the soldier.

"Me, too," says Sax. "I grew up there."

"No," says the soldier. "I mean he saw it last week. He was on a scouting mission when he got hit."

Sax springs to his feet and rushes over to Gyorgi, a youthful, friendly soldier with a bandage around his head.

"You were in Bé regszasz?"

"Yes sir," says Gyorgi. "We did some scouting, first around Budapest, and then up in the Carpathians. I'd be there now, but one of the sons of bitches got lucky with his grenade."

"Did you get into the city itself? What about the people? What about the Jews? Do you know anything about them?"

"It's just like here," says Gyorgi quietly. "No Jews left, none anywhere, in any of the towns. They took them away on trains and… I don't know."

Sax grabs Gyorgi and shakes him by the shoulders, shouting at a fevered pitch. "Where did they go?"

Aaron runs over and tugs at Sax's arm. "Take it easy, Ignatz. Gyorgi is on our side."

Then he turns to his Russian subordinate. "Gyorgi, we need you to tell us everything."

"Ok," says Gyorgi. "The Hungarians—they were rounding up the Jews. First it was the police and then the SS and…"

"German SS?" asks Sax.

"Germans *and* Hungarians. They call the Hungarian SS the Arrow Cross," says Gyorgi. "They're the new secret police—and vicious. They love doing all the 'dirty' work."

"And what is the dirty work?" asks Aaron slowly.

"Rounding up the Jews, and—"

"And?" Aaron persists, seeing Sax's rage building again.

"They beat them, shoot them, and put them on trains. Then the Germans take them away."

"Why? Where were they being taken?" Aaron asks.

Gyorgi hesitates. One of the other soldiers, who has been listening nearby, speaks up. "Tell them about the skeleton, Gyorgi."

"What skeleton?" snarls Sax.

Gyorgi remains silent.

"Gyorgi!" Aaron snaps, his patience also wearing thin. "Tell us about the skeleton."

"He was walking along the road," says Gyorgi. "He was just skin and bones—like a skeleton. They don't feed them in the concentration camps. He escaped from one in Poland. He…"

The other soldier speaks up. "He said the Germans are killing all the Jews in gas chambers—Jews from all over Europe. The children, their mothers, the sick and the elderly go first. He only lived because he was young enough for hard labor and wasn't yet weak enough for the gas chamber."

"Did he see what happened to the Jews from my town?" asks Sax. Gyorgi doesn't answer. "Did he see them?" screams Sax.

"I don't know. He was from the Carpathians."

"The Carpathians! Who was he?" cries Sax. "His name!"

"I don't know. He was very sick when we found him. He's dead."

Aaron's stomach turns over. Sax picks up his glass and hurls it against the wall with the force of a gunshot. The others stare at him as he stands, breathing hard. Aaron tries to comfort him but is himself overcome with grief. The Russian soldiers quietly disperse to other rooms to let the two men work through their dreaded realization.

"They're gone," whispers Aaron hoarsely. "How can it be otherwise?"

Sax shakes his head. Both are close to tears.

"What do we do?" asks Sax. "What do we do?"

Aaron has no answer. *Perhaps,* he thinks, *Bielka, being so small, has been overlooked by the Nazis. Perhaps there is still hope.* But he doesn't really believe it.

At ten o'clock, their brooding sorrow is interrupted by a knock at the door. Gyorgi goes to answer it.

"Kill them, whoever it is," growls Sax.

"But sir, it's—"

"If they're Hungarian, kill the sons of bitches, now!"

"But it's—"

Sax picks up his submachine gun and pushes past Gyorgi to the door. Standing there are Christina and Theresa, the baker's daughters, both dressed in their finest clothing. They shrink back slightly at the sight of the huge, hyperventilating man with a gun.

"Yeah?" asks Sax at last.

"We have presents for our new leaders," says Christina, the taller and seemingly older of the two. They hold forth baskets of baked goods and sweets. "We baked these. Our parents told us we should bring them to you."

Aaron and Sax exchange a quick glance, then Aaron takes the baskets from them.

"Thank you," says Aaron. "Come in."

The two girls enter warily but appear to be excited and curious as well.

"Want a drink?" asks Aaron.

The two nod, smiling widely and Aaron accommodates them.

"We've never been inside the Hodis' house before," says the one named Christina.

"Neither had we 'till this afternoon," says Aaron.

"It's nice," she replies. "Much nicer than the place where that jerk…" she giggles, and Theresa giggles with her.

"Jerk, huh?" says Aaron casually, pouring himself a drink. "What jerk?"

"Someone I was seeing before. You were asking about him," says Christina.

Aaron stops pouring. "I what?"

Christina casts a mischievous glance at Theresa. "A policeman. You were looking for the police."

Both Aaron and Sax lean closer.

"Yes, I was interested in that," says Aaron.

"Outside of town," Theresa says with an air of mischievous conspiracy. "They're hiding out. On the farms, the big ones. The farmers love them because they finally have someone to plow the fields, and for free."

The two girls giggle.

"They were such big shots, now they're in overalls," Christina says.

"They have some Germans, too," says Theresa. "Some of them are real Nazis."

Aaron and Sax nod.

"Have you seen the upstairs?" asks Sax suddenly.

The giggling stops.

"Of course not," says Theresa.

"We haven't seen it either," says Sax. "Would you like to?"

The two girls giggle again, finish their drinks in a gulp, and stand up. Sax and Aaron lead them upstairs to the bedrooms.

Early the next morning, while ground fog still swirls in the low-lying fields, the two men, hung over from the night before and accompanied by four Russian soldiers, smash down the front door of a sprawling farmhouse outside Gérjen. Rushing inside with their guns ready, they interrupt the farmer and ten young sturdy-looking farmhands at breakfast.

"Who is the owner here? Who owns this farm?" Aaron demands as the astonished men jump away from the table.

A stocky, silver-haired man speaks up. "It's mine, I'm the owner."

Aaron strides up to him and gestures to the farmhands. "Which of these are police?"

"None," says the farmer.

"You're lying," snarls Aaron. "Line everyone up against the wall!"

As the men are prodded to the wall, Aaron demands again, "Which of you are police? Which are soldiers? Which are spies?"

No one answers.

"We're not playing games, and we have no patience for this," says Aaron. "We are the new rulers of Gérjen. We are authorized to arrest or shoot anyone on the spot who lies. We need information from you. All of you." Still silence. "Alright, we'll give you one last chance. If you don't reveal yourselves, we're going to start shooting."

Still no one speaks until Sax aims his gun and fires a burst into one of the men, who collapses to the ground in a spray of blood.

Aaron is almost as shocked as the men, now visibly quaking against the wall, but he can see that Sax's temple has begun to pulsate, the rage within him bursting to get out.

Aaron then snaps, "Okay, who else wants to die?" He paces back and forth in front of them.

"Him!" says one of the men, pointing to another. "He is a policeman!"

Another man then points and screams, "This one's a German!" There is a flurry of finger-pointing. They are all police or Nazis, if all the accusations are to be believed—or none of them, if the denials are believed. Fear, like a noxious odor, fills the room.

"Quiet!" shouts Aaron, instantly causing the men to freeze. "Where are the Jews?" he asks. "I have been in this town for several days and haven't seen any Jews. There used to be Jews here. Where are they?"

He prods one of the men with his submachine gun.

"I don't know," the man stammers.

Aaron walks down the line, pointing his gun at each of the men. "Does anyone know? Something must have happened. We saw a kosher butcher shop, or what used to be a butcher shop, all burned up. We saw a synagogue. No one was there. We don't have kosher butcher shops and synagogues without Jews. Who can tell me what happened to them? To the Jewish women and children?"

By now, the men are trembling, afraid to look at Aaron as he paces and questions each one. All except the farmer, who is numb with shock.

Aaron surveys the group, then points to the one who has been identified as a policeman. "I've heard they were turned over to the Germans by good Hungarian policemen like you. Is this true?"

"I don't know," the man says.

"And they were put on trains to be killed."

"I don't know, sir."

"You? A policeman? Isn't it your job to know about crimes?"

Aaron stops by a cabinet displaying an extensive collection of fine china.

"I grew up in a little town in Czechoslovakia, and one day the Hungarians came in and they just took whatever they wanted from the Jews." He picks up a few plates. "Maybe some of this is ours." Aaron tosses them to the ground, shattering them.

"Then the Hungarians made us wear yellow bands and yellow stars and said we couldn't go out in public. My own mother couldn't go out in public."

Sax walks up to the man Aaron was questioning. "How would you like it if *you* couldn't go out in public anymore?" he grunts.

"No sir," the man stammers.

Sax aims his gun and shoots him once in the head, spraying blood and brain tissue over everyone nearby. Another man falls to his knees and vomits.

"See, Aaron? A Hungarian policeman doesn't need a yellow star. You can just look at his head. If he has a hole in it, he's not allowed in public."

Sax then fires at the kneeling man, blasting his head into pulp. Aaron watches as his friend's bulging neck turns crimson and seems to swell to the size of a tree stump. His eyes have the crazed look of a madman.

Aaron, his nostrils filled with the scent of blood, catches Sax's rage as if it's an airborne virus. His pulse quickens, and he grows ever angrier and more impatient with the prisoners' refusal to reveal themselves. With blood rushing to his brain, he is literally seeing red. He begins to pace frantically, then pulls a piece of wood out of the stove and holds it, flaming, in front of the remaining prisoners.

"I had a friend, Kimlit, from my home town. A very fine young man. One day he got sick, and you know what the Hungarians did? They put him in a barn with hundreds of other sick Jewish slaves and set it on fire." Aaron tips over a pan of grease on the stove and throws the burning wood onto the floor. Flames quickly engulf the grease and nearby furniture.

The men tremble as they watch the flames spread, terrified by what Aaron's next move might be. Sax wonders, too. Then Aaron himself falls suddenly silent, his eyes on the flames.

These are no longer flames in a farmhouse in Hungary. They are flames consuming his home in Bielka. They are flames consuming Helen's farm on the edge of the Carpathian Mountains. They are flames ignited by the hatred of the Nazis, hatred that spread like wildfire to their Hungarian minions and belch out onto his innocent relatives, neighbors, and friends. They are roaring, raping flames that destroy everything he knows and loves, laying it to waste and turning it to ash. In the midst of the flames, Aaron sees an image of one of the atrocities he had witnessed in Russia—the young Jewish mother he had watched being raped by the German SS. Could such a horror be happening to his sisters, to Helen or to his mother?

Unable to contain himself any longer, Aaron turns his gun on one of the men who has been pointed out as a Nazi and fires at him point blank. The man falls to the floor screaming. Aaron reloads his weapon and begins to shout above the screams. "Which of you bastards is next?"

"Please, no!" cries the farmer. "Please, please no, no more."

"Then tell us who they are, or the rest of them die!" screams Aaron.

"And then *you* die!" adds Sax.

Suddenly, three men step forward from what remains of the group. The first two admit to being Nazi officers. The other has been with the Hungarian secret police. Aaron orders two of his soldiers to put out the fire while he, Sax, and the other Russians tie up their prisoners, and put them on their wagon. They are taken away for further brutal interrogation to extract any useful information or intelligence to be sent back to headquarters.

During the days after that rampage, Aaron, Sax, and the troops make their rounds of other farmhouses, shooting at groups of men until those they want finally step forward or are rooted out. Then the two interrogate their prisoners. Any prisoner who refuses to give up the information demanded of him is beaten until he finally breaks down and cries out the answers. Any who are discovered to be Nazis or Hungarian secret policemen or Axis soldiers who committed atrocities are shot to suffer a slow painful death immediately after interrogation. At last, when Aaron and Sax finally finish their interrogations, they take their remaining captives away to the overcrowded prison camps in Päks, the town hosting the Russian commanding headquarters.

Their blood rage remains uncontrollable. The hatred the Germans and Hungarians have spewed forth on the Jewish people now seems to be belched back on them in all its ferocious intensity. Once the revenge killings begin, they feed upon themselves to the point where the usually cool-headed Aaron and his half-crazed partner take even the slightest hint of defiance as a pretext for punitive action. As the days go by, the redness of the two men's rage mingles with the redness of the river of blood it spawns.

As for the men who have been harboring these criminals, as well as those farmhands who are undoubtedly aware of their co-workers' identities, if, after repeated warnings they refuse to point them out, they are also found guilty, and their punishment is also justified, at least in the minds and hearts of Aaron and Sax.

However, Aaron is very kind to the townspeople. The townsfolk perceive Aaron and Sax, who do not wear Russian military uniforms, as political leaders, bulwarks from the raping, looting, and violent Russian soldiers, whom they've heard about from neighboring Hungarian towns. Aaron assures the townspeople that he will not allow the citizens of Gerjen to be harmed. All he asks of them is to reveal where the Nazi and Hungarian soldiers and police are hiding, to which the townspeople respond in kind.

The townspeople are at a loss as to how to further reward their saviors, Aaron and Sax, to demonstrate their deep gratitude. There is only a limited quantity of cakes and liquor they can send over. So instead, they send over their daughters to visit Aaron and Sax to entertain them during the evenings. And the young ladies are only too willing to accommodate their two new leaders. It is as if Aaron and Sax are being treated as a 1940s version of rock stars, as the women virtually throw themselves at the two men.

On occasion, some of the Hungarian young women begin to intimate how they would welcome marriage to Aaron, but Aaron deftly manages to refrain from such a commitment to them, because his heart belongs to one Helen Lazárovic. Aaron often wonders how Helen is surviving occupation under the Nazis and Hungarians and how desperately he wants to return home to protect her and his family. Little does he know that Helen and his family have long before been deported to the Auschwitz death camp.

On some occasions, when the two Jewish overlords complete their bounty hunting for the day, they and their band of Russian soldiers celebrate with a never-ending supply of vodka. The bigger the catch, the greater the celebration. And sometimes, when Aaron and Sax are too tired to transport their prisoners to Päks, these captives—bound hand and foot and tied to railings secured to the floor studs—are also present to witness the merriment.

On one of these festive occasions, Gyorgi blurts out, "Aaron—we've always wondered how you, sir—such a small man—has such great physical strength and power. No one would ever imagine it."

"Really?" asks a drunken Aaron, surveying the room until his gaze fixes on a burly looking prisoner, whose thick black chest hairs are peeking above the collar of his Nazi officer's uniform.

Aaron stands and stares at the German, who glares back defiantly. Although the prisoner is at least a foot taller, and must outweigh him significantly, Aaron cuts him loose with a butcher knife, then grabs him by the jacket and hoists him above his head with just one arm and parades him around the room while Sax and the Russians scream with delight.

Aaron then spots the burning coal stove used to cook the evening's meals, and with his grip still firm, lowers the prisoner onto the blazing fire. The Nazi writhes in pain and begs for mercy while Aaron holds him down, the cheers of the crowd now reaching an ear-shattering crescendo.

At last, Aaron says, "I think that's enough," and loosens his grip on the German, who tumbles in a heap to the floor.

While his Russian comrades continue to toast him, Aaron stumbles about the room in a drunken stupor. *"Na Zdróvia!"* they cheer, until at last, he finds a spot to pass out.

The next morning, he is roused from his sleep by an anxious Sax. "Aaron, I want to show you what you did last night."

"What are you talking about?" grumbles a perplexed Aaron, who gets up and follows Sax into the room where they had been celebrating the night before. Standing before him is the barrel-chested Nazi prisoner he'd punished, guarded by two Russian soldiers.

"Show him!" shouts a delighted Sax.

The two Russian guards rip off the German's shirt, revealing the hairiest torso Aaron has ever seen on a man, but a chest that is reddened and strangely hairless in large spots. "See Aaron?" says Sax. "You pulled out all his hair last night!"

"What?" asks a stupefied Aaron. "What are you talking about?"

"When you grabbed him by the chest and lifted him up," says Sax. "Now turn the Nazi scum around," he orders the two soldiers, "and take down his pants."

The Russians oblige.

The German's rump reveals burns ranging in color from black to red.

"You did this to him, Aaron—when you set him down on the stove, you burned his ass! That's better than anything I ever did in my whole life!"

"I don't remember a thing," says Aaron, quite hung over, with a quizzical look on his face.

"Then you got too drunk to enjoy it," says Sax. "Too bad. Anyway, our Russian friends have been calling me 'the big monster,' and you 'the little monster.' I'm starting to think it should be the other way around!" Sax snorts out a big belly laugh and walks away.

"I'm not sure I like that," Aaron mutters to himself.

About two weeks later, Aaron and Sax are prodding a ragtag group of ten German prisoners, hands on their heads, on the road from Gérjen to Päks. This group of prisoners holds special significance for Sax and Aaron. There are no Hungarians amongst them, only hardened veterans of the SS, the root of all the horrors that destroyed Sax's and Aaron's world as they knew it.

Aaron's vision, which has been flushed with red from days of killing, is now better balanced with the late autumn hues of the trees and the deep blue of the Danube River not far away. Although his pulse has slowed, he is still in shock from what he has done, how completely he has been gripped by a rage deeper than he ever could have imagined.

Just before the group reaches the outskirts of Gérjen, Sax orders the Russian soldiers to prod the prisoners toward an empty school building.

"What are you doing?" asks Aaron.

"Going to school," says Sax, who kicks down the front door.

"Why?" asks Aaron.

"To learn something." He pushes the prisoners through the open door. "These Nazi pigs haven't spilled a word all day. I think they must have been trained to take it without giving anything up. I want to learn how much they can really take."

Sax prods the men into a classroom and lines them up in front of the chalkboard while Aaron watches warily from the doorway, machine gun pointed at the Germans. The Russians point their guns at the Germans, too.

"All right—who's going to talk?" asks Sax, pacing before them. The prisoners remain silent, avoiding the big man's glance. "Come on, you Nazi bastards. I want information, and I want it now!" Without warning, Sax punches one of them in the face, breaking his nose. He then continues up and down the line, flailing away with his big fists, smashing faces and breaking bones as blood splatters, but the prisoners don't flinch.

Sax then tells Aaron and the Russian troops, "I see two private office rooms in the back. Aaron and I will take two of the stinking Nazis into one of the rooms. Meanwhile, you soldiers keep your guns pointed at the rest of the Germans. We'll take two prisoners at a time into the room for further interrogation until one of them spills the intelligence."

As Aaron and Sax prod the first two prisoners into the small room, Aaron suddenly shudders in an awful moment of recognition: The schoolhouse and Sax's brutality has taken him back to the schoolhouse at Novyi Oskol and the furious brutality the Hungarian SS had unleashed there upon Aaron and his fellow Jewish slaves. Aaron now realizes why Sax has chosen a private room for his "further interrogation." He intends to brutalize all the SS men in this catch with such savagery that he doesn't want the Russian soldiers to see.

"That's enough, Ignatz," Aaron says in a level voice. "Let's get the hell out of here and drop them off with the Russians."

"Haven't you heard?" asks Sax. "The Russians have more prisoners than they can handle. So we need to handle them ourselves." He picks up a heavy chair and begins beating the prisoners with it until it breaks, and then he uses the pieces as clubs to shatter their arms and smash their kneecaps with a greater ferocity than Aaron had ever seen from Sax. Through it all, Sax continually demands that the Germans answer his questions about military intelligence, but aside from an occasional grunt and groan, the prisoners make no sound.

Angered and frustrated at his failure to get even an utterance out of these two prisoners, Sax turns to Aaron and holds out a long piece of wood. "Your turn, Aaron. Go ahead. Smash their teeth out—like this!" Sax takes the wood and smashes one of the Nazis in the mouth. Blood and broken teeth dribble out. Sax stares at him for a moment, admiring his work, but the German does not cry out or utter a sound.

"Ignatz," an alarmed Aaron tries again. "We've already tried interrogating them. There's nothing more we can get out of them. Let the Russians take over. We're finished here."

"You're right."

Sax then announces to the Germans in the room, "Get out of this room, you two! And get back in line with the rest of your Nazi swine."

The two badly beaten prisoners cannot even stand up to walk out of the room.

Aaron calls out, "Gyorgi! Bring over one of your comrades to help get these two prisoners out of here."

Gyorgi and another Russian soldier prop up the two prisoners in the small room as Aaron directs the two other Russians to march the other Germans out of the schoolhouse. The remaining prisoners can barely walk, though they are not as brutalized as the two Germans in the room.

Aaron, Sax, and the Russians prod the prisoners, all of them savagely bloodied, into the schoolyard and toward the Danube River. When they reach the Danube, Sax unexpectedly dismisses the Russian soldiers, who salute and disperse, evidently perplexed. Aaron, too, is puzzled.

"This way," says Aaron, pointing toward the town.

"You're wrong. Follow me," Sax insists, herding the Germans to the bank of the Danube, where he ties each one to tall posts. He then sets his gun down, casually approaches one of the prisoners, and grabs the man's ear, tearing it clean off his head. Still, the prisoner makes no sound, even as blood splatters down from where his ear had once been. Sax then grabs the next man by the nose, twisting it until it breaks. On and on down the line he continues this brutality, ripping off ears, mutilating noses, pulling out lips and twisting them until the blood streams. Not a single soldier flinches. He then pulls his pistol from his hip, circles around the prisoners and begins shooting the fingers off their hands. Then he randomly starts shooting the noses and ears off their heads, the blood gushing and spraying wildly. Their refusal to cry out just makes Sax more and more frustrated, robbing him of the satisfaction of seeing and hearing his mortal enemies writhe and scream in agony, pushing him even farther over the edge.

Sax stops in front of an SS captain, apparently the commander of the group, who refuses to look at him. "Aaron," he says. "This Nazi bastard isn't even looking at me. Watch this."

Sax takes his knife and gouges out one of the captain's eyeballs, the man squirming in pain, his eyeball dropping to the ground, the blood gushing out of his eye socket, while Sax laughs uncontrollably, finally getting the reaction he's been seeking from this group.

"How does it feel to be a one-eyed Nazi pig?" he roars at the SS man.

Aaron simply watches as if in a trance, his gun now hanging at his side. He is transfixed not just by the violence—of which he's seen far too much to be shocked—but by the transformation of his friend. Sax's neck and face are deep red; his features are depraved as he decimates these men like a glutton devouring a table full of food. Sax then grabs an axe and swings the blade deeply into the torsos and necks of the prisoners, chopping them up into pieces, as their guts spill onto the ground, their blood gushing and spraying into the air.

Finally, he turns to Aaron, as if suddenly remembering he is not alone.

"Arón," he barks in Russian as if he is Aaron's superior. "You take the next one." He tears off an ear in demonstration, and looks back at Aaron, who steps forward even though he has no idea whether or not he would have the physical strength to perform such a feat.

Conflicting feelings numb Aaron's mind and body. Part of him feels that what Sax is doing—and he is about to do—is justified. The other part feels repulsed by the revolting form of revenge Sax has created, as if this is not part of "the plan." One thing, however, is undeniable: Sax has somehow seized the leadership role from Aaron.

Aaron stands directly in front of one of the Germans and looks him in the eye.

"Come on, Aaron. What are you waiting for?" Sax taunts.

Aaron grabs the German's left ear and yanks on it. Nothing happens. The man winces but does not cry out.

Aaron then positions his left hand on the German's head, determined to pull with all his might, when he catches sight of the Danube River and freezes. For a moment, he is not standing on the shore of a river outside Gérjen with a group of bloodied prisoners, nor in the company of a hideous beast who is also his friend. He is not on the brutal cutting edge of a monstrous war that has drained as much humanity from its survivors as it has blood from its dead. Instead, he is standing in Bielka by the beautiful stream running adjacent to his house, the stream that powers his neighbor's flour mill. Aaron's rage has built up and festered for five grievous years, and when it finds its release at last, it seems that nothing can stop it. Yet something does—and that something is, of all things, the vision of a peaceful farmhouse on the edge of a stream tucked away in a quiet corner of Eastern Europe. Aaron's memory proves stronger than any offense he has suffered. His boiling rage is suddenly quenched, and humanity, in the form of his memory of the cool soothing mountain breezes of Bielka, takes its place.

"Aaron!" thunders a voice that does not belong in Bielka. It is Sax, calling him back to the blood-splattered town of Gérjen.

"No," says Aaron, as he lets go of the German.

"What?" cries Sax.

"No more."

"Our families!" screams Sax. "My wife and two children—they killed them!"

Aaron points at the prisoners. "And we are not them, are we, Ignatz?"

"You don't want revenge?" bellows Sax. "The colonel said we can do whatever we want with these men. These are the fiends who killed, maybe raped your sisters, your mother! And Helen! Do it for Helen!"

"We've done enough."

Sax moves menacingly toward Aaron, his nostrils flaring. "If you don't do it to them, I'm going to do it to you!"

"You want to kill me, too, Ignatz?" asks Aaron. "Is that revenge? Is this what being a Jew means to you? Is this what your mother and father taught you?"

Aaron's words somehow reach Sax, who stops in his tracks.

"You are no better than a Nazi!" Aaron spits.

"And one more thing, Sax," says Aaron. "I'm the one who was appointed ruler of this town—so you are still my subordinate."

Sax's eyes flare with anger, but he does not move any closer to Aaron. The two remain transfixed in menacing confrontation while the Germans watch impassively.

At last, the silence is broken by another voice: "Aaron? Is that you?"

Aaron and Sax both turn. Limpy, looking much healed but distressed, is standing before them with a knapsack in one hand and a cane in the other, staring at the grotesquely bloodied and mutilated prisoners.

"They transferred me back to you. They said I would find you here. My God, what's going on here?"

"Ask Sax," says Aaron.

Sax's expression only grows grimmer. "Leave," he orders. "Both of you. I will take care of business since you won't."

But Aaron doesn't budge. He and Sax glare at each other for a moment. Then Limpy hobbles over to Aaron and tugs at his friend's arm.

"Aaron," he whispers. "Let's get out of here."

"I can't," says Aaron, his gaze still fixed on Sax. "I've got to stop him. He's gone crazy."

"You'll end up killing each other, and what will that accomplish?" says Limpy.

Aaron turns to Limpy and considers his friend's plea.

"Come on," says Limpy, pulling Aaron frantically by the arm as he begins to lead him back to town—but not before they turn to watch Sax dislodge the prisoners from the posts, and as the sun sets over the Danube, he shoots those Nazis who remain alive and kicks their corpses into the river, watching them float away, one by one.

That horrible afternoon was not the last time Aaron saw those bodies floating in the river. They came back to him that evening and for many evenings afterward in his sleep, their eyeless faces and toothless mouths wet with blood and water. They did not speak, but Aaron heard them nonetheless and heeded them, and from that day on, he stopped accompanying Sax on his killing missions, trying instead to escape the memory of the horror by inculcating Limpy with the task of requisitioning provisions for shipment back to Russia.

Yet, like the fingers of a poisonous fog creeping their way through the lowest darkest parts of the land, Sax's rampages spread across the countryside and scarred it, and scarred Aaron, too—for Aaron was closely associated with Sax in the minds of the Russians and the townspeople. The deeds they had done, morning after morning, and well into the afternoons and sometimes into the night, would be unimaginable in the minds of civilized people.

It was madness, consistent entirely with the madness of the world Aaron and Sax had endured for years. Yet Aaron did what he did because he had to endure the Novyi Oskol schoolhouse, the brutality of the slave labor camps, and the atrocities he witnessed committed against so many other Jews; he felt justification for his execution of the many hundreds of Nazi war criminals who committed atrocities against innocent Jewish women and children; but he had a reckoning between the crimes against humanity the Jewish people had suffered, many at the hands of his prisoners he captured in Gérjen; versus those Nazi and Hungarian captives who may have not fully participated in these atrocities.

That day by the Danube was where Aaron began to see the indiscriminate revenge killings as madness, but Sax did not. Yes, Aaron and Sax had both endured grievous wounds at the hands of their enemies; and so did countless other Jews;. And yes, their persecutors deserved punishment. But now Aaron began to ask, "What have I done? Did I punish some of the prisoners more than they deserved?" He searched for answers and could find none. But Aaron's realization of his own possible wrongdoing, and his cessation from it, was not enough, as long as Sax continued his frenzied campaign. Aaron continued to appeal to him not to become one of the monsters they'd both endured for so long, but Sax's own anguish and anger were too unfathomably deep; and such revenge is a cold emotion not influenced by sentiment or reason. Surely, Aaron told Sax, they could deal with their captives as they had done in the past, taking them to Päks or holding them in their own temporary jails; then at least burying the dead ones in fields far from the city limits. But Sax would have none of it. He continued kicking corpses into the Danube River. Aaron became increasingly aware that, sooner or later, the townspeople would discover Sax's burial ground in the river, and that many corpses, several of which were Hungarian and some of which may possibly have been residents of this town, would eventually float to the river's surface. Then what? Aaron also realized that one day, Aaron, too, might be a target of Sax's unbridled rage, especially after he threatened him at the river.

When Aaron's appeals failed, he tried to contact his colonel—but unfortunately, the colonel had moved on to the front, deeper into Hungary; so he spoke to their other superiors in the Red Army to intervene. Their response was worse than no action at all: When apprised of the full dimension of Sax's activities, they voiced approval and encouraged him, especially since he had now become fluent in Russian. Sax was punishing the enemy in a way that the Russians wished they could do. This served also to undermine whatever authority Aaron had left, for Aaron had from the start been appointed by the colonel as the "brains" of their operation, the leader, and Sax the brawn, the enforcer. Now that Sax was doing the "dirty work," the Russians preferred putting their weight behind him, while Aaron had become in practice his subordinate. The only comfort Aaron took was the knowledge that Sax's murderous rampages did not extend to women and children. As insane as he had become, he had no interest in targeting children, and as for the women—he had "other plans."

Rumors of Sax's experiences only piqued Limpy's interest. When Aaron visited with him, he complained of being cooped up at his administrative quarters on the far side of town and pleaded with

Aaron to allow him to join Sax, as he'd always wanted vengeance—after all, it was the Nazis and Hungarian soldiers who disfigured him. Aaron refused, for fear of putting him at risk, especially with the dangerously unpredictable Sax. Aaron made it clear to him that he must stay behind, so that he could attend to the important daily business of running the town and being accountable for all the supply shipments being sent to Russia. Because he was doing so well in this position, Aaron assured him he would be richly rewarded, perhaps to eventually run a big city. At that, Limpy and Aaron heartily laughed and then embraced.

Although Aaron had hoped he could wait out the war in Gérjen, and then return home to face whatever truth awaited him there, he started to conclude that Sax was too great a threat to that plan, that the fury he had unleashed would surely come back to haunt them.

Aaron had but one course of action—he had to get away from Sax, even if it meant slipping off into the woods again to live off the land and his own guile. By the end of January 1945, Aaron secretly began to plan his escape.

CHAPTER 17
ESCAPE FROM THE RUSSIANS

BY AUTUMN 1944, ALLIED forces begin closing in on Nazi Germany and her allies. On the Eastern Front in Hungary, the Red Army, with a sizeable portion of its forces already west of the Danube River south of Budapest, launches a new offensive toward the city late in 1944. But the city changes hands a few times over the next several weeks before Hitler's obsession with holding Budapest finally allows his forces to recapture the city with crack SS troops in early 1945.[11]

A senior German intelligence officer with a broad inelegant face, pale skin, white hair, and cold tired eyes stands before the map of Hungary posted on the wall of his substantial office at German Operational Headquarters in Budapest in January 1945. The map shows units of the Red Army filled in with great detail everywhere except in the vicinity of Gérjen. A nervous bespectacled junior officer stands before him.

"You'll notice a gap in the one sector."

"Yes."

"We seem to have very little information about Red Army units in this area. I was wondering about this gap. Herr Eichmann was as well. Do you know why there is a gap here?"

"Sir, we've had our eyes and ears taken from us."

"How?"

The junior officer shifts nervously, then tries to explain: "Two men. The Russians have placed them in charge of the town and its surroundings. They have been very ruthless and very effective. That is what our reports indicate."

"Who are they?"

"We don't know. But they seem to be partisans, or possibly former slaves."

"Slaves?" shouts the intelligence officer. "You mean they're Jews?"

"Yes, sir, they appear to be. They have gone on a rampage of terror and killing."

The intelligence officer sits down at his desk. "That should not be surprising. Wherever there are atrocities committed, you can bet there are Jews behind it. Why haven't you stopped them?"

"Sir, most of our battalions are below company strength. It is all we can do to guard the shores of the Danube. We do not have the resources to attack across the river all the way to Gérjen to neutralize them."

"You need to launch an offensive to take out two Jews?"

"We had been hoping some of our spies would be able to do the job, but we hear that these Jews have managed to capture or kill nearly all our operatives."

The intelligence officer is now furious, and his face turns beet red. He stands up and points directly at the junior officer and shouts, "Why haven't you ever told me about this before? I could have you court-martialed for this!"

The junior officer stammers and at last he responds, "Sir, I was afraid to admit that we had been outmaneuvered by Jews, but these two are very crafty."

"Don't ever say that! No Jew is crafty!"

The senior intelligence officer sits down and begins scribbling on some documents on his desk, then hands them to the junior officer.

"I can spare you Lieutenant Kraft and three of his hand-picked men."

"Kraft? Of the SS?"

"Yes. Use him well. They should be able to make contact with the intelligence sources we have remaining around Gérjen, and I expect it will not be difficult to remove this Jew problem. I want this gap filled in within two days."

He points to the map.

"Yes, sir."

In Gérjen that evening, Aaron is busy packing. He is doing it quietly, to avoid suspicion. He decides to go separately on patrol the following day, then slip away from the Russian soldiers to go into hiding and wait out the war. In preparation, he has been building up a cache of cigarettes, liquor, and various dry goods to use for trading purposes once he is on his own. He makes sure to include as much as possible of the voluminous amounts of cash and jewelry he had stolen along with the Russians when they raided the wealthy Hungarian villas several months earlier. Aaron was hoping to give some of this treasure to his beloved sweetheart, Helen, as a wedding gift with the remainder to his mother and sisters in order to bring some hope and sunshine back into their lives, as fleeting as that might be. Now Aaron fears that he will need to use some of this cash he intended for Helen and his family gifts in order to bribe officials.

His task is interrupted by the appearance of Sax, drunk and blood-soiled, with two young women. The two men are hardly speaking by now, and Sax doesn't even offer one of the women to Aaron, who had long stopped indulging in their company. Still, one of the women, a petite blonde, looks longingly at Aaron and begins to approach him before Sax puts a meaty hand on her arm and drags her back toward him.

When Sax sees Aaron shaking his head in disgust, he stops.

"What's the matter with you? Don't you want this little one over here?" Sax taunts, pointing to the petite blonde. "Better hurry. She's not gonna be around for you once I get through with her."

"No Sax," says Aaron. "I'm finished with all your madness. This whole thing has got to stop—it's gone on way too long as it is!"

"The hell with you!" cries Sax menacingly. "These Hungarian whores are ours. If you don't want them, I'll take all the bitches for myself!"

After Sax disappears upstairs with the women and a bottle of vodka, Aaron lies down on the couch to catch some sleep. Before long, his rest is thwarted by the screams of the women and the roaring drunken laughter of Sax. Aaron wonders: *What the hell is Sax doing with these women?*

It is almost dawn when Sax comes downstairs in a drunken haze. He bellows to Aaron about all his accomplishments the day and evening prior, including lurid detail about his sexual conquests of some of the women. Aaron endures it all wordlessly.

After Sax spends himself with his boasts, his demeanor changes. He sits beside Aaron and begins speaking to him quietly, like a close comrade.

"You're right, Aaron. I am too hard on these women. We...well, I...should treat them better."

Aaron looks at Sax skeptically.

"Yes," Sax says. "I know I have been wrong. We shouldn't see them as whores. We should see them as *mothers*. That's the best way to get our revenge."

"Mothers?" asks Aaron, incredulous. He points to Sax's vodka. "You should put that down."

"No! Listen to me and don't judge. The people of this town have been sending their daughters to us, even bearing gifts to buy them favor."

It is true, for power has its appeal, even when wielded in such a grotesque way.

Sax continues, "Now is the time for us to get as many of their women pregnant as we can. That will *really* punish the Hungarian people and their families for what they've done to us."

Aaron stands up, astounded. "Deliberately getting the women pregnant? They'll be scorned and mocked. No man will marry them. Their children will be treated as lepers. You are making innocent women and children victims of this war. Who are you, Ignatz? What has happened to you? You've lost all sense of decency. You've become an animal."

Sax's eyes take on the same fire Aaron had seen when Sax was about to act in a murderous mood. "Are you nuts, Aaron? You've done nothing here for weeks. Are you weak? Afraid?" he barks, then catches himself and calms down. "You must do this with me, Aaron. We rule this town, so we've got to stick together. We're getting revenge for what they've done to us, these Nazis and Hungarians; revenge with bullets and fists and clubs. Now we can vengeance with lifelong disgrace and shame. Imagine how these people will feel when they realize all their daughters are swelling up with Jewish children inside." Sax starts to smile. "And maybe some will expect marriage, even to a Jew, but…" he pauses for a big belly laugh, "by then we'll have vanished, and they'll have to harvest the crop we've left behind for them!"

Aaron shakes his head 'no.'

The wide grin disappears from Sax's face. "This will be the ultimate revenge, Aaron, the righteous vengeance of the Jewish people. *Our* revenge."

"Absolutely not!" says Aaron.

Sax spits on the ground and pours himself another drink, burning with anger at Aaron's dismissal of his latest twisted notion for vengeance.

Later that night, Aaron is awakened by the petite blonde he'd seen earlier with Sax, who has snuck into his room. That her face was freshly bruised is evident even in the dim light, though Aaron has seen worse.

"You don't have to—" says Aaron. "Go home."

"No," says the woman. "I came here for you—not for what you think. I have heard you are a good man."

Aaron sits up.

"I need your help," she continues. "This monster, this Sax, he has my two brothers. He has beaten them badly. They are not bad people; they were just soldiers. They never said a bad word about Jewish people." She begins to cry. "They do not deserve to die. He is going to kill them in the morning."

"Where are they?" Aaron asks.

"In a barn, just down the road. He has a Russian soldier guarding them. I know the soldier will listen to you if you tell him to let them go."

"What did they do for the Jews in this town? Did they try to stop the deportations, the atrocities? Did they lift a finger to help? I was tortured by many Hungarian soldiers. Why do your brothers deserve leniency?"

"They did nothing," she says, tearfully again. "Neither bad nor good. They meant no harm. There has been enough killing. Please help them."

Aaron is wary—is it some sort of trap? If not, what would he do about Sax's wrath in the morning? *Sax is a monster,* Aaron thinks. *She called him a monster, and that is what he has become. A Jewish monster. Do Jews not hold themselves to a higher standard?* He picks up his gun and decides he can handle Sax when the time comes. After all, he has survived many more substantial dangers.

A few blocks away, Aaron finds the Soviet soldier half asleep outside the barn and dismisses him. He then leads the girl inside, where the two badly bloodied young men are tied to a post. Their sister weeps at the sight. As Aaron frees them, one of them mutters a "thank you" through broken teeth. The woman guides them to the door, urging them to go home and hide.

"How can I repay you?" says the young woman to Aaron.

"It is a gift. If you repay someone for a gift, it's no longer a gift, but a debt," Aaron replies.

The woman nods tearfully and continues walking back toward the headquarters with Aaron.

"Why aren't *you* going home?"

"I'm afraid if Sax does not see me when he wakes up..."

Aaron stops her. "I'll tell him I had you after he did."

The woman looks into Aaron's kind eyes, then mutters a "thank you" and disappears into the night.

The next morning, Aaron agrees to join Sax in making the rounds to distract him from remembering his appointment with the two brothers. By afternoon, Sax remembers it, but Aaron lies and tells him he has finished them off before dawn, because one was almost dead, and the other had died, and the body was creating such a stench that he decided to dispose of them both.

In the pre-dawn hours that day, a few miles away, four men in farmers' clothing row across the Danube and climb ashore, where they crouch, sorting through their baggage, their movements swift and crisp. Among their sacks and suitcases are weapons of various kinds—one rifle with a scope, and several automatic weapons. The man with the scope, Lieutenant Kraft, orders his other SS soldiers to check and conceal their guns, then leads them quietly inland.

By mid-afternoon, after Sax, Aaron, and a squad of soldiers have confiscated a considerable amount of property and taken a few prisoners, Aaron makes an excuse to return early to their headquarters. On the way, he stops by Limpy's quarters to say goodbye before he makes his escape from Sax and the Russians.

"I know the Russians are backing Sax now," says Limpy. "But my loyalty is to you, Aaron, now and always. You saved my life, and you've made me a king here. Please take me with you."

"Not this time, my friend," says Aaron. "This time, I go alone. I cannot put you in the kind of danger I'll be facing. You'll be safer here. You've done a good job for the Russians. You've sent them plenty of supplies, more than Sax and I ever did, and you've committed no wrongdoing. They should give you a 'Hero of the Soviet Union' medal." Both men laugh heartily at that notion, then hug and bid one another farewell.

Aaron never sees Limpy again.

Back at his own headquarters, Aaron secures his store of cigarettes and other supplies and is packing an extra coat when an urgent knock on the door causes him to freeze. He waits, hoping his unknown visitor will go away, but the knocking persists. Aaron cocks his weapon.

"Who is it?"

"Theresa," says the voice. "Please open the door."

Aaron opens it and finds the young blonde woman standing there with one of her brothers—the one with the shattered teeth.

"What is it you want?" asks Aaron impatiently.

"Let us in, quickly!"

Aaron lets them inside and closes the door.

"They are coming!" says the brother in a loud whisper.

"Who?"

"The SS. A squad of Germans. They mean to assassinate you and Sax."

Theresa chimes in. "They arrived in town this morning and were asking around. We know they're waiting. They are expecting you. They'll kill you."

"We've learned that their commander is an SS marksman named Kraft," says the brother.

Aaron goes to the window. "How many?" he asks.

"Four in all. Dressed like farmers," says the brother.

"Where?"

"One kilometer, down by the square. They've been told that's your usual return route. They'll ambush the wagon and kill everyone."

Aaron turns to his two saviors. "I don't know how to repay you."

"It's a gift," smiles Theresa.

"We'd better go," says the brother.

Aaron leads them through the rear garden for a covert getaway. As he does so, he weighs his options. Four against one—and one of the four is apparently a sniper. Even though Aaron had won recognition as a marksman in his Czech army days, as well as during more recent firefights against the Germans, he does not have a sniper rifle or scope, and would be clearly outgunned and outclassed. His only advantage lay in the element of surprise.

Yet Aaron also realizes that he has a much safer option—his own way to freedom is now clear. He can make his escape into the woods to wait out the war while Sax and the Nazi assassins are preoccupied with each other. True enough, Sax would probably be killed, but perhaps the world would be better off without him, given what he had become. And perhaps death would be better for him, too, rather than a life in which he would have to bear the burden of his ghastly actions, or the torture of his own thirst for vengeance.

Sax's life and his own weigh in the balance, but to Sax's life, Aaron is forced to add the lives of the loyal Gyorgi and the other Soviet troops accompanying him, for they, too, could be killed. That means five lives at stake, not just one, which tips the scales in favor of action.

Aaron makes his decision just as he lets Theresa and her brother out the rear gate. He stops her.

"Can you drive a wagon?" asks Aaron.

"Yes."

"I need your help—one last time."

A short while later, Theresa is driving a one-horse wagon filled with straw through the quiet town square. Hidden beneath the straw lies Aaron, along with his submachine gun, a Soviet army rifle, hand grenades, and several extra clips of ammunition. He has considered warning Sax and the others of the ambush but is unsure which route they will take to get to the town square, perhaps exposing them to even greater danger. He has also thought of trying to get more Russian troops to help him but decides against that plan for lack of time. This is a problem Aaron will have to solve alone and soon.

Theresa drives the wagon in a slow deliberate circle around the square, allowing Aaron to mark the SS assassins one at a time while peering through the slats of the wagon. Two have chosen vantage points in the upstairs windows of shops. Aaron almost fails to spot Kraft, who has chosen the roof of the highest building on the square—a three-story bank. This makes sense ever since Aaron learned in the Czech army that the most expert of assassins generally try to obtain the highest vantage point, and Aaron feels he has Kraft in view. The fourth German, Aaron is not able to make out at all.

After their wagon drive around the square, Aaron whispers to Theresa to stop the wagon on the edge of the square in a place with a commanding view of the locale, then tells her to get out slowly, walk away, and not come back. This she does with deftness, after whispering good luck to him.

Aaron knows that if he takes out Kraft first, the odds of his survival will go up considerably. If he can take out two before his position is discovered, he would be down to two against one—not good, but no worse odds than he has already beaten during his long sojourn on the Eastern Front.

As the sun begins to set, he silently aims his rifle at Kraft couched on the roof of the bank. It's now or never. If he waits any longer, he might be discovered, or Sax and his men might show up, rendering his pre-emptive surprise attack moot.

With the crack of Aaron's rifle, Kraft's head disappears from view. Aaron doesn't even have a chance to check if his shot hit its mark when the horse, surprised by the sound, rears and bolts across the square. Aaron holds on tightly, doing his best to stay hidden, but the wagon tips over and he and his weapons go sprawling across the cobblestones while the horse breaks free and gallops away.

Retrieving his automatic weapon as quickly as possible, Aaron takes cover behind the overturned wagon and fires a burst at one of the Nazis he had spotted in the window. This soldier disappears in a shower of broken glass.

Immediately, the other SS soldiers, who had holed up behind other windows, begin to fire back. Aaron, now trapped behind the wagon, has no choice but to hunker down while bullets shred the wooden baseboard and ricochet closer and closer to him. He manages to reach out and seize two smoke grenades that have spilled from the wagon. Obviously, things are not going well—at least two of the assassins are still alive and know where he is. Still, with all the noise, Sax and the others would surely be forewarned and avoid the trap. He decides his own retreat is now imperative.

He pulls the rings on the two smoke grenades and hurls them over the wagon, where they burst instantly into clouds of thick white smoke. The Nazis continue to fire blindly into the smoke, while Aaron sprints behind the corner of a stone building, where he collapses, out of breath.

He hears footsteps behind him and spins around, gun ready—only to see Sax, the Russian soldiers, a horse-drawn wagon loaded with captured weapons and stores, and about a dozen prisoners in farmers' clothes.

"What's going on?" growls Sax.

"Ambush. German SS troops. At least two, maybe more."

"Where?" says Sax.

"Not sure," says Aaron, still out of breath. "One in a second story window to the right. Another on the roof maybe. The others I don't know."

Sax nods. "Let's find out." He runs to the wagon and begins yanking the ammunition clips from confiscated German weapons.

As Aaron watches, Sax hands the unloaded weapons to the bewildered prisoners.

Sax then cocks his own automatic weapon. "Run! Out through the town square!" he bellows to his captives.

The prisoners, shocked, don't budge. Sax fires his gun at one, dropping him to the ground. "Now!" he cries.

The terrified prisoners immediately rush into the square, where the white smoke is already dissipating. They are immediately met by a hail of automatic weapons' fire, which cuts down half a dozen. Aaron, Sax, and the Soviet soldiers take advantage of the misdirected fire to locate the now-exposed SS troops in the building and dispatch them in a hail of bullets.

As soon as the hit squad is silenced, Sax and the Russian soldiers gun down the last few prisoners, who are trying to escape. Aaron then leads the Russian troops first to the roof, and then to the second story window, where they find Kraft and the second Nazi soldier, sprawled out dead. Aaron's first shots had indeed found their targets.

"What the hell were you doing?" asks Sax as he picks up Kraft's sniper rifle.

"Saving your hide," says Aaron.

"Thanks," grunts Sax.

In Päks, in February 1945, at an improvised headquarters of a forward operating unit of the NKVD—pronounced EN—ka—vee—DAH—the precursor to the KGB—two young intelligence officers hurry into the office of a major general carrying documents containing a daily intelligence briefing. The major general—a tall, smooth-skinned, sandy-haired man in full dress uniform who seems young for his rank—receives the dossiers and flips through them.

"What is going on in Gérjen?" he asks, looking up.

"Going on, sir?"

"Even though it's been a quiet sector for the last few months, it has generated the most prisoners of any comparable district. We also seem to have drawn a substantial amount of material goods for our war effort from there, as well as significant amounts of enemy intelligence. What is the secret?"

The two underlings exchange glances. "The two Jews, sir," says one of them.

"Which Jews? What do you mean?"

"I believe they are called Sax and Gershkovitch," says the underling, using the Russian translation of Aaron's last name. "They were Hungarian slaves. Now they are Hungary's bane and the Germans' too, from what we know."

The major general nods. "My superior is most interested in this case. Please bring me their files."

Early the next morning, a black truck with a red star on it growls its way through the quiet early-morning streets of Gérjen, scattering a herd of sheep being led out to pasture, rolling past downtown shops just opening for the day, and finally squeaking to a stop in front of the villa where Aaron and Sax hold court.

Aaron is in the kitchen preparing a pot of coffee when he looks out the window and sees the vehicle pull up. He has awakened early, intent on carrying out his escape. The arrival of the truck, and the four men who climb out of it—dressed in sleek black uniforms and spit-shined shoes and equipped with automatic weapons—make him uneasy.

"NKVD," whispers Gyorgi. "Secret police."

The men enter and the commanding officer, a tall, youthful firebrand with a well-trimmed moustache, stands before Aaron.

"Are you our comrade appointed as overlord of this town?"

"Yes," says Aaron. "Gershkovitch. Arón."

The officer grins and holds out a hand. They shake.

"You are requested by the commandant. Where is Sax?"

"Upstairs," says Aaron.

The commander nods to one of his men, who heads for the stairway. At that moment, footsteps can be heard descending, and a young woman appears, her hair and clothing in disarray. She glances briefly at the men, and then slips out the front door.

Before the NKVD agent can ascend the stairs, a second woman appears, her condition similar to the first. She likewise departs, and the man at last walks up the stairs.

"Coffee, sir?" asks Aaron.

"No, thank you."

"Why does the commandant want to see us?"

The NKVD commander shakes his head slightly.

"We have been doing as ordered," says Aaron. "We have been rounding up prisoners, interrogating them, confiscating property for Mother Russia. Some we have executed, with justification. We fought off a vicious Nazi ambush yesterday."

"Your activities are well-known to us," says the commander.

Sax lumbers heavily down the stairs, still buttoning his shirt, the NKVD agent close behind. Sax throws a worried look to Aaron, who throws it back to him.

"We have our headquarters here," says Aaron. "Under orders. Soldiers to command, missions underway. It is difficult for us to go away now. Here, let me show you my papers."

Aaron gives the NKVD commander his papers from the Russian colonel who had put him in charge of Gérjen, as well as his Soviet ID papers. The NKVD agent crushes the papers in his beefy hand and stuffs them into his pocket without even looking at them. At that moment, Aaron realizes he is in serious trouble.

"This way, please," says the commander, gesturing toward the door.

Aaron nods and reaches for his submachine gun.

"You may leave your weapons here."

Aaron stops. "We'd prefer to—"

Two of the NKVD agents lift their guns ever so slightly. The commander nods to the door. Aaron and Sax are led outside and into the truck, and from there are taken on a long journey back to Päks. Sitting on a bench opposite Sax as the truck rumbles along, Aaron silently blames his partner's behavior for whatever new calamity now lay in store, and Sax, equally silent, gauges the size and disposition of these NKVD agents in the event a struggle might be called for.

At the NKVD headquarters in Päks, the two are led to the office of the major general, who sets down the papers he's been reading and leans back in his chair, smiling.

"My apologies for taking you away from your duties so abruptly. Drink?"

Aaron and Sax both decline, but the offer of a drink is an unexpectedly good sign. Aaron relaxes slightly.

The major general gets up and pours one for himself, then circles the two before sitting down again behind his desk. He stares at them for what seems an eternity, swirling his vodka before sipping it. At long last, he speaks.

"I wanted to see how big you were. You are big, at least one of you is, but not quite as big as I've heard." He smiles. Aaron and Sax are mystified. "You are legendary among my men. War heroes; the intelligence you've been extracting from your prisoners has been of great service in our campaign to oust the German and Hungarian invaders from Mother Russia, and now you've been invaluable in our conquest of Hungary; no doubt your work will help us with our invasion of Germany." He points to the paperwork on his desk. "You send us lots of work. Excellent interrogations. Though not so many the last few weeks, and the ones we get are sometimes not much use to us. Difficult to speak without any teeth."

Sax nods almost imperceptibly.

"Great men like you are too big for a little town like Gérjen," continues the major general. "Not when the needs of the Soviet Union are so great."

"Thank you, sir." Aaron's fears ease considerably. They are headed for a bigger town—could it be Budapest? He can't imagine being assigned to run a city that large. And besides, he had thought it was still in German hands. Perhaps he can secure a new assignment separate from Sax.

"It's *we* who need to thank *you*. That is why I have a promotion to offer you with a much more important assignment. You now get to become spies."

Aaron's spirits sag as quickly as they have risen. Sax looks surprised.

"Spies, sir?" asks Aaron.

"Yes. You speak German, Russian, Hungarian, and Czech. You're smart and resourceful. Only the best can do something so challenging as spying, and you two are among the very best I've ever seen. You sure you don't want a drink to celebrate?"

Aaron is tempted to drink—although not to celebrate—but again declines, and Sax takes his cue from Aaron.

"We don't know anything about being spies, sir," says Aaron. "We've never done that."

"You think we would send you unprepared? We have an espionage training program in which you will learn everything you need to know. I have all the instructions and documents you need. Tatiana will show you." He picks up a pile of documents from his desk and calls to his assistant who is seated in the hallway outside. She is an attractive woman in a colorful full-dress uniform. As the major general begins to converse with her, Aaron and Sax exchange worried looks.

"We are Jews," says Aaron.

The major general interrupts his conversation. "So? Many of my men are Jews. We are not prejudiced like the Hungarians and Germans."

"I mean, sir, we'll be tortured and killed if we are captured—not just as spies, but worse because we're Jews."

"They torture and kill Russians, too!" The major general says impatiently, then catches himself. "Who says you would be captured? Two smart men like you will not be captured."

The major general pauses, and then says, "I tell you what we'll do. We'll supply you with poison vials to use if you think you are in danger of being captured. Besides, we don't want you giving away *our* intelligence under torture."

Aaron exchanges looks with Sax, and then asks, "What kind of mission would we have?"

"I don't know. You will get it when you get it. We are preparing to invade Germany. And we won't be able to secure Budapest until we quash Hitler's counter-offensives. We need spies; we need your help."

"Of course, sir, but I'm no longer such a healthy man for this," says Aaron.

The major general quickly looks him up and down. "I don't have any doctors to examine you, but you look healthy enough to me."

"It is a difficult decision, sir," says Aaron.

"Decision?" barks the major general. "What decision?"

"We want to help Mother Russia, sir, but if we don't understand what kind of mission—"

The major general, realizing that spies who are intimidated into spying would be less reliable, sits back down. "Let's say, for example, we parachute you into Germany. You take advantage of your language skills. We give you the probable addresses of certain Nazi officials, and you track them down and interrogate them before you assassinate them. You then report the information back to our people there, either by radio or other covert arrangements."

Aaron's morale sinks even lower. He has already endured many scrapes with death at the hands of his old enemies, and now he faces the prospect of certain death at the hands of his new "friends."

Now clearly frightened, Aaron calmly says, "That sounds like a worthy assignment, sir. We would like to spend the night thinking about it and report back in the morning."

"In the morning?" asks the major general.

"Yes, sir. We can go back to Gérjen, take care of our duties for the day, and return here tomorrow at first light."

The major general looks at them for a moment, then picks up his phone. "I will spare you the trip."

Aaron and Sax are led into a small, bare room lit by one bulb. The two are given pens and paper and told by the major general to write out their complete personal histories, and have them ready by the following morning, to be delivered with their decision.

"Just watch out that you tell the whole truth in those papers," warns the major general. "If not, you will surely fall into my hands again, and this time, it would not be good for you."

He turns and leaves, followed by the two guards. The heavy wooden door slams shut with a loud thud.

After the sound of footsteps recedes, Aaron tries to open the door, but it is locked. Their previous stature as absolute rulers over the people of Gérjen is now completely deflated. Sax in particular seems troubled by the abrupt loss of power. At last, he speaks up.

"We could parachute in and hide in the woods in Germany until the war is over," he says.

"What if they drop us in a city?"

Sax shrugs. "We could hide in a park."

"There would be no one to help us—no farmers, no farmers' daughters," says Aaron. "We'll starve to death. If we're found, we'll either be shot as deserters or as spies. Or worse—if they strip us down naked and take a good look at our circumcised bodies, they'll hang us as Jews, and even worse, as Jewish spies."

"We say 'no,' they might shoot us right here," says Sax.

Aaron shakes his head. "I can't believe they would do that, not after everything we've done for their cause."

The two fall silent. At last Aaron picks up his pen and begins to write. Sax does likewise. They spend the night going into great—if somewhat sanitized—detail about their exploits as the rulers of Gérjen and heroes for the Soviet cause. Aaron hopes the overwhelming weight of their positive impact on the Russian war effort will counterbalance any temptation the major general might have of ending their war effort permanently, by just using a bullet.

Early the following morning, Aaron and Sax—weary after a sleepless night—are marched again into the major general's office by three NKVD agents wielding automatic weapons. One of the agents hands the histories Aaron and Sax have written to the major general, who glances through them.

"Well?" he says at last.

"I'm afraid," says Aaron, "After much careful consideration, we have decided we could best serve the cause by remaining in Gérjen and continuing our prisoner roundups and interrogations, sir. Our answer is 'no.'"

The major general does not react at all. He continues to leaf through the histories, and then at last looks up at the two.

"I understand why."

Aaron and Sax both breathe a barely audible sigh of relief. "Thank you, sir," says Aaron.

"Yes, I understand why you do not want to become spies. It is because you already *are* spies."

Aaron looks at him, bewildered.

The major general smiles. "For the Nazis, of course."

Aaron and Sax are stunned. "No, sir—that's impossible," says Aaron. "You can see from our histories what we've done for the Soviet cause."

"Yes, lies. You are both very good liars."

Aaron pleads, "You can ask any of the Russian soldiers and officers we have worked with for the last several months."

"You can fool them with your trickery, but you cannot fool us, you Nazi pigs."

Aaron senses his future growing darker than it had been at any time since he was a slave laborer. He stammers onward, "But we're Jewish, sir, and you know what the Germans think of us."

"You have lied about that as well. You did not want to attend our espionage school because you have already been superbly trained. You lie most persuasively. You will be taken away now and receive a lesson in counterespionage. During that lesson, you will be given an opportunity to rewrite these"—he gestures to the histories—"this time telling the truth."

"We have told the truth, sir, every word is true!" says Aaron.

The major general casually unholsters his pistol and begins to whip Aaron with it until he sinks to his knees, his face bloody. Sax begins to react, but the other agents cock their automatic weapons and hold him off.

The major general then barks at Aaron, "You ungrateful stinking Jew! We made you a king here! We made you the ruler of a Nazi town! And this is how you show your gratitude? By refusing to carry out an important mission?" He grabs a club from one of the guards and begins beating Aaron over the head, screaming, "Jew-pig!" until Aaron slumps to the floor, unconscious. Aaron realizes only too late that the major general's "offer" of a promotion was in fact an order—an order that he has disobeyed.

Sax moves to try to help Aaron, but the major general motions the guards toward Sax, and they begin beating him while several other agents are called over to hold the big man down to the floor. At last the beatings stop.

Before he leaves, the major general says, "I look forward to reading proper confessions from you two very soon, with details about your contacts and how much you know. The sooner you begin your confessions, the sooner the beatings will stop. You better tell us the truth, or you will go to the gallows. You will be hanged. At least if you talk, we can make a deal."

Aaron is pulled to his feet, and he and Sax are blindfolded and prodded down the corridor and into another room, where they are strip-searched and beaten again. As Aaron endures this, he thinks about the cache of valuables and riches he had saved up intending to bring them home for Helen and his family, which he now has involuntarily abandoned. He thinks about his preparation for his escape into the woods, and how his timing—so good and so central to his survival until now against impossible odds—has finally let him down. In a sense, it was his own compassion—his rescue of the Hungarian woman and her brothers in distress, and of Sax and the Russian troops—that had delayed his escape and ultimately doomed him.

Aaron begins to lose track of time, as the days of beatings stretch into weeks, perhaps even months. He and Sax are thrown into separate jail cells in a ghastly Russian gulag, constantly hearing the words "liar, liar!" and "dirty Jew!" with nothing to eat but leftover food from the guards.

After yet another brutal beating, Aaron and Sax are prodded out into the courtyard in the darkness of night, where they are loaded onto a truck. For more than an hour, the two sit blindfolded in the back while the vehicle crisscrosses the Hungarian countryside, leaving Aaron disoriented. It does not finally matter to Aaron where he is, because he knows where he is going—either to be hanged, shot, or sent to some prison, perhaps a gulag in Siberia, to waste away his life, unable to get word to his family or to Helen, if by some miracle they had survived the war.

As the night wears on, however, the cloud of despair begins to dissipate as Aaron refocuses on survival. He surmises there are only two NKVD agents in the truck—one driving, the other in the back serving as a guard. Just two against him and Sax—the odds are not bad. He can tell from their voices that they are quite young. And, most important of all, he begins to realize they are lost.

As they pull up to an intersection and begin to curse, Aaron senses an opportunity and believes it worth risking another beating.

"Excuse me, sir," he says through the blindfold. "I speak Hungarian. If you need directions, I can ask one of the locals for help."

He braces himself for some form of physical retaliation for speaking up, but none comes. Instead, one of the agents removes his blindfold, and as soon as Aaron's eyes adjust to the light, he makes another important discovery: by observing their uniforms, Aaron realizes that the guards are not NKVD agents. They are Russian soldiers who look so young, that by all appearances, they are recent recruits. The driver stands at the side of the truck while the other soldier sits right across from Aaron.

"You know how to get to Nyiregyhaza?" asks the guard.

"No, because I do not know where *we* are. But I can ask someone who knows both where we are and how to get to Nyiregyhaza from here."

The guard looks at the driver, who nods and gets back into the cab. The truck drives on for several more miles until they pass two women and an old man leading a pair of cows along the road. Aaron nods to the guard, who pounds on the top of the cab. The truck slows and Aaron gets out.

"Excuse us," he says. "These soldiers are trying to take us to Nyiregyhaza, and they want me to ask you how to get there. But please, please tell me the wrong directions—tell me the opposite way—they do not speak Hungarian. They will kill us when we get to Nyiregyhaza."

The three glance up at the truck and can see Sax, still blindfolded, and the Russian soldiers armed with rifles. The old man nods and begins to give detailed directions, gesturing with his hands, while the Russian soldiers watch.

"Thank you," says Aaron.

"It is my pleasure," says the old man. "If Nyiregyhaza is a danger to you, you will be safe now."

Aaron gets back in the truck and as the Russians proceed to follow the directions, they become increasingly lost, stopping twice more for Aaron to ask the locals for help. Both times, Aaron persuades the townspeople to send them astray. The Soviet uniforms on the soldiers tell the whole story. Given the brutality and rape the Hungarian civilians have been suffering at the hands of their Russian enemies now invading their country, it is easy for Aaron to get the wrong directions he seeks.

As night falls, they stop at a farmhouse, where the Soviet agents order the occupants—an elderly man and woman—out for the night. Aaron and Sax are locked in one of the bedrooms, and by now, they are no longer wearing blindfolds. They can hear one of the Russians pacing on guard duty on the other side of the door.

"When he falls asleep," whispers Aaron to Sax. "We go." He points to the window.

Sax nods.

At last, with morning light already appearing in the sky, the pacing stops. Aaron turns to Sax—who is deeply asleep—and tries to rouse him without making too much noise, but soon enough the door opens, and the driver appears, rifle in hand, and orders them out. After considerably more prodding, this time by the Russian with his rifle barrel, Sax at last awakens. Aaron and Sax are then ordered to sit outside on the steps, where the driver gives them a small ration of dry *kasha*—buckwheat groat—while the other soldier remains asleep inside.

As they munch on the cereal, which tastes like sawdust, a Hungarian woman walks by on the road out front with a milk pail in her hand.

"I want some of that for breakfast," says the driver, his eyes lighting up.

Aaron tosses a furtive glance to Sax, and then stands up. "Let me get some for you."

The driver nods enthusiastically, and Aaron heads out to the woman.

"Excuse me, madam," he says.

She stops and looks at him warily. Her pail is empty.

"I am Hungarian," says Aaron. "My friend and I need your help. These Russians are going to take us somewhere to kill us. I need you to point to that barn behind you and keep walking toward it."

She begins to back away.

"Please," says Aaron. "They don't speak Hungarian, so they don't know what I'm telling you. Doing this may save our lives."

She points to the barn, then quickly heads away.

"Thank you," says Aaron as he runs back to the Russians. "She's got plenty in the barn. Sax and I will get it for you."

Instantly, Sax and Aaron rush off in the direction of the barn.

"Wait!" calls the Russian agent.

They ignore him and sprint past the woman, rushing down the country lane, which is bordered on both sides by high stone walls.

"Halt!" cries the Russian. Aaron glances back. Instead of pursuing, the soldier rushes back into the house to rouse his comrade from sleep, giving Aaron and Sax just enough time to disappear around a corner and out of sight.

Still, they are in a lane with high walls on each side. Closed iron gates bar the way to other roads.

The pop of a gunshot, then another, breaks the morning silence. Aaron veers sharply left into an alcove by one of the gates, followed by Sax, who grabs the gate and tries to shake it open, but it won't budge. Another gunshot. Aaron and Sax are just about to sprint farther down the lane when a loud, rusty creaking erupts behind them.

The gate is opening, all by itself.

Aaron and Sax look on in disbelief, then up to the sky. Is this a gift from God at their most needful hour?

All along the lane, gates are opening as if by magic. Then comes a cacophony of squeals—herds of pigs are being led out into the fields. It's that time of day for all the gates of the town to open for the pigs to feed. For a fleeting moment, Aaron thinks that God has finally shown His kind and merciful face through this miracle.

But then Aaron thinks, *No, this is not God. This is my good luck that the gates opened at the very moment the pigs grazed.*

Aaron and Sax dash through the open gate and down the street, scattering scores of pigs and their bewildered shepherds. They pass through another gate and onto a different street. Then they jump over a fence so high that afterward, Aaron doesn't know how he had cleared it.

Looking back, he sees the Russian agents chasing and shooting at them, yelling for them to stop. Then Aaron notices all the gates begin to close, including the one right in front of the Russians. The soldiers are momentarily stymied. They have to stop to unlock the closed gates.

Aaron and Sax now have a few minutes' advantage and sprint far ahead.

"To the woods!" cries Aaron, gesturing to a stand of trees in the distance. It is the most beautiful green forest he has ever seen, stretching far across the horizon. For Aaron, is this the Promised Land, his freedom? Can they reach it in time? For a moment, Aaron asks himself again, *did God place this forest before him, so that he could disappear into its safety? But no, Aaron realizes, it's not God. It's his own dumb luck that the dense green forest lay before him, beckoning him to reach it while he could still run.*

The two fugitives run toward the cover of the forest. But as freedom nears, Aaron hears shooting behind him, and bullets again zip through the air. In his fear, it seems like they are coming from all directions.

Aaron and Sax keep running, leaping over more fences, clambering through farmhouse yards, and dodging animals as the gunshots continue, whizzing by them as the chase grows more and more desperate.

They run for what seems like an eternity. Aaron's lungs are screaming, the muscles in his legs are burning, but he forces himself to keep going. *Who cares if I hurt?* Aaron asks himself. *If they catch me, I'll be dead and then I won't feel anything.*

To keep himself going, he focuses his eyes on the beautiful forest ahead, filled with acres and acres of trees to hide behind.

The Russians are still in pursuit, not gaining any ground, their guns waving in the air when they are not shooting wildly. The townspeople stay in their homes, avoiding the gunfire. Aaron and Sax manage to stay ahead, building on their head start and the speed that comes from blinding fear.

At last they pass the outskirts of town and find themselves in an open field. The forest is right before them.

Faster, Aaron says to himself. *Faster.*

The soldiers can't catch them, but they don't stop either. Then, just as Aaron and Sax near the edge of the forest, the Russians stop for a last attempt to shoot. Aaron and Sax are easier targets in the open field, and the bullets keep whizzing by, some of them barely missing.

Aaron keeps his eyes on the trees. He knows if they make it into the woods alive, they will be safe.

At last, they reach the forest, but they keep on running, tearing through the underbrush, heedless of any obstacle or pain. The sound of the gunshots grow fainter. Finally, they come to a clearing deep in the forest where they allow themselves to collapse, their lungs burning, unable to go another step. Lying on the ground, they listen intently—and hear nothing. It's just as well because neither man can move. They are spent. Aaron feels a pain in his chest grip him, while he hears belching sounds from Sax. Both men vomit from the ordeal.

"What happened to that milk?" asks Sax.

Aaron cracks a smile. "You want it? Go get it."

Sax waves him off.

The Russians do not follow the two men into the forest, as they are deathly afraid of anti-Russian partisans hiding there. The two remain in the clearing, listening carefully for several hours, sometimes awake, sometimes nodding off, gathering their strength, until night draws near. When they finally awaken at sunrise, they have no idea what day or time it is. They only know that the crunch of approaching footsteps means that someone is nearby. Though instantly alert, neither has the strength to do anything but lie there frozen.

"If they want me, they can have me," whispers Aaron, resigned to being captured. Perhaps he could gather his strength for one last fight. Perhaps the intruder would not see them in the heavy brush. But the sound grows closer; birds fly from the clearing, and insects grow quieter. At last the footsteps stop. Aaron glances up and sees an old man with a long gray beard and even longer gray hair peering down at him in the morning light, leaning on an axe.

"You boys hungry?"

Rescued by the partisans, Aaron and Sax are given food and shelter for several weeks—until word comes to the forest that the Soviet secret police had price tags on their heads—and that anyone harboring them would be severely punished as well. The partisans fear that the Russians might soon invade the forest to recapture them, and grievously harm the partisans as well. Aaron and Sax don't want to put their friends in jeopardy, so they thank the partisans for their kindness and depart the forest. With the war still raging, they decide to return to the one place where they could feel secure—Gérjen— and hope the NKVD have been long gone, moving onward to the front. The two men hope they can hide there with Limpy and some friends until they get word that the war is over.

---

11 See the map page 299 (German-Held Territory January 1945).

CHAPTER 18

ONCE THE POWERFUL, NOW THE POWERLESS

AFTER THE RUSSIANS REPULSE Hitler's last futile attempts to retain Budapest in March of 1945, the German garrison in the city finally surrenders to the Russians.

The Red Army then begins a massive offensive of its own, which propels Russian forces through Eastern Hungary. Meanwhile, in Poland, Russian forces commence the invasion of Germany from the east, while the Anglo-American Allies cross the Rhine River to invade Germany from the west. Ultimately, when Hitler would realize the end was near, he would soon put a gun to his head.[12]

At the same time, Aaron and Sax are carefully making their way back to Gérjen, where they hope a warm welcome will await them. They sit hidden in an underbrush on a hill overlooking the town. It is dusk, and they have been keeping watch all day without seeing any NKVD agents or Soviet troops.

Two young women stroll past, unaware that they are being observed.

"Mine," says Sax. "The one on the left, at least twice."

"Congratulations," scowls Aaron, as he stands up moments later.

"What are you doing?" asks Sax.

"Going to find some dinner, maybe find a place to sleep."

Sax gets up and joins him. The two walk cautiously toward the center of town.

"It was vengeance, every bit of it. We earned it, they deserved it," says Sax, even though Aaron hasn't said a word. "Think about your family, your mother, and Helen," he continues.

"Think about what the bastards must've done to them. What we did was just, what I did they deserved, so don't be so self-righteous."

Still, Aaron says nothing, but shaking his head "no," which only seems to make Sax angrier.

A few townspeople walk past, giving them a wide berth.

"They still respect us and fear us," says Sax. "This town is still ours."

One of the young women Sax had slept with walks by, pauses and stares as they approach, then darts away.

Aaron and Sax stop some distance from their villa. A truck is parked in front, and a Soviet soldier is moving supplies from the villa to the truck. Aaron and Sax wait until he goes inside, then rush to hide in the shadows of the house. When the soldier emerges with another load, they recognize his familiar face.

"Gyorgi!" says Aaron, in a whisper.

Gyorgi almost drops his load. "What are you two doing here?"

"We need help!" says Aaron as he and Sax emerge from their hiding place.

"You sure do! You've got a price on your heads!" Gyorgi looks around quickly, then leads them back into the house.

"What price?" asks Aaron.

"Fifty thousand rubles for you. A *hundred* thousand for him," he says as he points toward Sax. "The Soviet government wants you both, and the new Hungarian government, too. You can't stay here."

"Any Russian soldiers or NKVD around?" asks Aaron.

Gyorgi shakes his head 'no.' "Haven't you heard? Everybody's clearing out. I'm one of the last. But you both must steer clear of the new Hungarian police, hand-picked by the NKVD.

"Where's Limpy?" asks Aaron. "Maybe he can hide us."

"They transferred him weeks ago to help run a bigger town farther east. Budapest fell last month, Vienna yesterday. The war is almost over. My advice is to get out of town and lay low for a little longer, and then go home."

Aaron and Sax look at one another, stunned by the news, though Aaron is happy for his friend, Limpy.

"Béregszasz? Liberated too?" asks Sax.

"I don't know. Probably. But the Germans are kaput."

"Can you spare us some food?" asks Aaron. "Maybe a weapon?"

"Weapon, no. Take whatever food you can carry but be quick and don't let me or anyone else see you do it. Goodbye, comrades."

They shake hands. Gyorgi leaves the room, and Aaron and Sax take all the food they can stuff into their pockets before heading out the door and quietly moving back down the dark streets toward the open fields.

"Why a hundred thousand for me and just fifty for you?" grunts Sax.

The baker appears on the road ahead with his daughter Christina. But instead of shrinking away from Sax and Aaron, they come right up to them.

"You got me pregnant!" Christina shouts at Sax. "And then you disappeared. Now what are you going to do about it?"

Sax backs up. Aaron is surprised to see the man who had stared down so many dangers seemingly flinch before the angry glare of this young girl and her portly middle-aged father.

Sax finally replies, "I don't know."

"I know," says Christina's father. "You will marry her!"

"Okay," says a curiously docile Sax.

Soon more women and parents begin to gather around Sax, several demanding marriage. Sax just stares at them, uncertain how to respond. Apparently, word has gotten out that the two erstwhile rulers of Gérjen are back.

Aaron is almost amused by his partner's predicament, until he finds himself wondering when the new Hungarian authorities under the Soviets will learn they are back; it is just a matter of time—unless they move quickly.

"We will be back, and we will make this right," says Aaron to the townspeople, as he and Sax try to push their way through the crowd toward the edge of town.

"Back? Where are you going?" shouts Christina.

"We will be back later tonight," says Aaron. "Meet us at the villa."

"Nonsense!" cries the baker.

A truck approaches from behind, headlights glaring.

"It must be Gyorgi!" whispers Aaron. "Let's get on!"

Sax nods and the two begin to reverse course, then break away from the crowd and rush toward the truck, which screeches to a halt. But just before Aaron and Sax could hop in, six armed Hungarian gendarmes clamber out and aim their weapons at the two fugitives.

Wrong truck.

Again, the crowd surges around them as the lead gendarme holds them at gunpoint.

"Sax and Hershkovitch?" he asks, using the Hungarian idiom for Aaron's last name.

Many voices shout affirmation of their identities.

"You are under arrest."

The crowd continues to jeer as the gendarmes lash their prisoners' hands behind their backs and escort them into the back of the truck. As they drive away, several of the women hurl stones at them.

The two prisoners are driven deeper into Hungary, to a larger town that has its own police station, which is marked by a large Soviet flag indicating the town has been liberated by the Red Army and is now under Russian control. Once inside, Aaron and Sax are untied and led into separate cells.

Early the next morning, they are brought before the police captain, a wiry man in his mid-forties with a well-pressed uniform and leather gloves which seem out of place indoors. One of the young gendarmes stands next to his desk and reads down a list of Aaron's and Sax's rampages in and around Gérjen, their having been taken as spies by the NKVD, their subsequent escape, and the price on their heads. When he is finished reading, he sets the document on the captain's desk. The captain sizes up the two men before him and shakes his head.

"You are twice as big as he is," says the captain to Sax. "Are you worth twice as much?"

"We are not spies," says Aaron. "We are Hungarian. We fought for the Red Army. We are Jews. How could we be spies?"

"How could you be Hungarian Jews?" asks the captain. "All the Jewish men your age were sent to labor camps."

"We *were* slave laborers," says Aaron. "Before we escaped to join the Russians!"

"How can I believe you?" asks the captain. "Where were you slave laborers?"

"All over Russia!" shouts Aaron. "In Novyi Oskol, in Pinsk, in Vóronezh!"

"And Minsk and Dubno," adds Sax.

Aaron begins unbuttoning his shirt, and the youthful gendarme starts to raise his weapon, but the captain stops him. Aaron pulls up his shirt, exposing his scarred back.

"Scars from carrying a machine gun and being beaten for it. Hundreds of miles I carried it."

The captain quietly nods. Aaron pulls his shirt down.

"What more can we do to prove it?" Aaron asks. "I cannot show you the friends I've lost."

"I believe you," says the captain, pulling off his gloves with his teeth. He holds up his mangled hands with blackened stumps where several fingers should have been. "I was at Novyi Oskol. They hung me up by my hands for hours in the cold. Then they took my gloves. Russian winter; very harsh."

Aaron stares, recalling the same peculiar torture he had seen inflicted by the Hungarians against other slaves.

"You are Jewish?"

The captain nods.

"Then you know. You know everything," says Aaron.

The captain nods again. Aaron and Sax breathe sighs of relief that somehow they have made another improbable escape.

"I am from Bielka, in the Carpathians," says Aaron.

"And me, from Bé.regszasz," says Sax.

"We are hoping that our hometowns may have been liberated," says Aaron. "We need to go home and find our families."

"How will you get back there?" asks the captain.

"Any way possible; on foot, most likely. It doesn't matter."

"How will you do that if you are prisoners?"

Aaron's heart sinks again. "But we told you, we are not spies. The charges against us are false."

"I believe you," says the captain. "But I am not the law, only a servant of it." He gestures to the posters of Lenin and Stalin pasted on the wall, then signals to the gendarme. He, in turn, calls out to two more policemen waiting in the hallway, who promptly enter and once more tie the prisoners' hands behind their backs.

"Have you forgotten who you are? Have you forgotten your people?" cries Aaron.

"Traitor!" barks Sax, spitting on the floor as they are led away.

Darkness falls on Aaron at midday as a blindfold is placed over his eyes. The gendarmes then march him through numerous corridors until he suddenly feels the warmth of the springtime sun on his face. He is then prodded onto the back of a truck, and only when he hears one of the guards instruct someone else to step up, does he realize that Sax is still with him.

The two sit in silence for what seems like an eternity as the truck twists and turns along roads they cannot see.

"If you get lost, I can help you. I'm good with directions," says Aaron at last to no one in particular. He can sense Sax's grin without seeing the big man's face.

"Why don't you get us some milk? I'll help," comes Sax's reply.

There is no response from whoever is guarding them.

After several hours, the air grows cooler, and Aaron figures it is evening. At last the truck comes to a stop, but its engine continues to run. Aaron waits tensely to find out what will happen next. Will they take off his blindfold before they shoot him? Will he then enter into eternal darkness?

After a moment, a guard lifts the blindfold from his eyes. Aaron blinks in the dying light, surprised to see the youthful face of one of the gendarmes who had first arrested them. Then the gendarme pulls the blindfold off Sax and prods the two men out from the back of the truck. They have stopped on a country road with only a few scattered farmhouses visible in the distance. Have the two men been taken here to be shot?

With only the driver and the gendarme, it seems to Aaron that there might still be an opportunity to escape. That prospect becomes even more likely when the gendarme unfastens their hands.

"There is a railroad station in the next town," he says, pointing down the road. "But the captain suggests you not travel together anymore, since people will be looking for a hundred thousand ruble one," he indicates Sax's big size, "accompanying a fifty thousand ruble one."

Aaron and Sax are too astonished to speak.

"Thank you," says Aaron at last.

"Thank the captain," the soldier smiles as he climbs back into the truck, which immediately turns around and speeds away.

Aaron and Sax regard each other across the dirt road as the dust settles and silence falls.

"Another escape," says Aaron.

"Easier than from the NKVD," Sax says. "Or from the German and Hungarian armies."

Aaron nods. "Think it's the last?"

Sax shrugs his broad shoulders. "No."

"Maybe the last for us as a team," says Aaron. "I think the captain is right; we must go our separate ways."

Sax nods. The two men put their arms around each other and hug goodbye, as tears well in their eyes. In that brief moment, Aaron can remember Sax coming to his aid as he struggled with the field kitchen buried deep in the snow. He can see himself sharing secret meals with Sax to keep him strong. He relives the incredible loyalty this man had shown him in their days of combat together. This life-saving friend, who grew into a monster, is now a human being to Aaron again.

"I could not have made it without you, Ignatz" says Aaron.

"Nor could I without you, Aaron."

"Béregszasz is not so far from Bielka," says Aaron.

"Nor Bielka from Béregszasz."

"So you will come visit, after you have had time to settle in at home."

"And you will, too" says Sax.

"Yes."

"Good luck, my friend," says Aaron.

"Same to you."

They draw apart, and Sax looks up the road. "He said the train is *that* way," he says as he points.

"Why don't you go there, then?" asks Aaron.

"Me? No. You go. I'm hungry." Sax grins slyly and points to a farmhouse in the distance.

Aaron smiles and starts down the road. After a while, he turns to look behind him, but Sax has disappeared. As he walks onward, Aaron's vague sense of regret for leaving his great war-torn comrade is tempered by the new world he can envision emerging ahead. Somehow, from what seems like the distant past, he can conjure up the future: A world at peace. He knows that in such a world, the qualities that had made Sax an indispensable comrade would be a hindrance. He knows that the need for survival skills such as scavenging for food, of ruthlessness and cunningness, of killing instantly or risk being killed, would be replaced by a need for other skills: A capacity to work peaceably with others, to nurture relationships, and to work within the law, for law would undoubtedly be re-established to secure normalcy.

Although Ignatz Sax had grown up in such a world, Aaron does not believe he could ever return to it without consequences. The demons unleashed by war, enslavement, humiliation, brutality, and the ghastly murders of his wife and two children have dug their claws deep into him and would never let go. Association with Sax therefore risks association with those demons, which could threaten Aaron's freedom and his life when peace returns.

Thus, Aaron begins to put Sax out of his mind and Sax disappears from his life almost as suddenly as he had appeared that snowy morning nearly two years before. It is not until years after the war that Aaron would begin to think about Sax again and would try to determine his fate, but by then it will be too late. He would never hear of or see his old comrade again.

The morning sunlight peeks through the Carpathian foothills, dispersing the gloom through which Aaron's train has traveled all night, waking him from a restless sleep. It is a train crowded mostly with emaciated, ragged refugees, but at least it has seats and is designed for people, not cattle. It has been six long years since Aaron was taken from his home on a train into slavery.

He has spent a nerve-racking night, not from fear of being captured again, as that fear seems to fade with each mile he draws closer to Bielka, but because he will finally find out whether Helen and his family, whose memories helped him survive his ordeal, have in turn survived theirs. Maybe they've had the same luck that Aaron did. Maybe a Christian neighbor had hidden them. Maybe they'd jumped off a train on their way to a concentration camp or escaped to another country.

He gets off the train before it reaches Bielka, having decided to first visit Helen's farm.

He makes his way through the fields and climbs a fence that hasn't been there before. Ahead of him, he can see that the house has been burned to the ground. Although it no longer smells of smoke, there is no way to determine how long it has been gone.

He slowly works his way through the wreckage. There is no evidence of bodies, but at the same time, there is little evidence of anything else. He decides the house might have been emptied before it was burned.

After he has inspected the ashen ruins, he wishes he hadn't gotten off the train where he did. Now he would have a long, lonely walk to town, one that promises to be heavier than any he has ever taken before.

He makes it to Bielka a little before noon. The town is cheerless. The Jewish shops are either boarded up or occupied by Hungarians. The streets look careworn and neglected. Where merchants and farmers should be selling their wares and produce, very few are stirring.

At last, Aaron sees his house in the distance. Like everything else, it seems quiet and empty, but is still standing. The closer he gets, the emptier it appears, until he reaches the door. He goes inside to see that the house has been stripped of everything except its bare walls.

He lies down on the floor and closes his eyes, barely moving, just waiting until the sun goes down.

Soon after nightfall, the flickering light from an unsteady lantern is casting shadows on the walls, and he can hear footsteps approaching. A figure appears in the doorway.

"Aaron?"

The figure revealed in the lantern's light is Ivan Kwok, the Herskowitzes' next-door neighbor. The Kwok family was Ukrainian and had worked for Aaron's family all their lives. The Herskowitzes had rewarded the Kwoks for their loyalty by granting them a home of their own on the family estate.

"Aaron! It *is* you!"

Aaron nods. "Hello Ivan."

"Pauli said he thought he'd seen you, so I wanted to see for myself. Here." He pulls a package of cheese from a sack and hands it to Aaron. Then he pulls out some of Aaron's personal bed coverings he'd saved and places them on the floor.

"Thank you," Aaron sighs. Then he whispers, "Are they still alive? My mother? My sisters? Helen Lazárovic?"

"For sure, I do not know," Ivan says. "The Hungarian police arrested your family and Helen's family. They arrested all the Jews about a year ago, on your holy night of Passover."

Aaron nods silently.

"They were sent to Beregsasz where they were put in a ghetto. I saw them many times during the next six weeks there. Two or three times a week, I would walk there and bring your family a satchel of food I carried on my back. The Hungarians, they barely gave them anything."

Aaron nods again. "Thank you, Ivan. When did you see them last? Could they still be in Béregszasz?"

"That was just a temporary place. The Germans took them all away on a train about a month later. We thought they were going to family labor camps, Aaron. That's what we all thought." Ivan's voice begins to tremble. "Death camps," he whispers. "They sent them all to die at a place called Auschwitz in Poland. A few have straggled home. Simcha says he saw your younger sisters, Leah and Rachel, just a few weeks before the Americans liberated their camp at a place called Bergen-Belsen in Germany. They should have been home by now. A few survivors show up at the train station every day. You may want to check there for a while."

"The Lazárovic family? Helen Lazárovic?" he asks quietly.

"I haven't heard anything."

Ivan's wife, Olana, enters the house with a tray of tea and sweet cakes, which she sets before Aaron, who thanks her, but does not take any.

"They parceled out your land to eighteen different Hungarian families," Ivan continues. "We got your house so we could hold it for you and your family, hoping you would return. We also have your mattresses and pots and some furniture. We knew that no one could steal from an empty house."

"Thank you," says Aaron.

"I will have my son, Steffan, help me bring the rest of your things back here tonight. I can transfer the property back to your name as soon as the district government office reopens. We can team up and start to plow the fields together. There is still enough farmland owned by your family to make it worthwhile. Steffan can help while you get your strength back."

Aaron nods slightly but does not speak a word.

"Go get Steffan," Ivan says to his wife.

"Please, no," says Aaron suddenly, in a voice sounding as dry as dust. "I thank you both for your thoughtfulness and kindness, but I do not think I can stay here. The property is yours."

"Give yourself some time, Aaron. We realize this is very difficult for you. You can stay with us as long as you like."

Aaron nods and bids them good night. After they leave, he remains seated, occasionally sobbing late into the night, until the lantern they've left behind burns itself out and the darkness is complete.

Aaron takes Ivan's advice and goes to the train station the next morning, and there he stays for more than a week, waiting for his family's return; waiting for a glimpse of Helen. The train station becomes Aaron's new home. Ivan and Aaron's other Christian friends provide him with a blanket and each day bring him food and drink. Every day, stragglers return from the concentration camps, but no one from Aaron's family is among them. These survivors tell Aaron how it was at Auschwitz: Older people and young women with children went straight to the gas chambers, while some of the younger, more able-bodied inmates were allowed to live on, many doing menial labor until they dropped from deprivation.

Each time the train pulls into Bielka and people disembark, Aaron's hopes to find a loved one flicker, though briefly.

After nearly two weeks, Ivan at last convinces Aaron there was no longer any point in staying at the train station. Aaron does not go home with him, though. Instead, he writes a note to his brother in New York:"Dear Harry, I have survived the war, but I don't think Mother or our older sisters made it. Our younger sisters? I don't know, I'm still searching for them. For me, I can't stay here. Can you, or Izzie, or Sam help me escape Europe and come to America?"

Aaron does not have Harry's address anymore, so he simply writes on the envelope: "Harry Herskowitz, New York City, USA," on the envelope, then seals it and sends it off, hoping by some miracle, that the letter would reach Harry.

Aaron then gets on the train in Bielka—they are free at that time, owing to the great many penniless refugees making their way across the continent. Ivan has given Aaron a small amount of money, and with that, he begins to rely on his well-honed survival skills, first working the black market, which is thriving in the chaos of post-war Europe. He deals in a great variety of once common, now rare, household goods: Cigarettes, matches, soap, heating oil, and most of all, exchanging monies for profit between the different Eastern European currencies. Soon Aaron carries bags and suitcases filled with goods and money. Aaron returns many times to Bielka, giving cash to Ivan and his wife as a means of thanking them for their own steadfast generosity and good will, and especially for Ivan's kindness in carrying food to his family at the ghetto for six weeks. Ivan asks where Aaron was getting all this money and Aaron tells him he got very lucky in the Eastern European markets—he just doesn't tell him it is the black market. All during this time, Aaron queries with whomever he could as to the fate of Helen and his sisters, searching for some news. His questions remain unanswered.

Aaron eventually finds remarkable material prosperity, but he is still alone, without his family or his God. One particular day in

Czechoslovakia, he wanders into a church and asks the priest if he could convert from Judaism to Christianity. The priest tells him it is impossible. Aaron was born Jewish and must remain Jewish.

His loneliness is finally relieved, several months after the war by another miraculous encounter: he finds none other than Max, his childhood best friend, who is working a farm in the Sudeten part of Czechoslovakia, where the German families Hitler had moved in had now been ousted. The land has been returned to Czech families, and Max got one of the farms. Max had lost his wife and children in the death camps, but he is trying to make a new life for himself. Miraculously reunited once again, Aaron takes a break from the black market and he and Max soon become partners, working the farm together.

But Aaron's new attempt at a more stable life is overshadowed before long by news that the Soviet Union will soon be establishing an iron hegemony over the nations of Eastern Europe, including Czechoslovakia. As far as Aaron knows, he still has a price on his head, so it is time for one last escape. He prepares to make a final trip to Bielka, to bid goodbye forever to Ivan and Olana and the few friends he has left there. Then he would leave for Palestine.

---

12   See   the   map   page   300   (Defeat   of   Germany).

CHAPTER 19
A CHANCE WEDDING

AARON SITS QUIETLY ON a train heading east in a remote area of Czechoslovakia, his pockets and baggage bulging with money, cigarettes, soap, and other small, tradable items he hopes will be enough to get him through the long journey to Palestine. He has heard rumors that thousands of Jewish Holocaust survivors have been trying to flee to Palestine to escape from the ruins of Europe, only to be intercepted and left stranded on boats in the Mediterranean Sea, in European displacement camps, or on the island of Cyprus. The British are still in control of Palestine, and they continue to bar entry to Jewish refugees in order to please the anti-Semitic oil-rich Muslim countries. Nevertheless, Aaron feels confident that if he is alone and traveling over land, his wartime experiences and resourcefulness will allow him to sneak across the border unnoticed. He wonders about the road ahead and what he will find once he gets there. He hears there has been combat, something of which he has seen far too much, this time between Palestinian Muslims and Jews. He knows it will be a rustic existence, yet he is just getting used to sleeping in a bed again. Still, sleeping on the ground in a kibbutz or in a Jewish military camp in Palestine is preferable to occupying a stout bed in a Soviet prison.

While Aaron is contemplating these possibilities, the train begins to slow as it approaches the small Czech town of Léborets. He's overheard a few of his fellow passengers talking about a wedding that is to take place there that afternoon. As the train stops temporarily at the remote town, Aaron hears the faint sounds of something he hasn't heard in many years—Jewish wedding music. At this time in Europe, any Holocaust survivor attending a Jewish wedding is automatically considered a guest, and Aaron wonders whether or not he should get off and join the festivities in an effort to find an occasion that brings joy; something he's had little of for so many years. He has enough money—for now—but a free wedding meal is a free meal, and any money he saves now might come in handy later if he needs to bribe a border guard or an immigration official.

Nevertheless, he has just decided against interrupting his journey when the conductor comes through to announce that track work ahead will delay the train for an hour. As the conductor moves to the next car, Aaron can hear the sounds of wedding music drifting more clearly through the open windows. He has always loved music—he had played the mandolin in his youth—and the prospect of food, music, and the idea of a celebration seems far preferable to a lonely wait on a stalled train. He lifts his baggage and begins to follow the music, coursing his way through the town.

When he arrives at the house of celebration, the wedding ceremony has already taken place. The gathering is comprised mainly of Jews in their twenties and thirties, with those older and younger having suffered disproportionately in the death camps and ghettos. It is the first time in many years that Aaron has heard the joyous sounds of Jewish wedding music; the first time in years he has seen Jews dancing for joy, the first time in years he has smelled the tantalizing aromas of a Jewish wedding feast.

As Aaron steps up to the buffet table, he is stopped in his tracks by a single word: *"Chaia!"*

Someone is calling out the name *Chaia*. In Hebrew, *Chaia* means life, and in those life-affirming moments, it is an appropriate word to say. But it also has another meaning for Aaron. Translated into English, it is *Helen*.

He hears a woman's familiar lilting laughter. And there she is, standing across the room, her face aglow, chatting with friends. He is not in some faraway vision of the Carpathian Mountains. He is not, this time, destined to find himself withdrawn from her presence so as to slug along for another day carrying a machine gun or rucksack on his back. *"Chaia!"* he calls out, stunned and overjoyed at once.

"Aaron?" she replies, incredulously.

The two stare at each other across the floor. As they begin to approach one another, the room becomes quieter.

"I thought you died in Russia," she says, walking toward him.

"I feel like I did—a thousand times."

"Me too," says Helen. They both pause, feeling the pain of all that was lost.

"What on earth are you doing here?" Aaron asks, once he recovers his voice.

"It's my cousin's wedding. I came from Carlsbad, where I've been living with some of my family, to help her prepare the food."

They stare at each other, she with a beguiling smile, he, dumbfounded. Several people from Bielka recognize Aaron and come over to greet him, but he has eyes and ears only for Helen. He has seen her many times in his thoughts, of course, and in those visions, she was beautiful, yet not as radiant or beautiful as the woman he sees before him. They move toward one another, the space between them growing more intimate.

Aaron thinks back through what seems like centuries. "I was thinking I had lost you forever, but memories of you sustained me through the worst," he says as he gently takes her hands and they gaze into one another's eyes. The room now falls silent, at least to them.

"It's a miracle," Helen says, "that we've found each other in the middle of Czechoslovakia."

"Only soon I must leave again, Helen. Come with me to Palestine and we can start over."

"Palestine?" Helen smiles. "Why Palestine? We could have a life with my family in Carlsbad. Some of my brothers and sisters survived."

"I'm afraid I can't stay in Czechoslovakia. It's a long story."

Helen frowns. "You look hungry, Aaron. Let me get you some food. I'll serve you myself."

They talk late into the night about what might have been and what still could be. Helen tells Aaron how she survived starvation and beatings at the concentration camps. She describes to Aaron how she saved her little sister Gitu's life several times and how she and Gitu survived by taking great risks, secretly planting the seeds of potatoes in non-descript areas on the grounds near the Leipzig slave labor factory.

"Gitu and I made a pact when we escaped from the Nazis at the end of the war, Aaron," says Helen. "We swore to each other that for the rest of our lives we would each cook baked potatoes every night for our families to commemorate how we survived."

"I can't wait to taste your baked potatoes, Helen," says Aaron, smiling.

"I made some for dinner, but our guests ate all of them early on; so you *will* have to wait, Aaron."

Helen tells Aaron that she saw his two younger sisters, Leah and Rachel, near the end of the war near the Bergen-Belsen concentration camp, crouched in the back of a truck with other Jewish women, though they looked very ill and emaciated.

"No Helen," says Aaron with his head down in sorrow, "If they haven't come home by now, they are gone."

Aaron tells Helen about the harshness and atrocities while a slave laborer under the Nazis and Hungarians, and the incredible luck of his escape to join the Russians. But he can't bear to tell her about his own violence in Gérjen, and he never would.

Having long since missing his train, Aaron has already abandoned his plan to immigrate to Palestine, at least temporarily. Instead, he would continue trading in the black market and helping Max work the farm until he could figure out what the best path would be to make a life with Helen. At last, it is time for him to catch the next train back to Bielka where he plans to bid his final farewells to Ivan and Olana. The two embrace tightly as Helen whispers, "Don't keep me waiting for years this time, Aaron." The two lovers smile at each other.

When he is back on the train, however, Aaron overhears talk from native Czechs that the Soviet Union has already annexed his home province of Transcarpathia, based on their subterfuge that many Ukrainians live there, and Ukraine has been a province of Russia for centuries. He fears the worst if the Russians capture him again, as the train is rapidly approaching the Carpathians. He jumps off the train and resigns himself to never seeing his home town again.

Instead, he goes to Romania in an attempt to sell goods from his black market business before returning to Helen in Carlsbad. From each stop he mails her a letter expressing a passion and love he didn't know he had in him anymore, and a lust for life he thought he could never feel again. He writes her beautiful love letters and poetry expressing himself in all the languages they share: Czech, Hebrew, Hungarian, Yiddish, and Russian.

Overcome by this avalanche of emotion, when they meet again a few weeks later, Helen joyfully accepts Aaron's proposal of marriage. With her hand thus assured, he sets off once more to raise the money he will need to smuggle both of them out of Eastern Europe.

However, their wedding plans are not so quickly realized as Helen's oldest surviving brother, Meyer-Joseph, has taken on the role of surrogate father to his surviving siblings, and he has other plans for her.

"Helen," says Meyer-Joseph. "It's time for you to get married, and I have some fine suitors for you."

"I don't need any suitors," says Helen.

"Yes, you do. And one of them—David—you already know from home."

"David?" asks Helen. "From Bielka? He smells!"

"Never mind things like that, Helen. As a wife you will learn to accept such things."

"Perhaps *you* would accept them if *you* were a wife, but not me," Helen retorts.

"If not David," says Meyer-Joseph with a sigh, "Then there is Michael."

"Have you seen his teeth?" asks Helen.

"We are finding a suitor for you, not a horse."

"I don't need either. I already have—"

"You have Isaac," says Meyer-Joseph at last. "Isaac, I know the best. We volunteered with the Czechs held in Siberia to serve together under the Russian army during the last year of the war."

"No, Joe—Aaron has just proposed to me."

"Don't be ridiculous. Forget about Aaron. He is a black marketer. My friend Isaac is tall, respectable, and well-to-do. He will make you a fine husband."

"But Joe, he hasn't even proposed," says Helen.

"That's because you are the most beautiful woman in Czechoslovakia, and he's so in love with you that he doesn't dare say 'boo' to you. Don't worry, Helen. Any man would take a beautiful woman like you for his wife."

"No, Joe. I love Aaron."

"Helen, I am now the head of this family," says Meyer-Joseph firmly. "I'm the one who knows what's best for you, and you must follow our traditions. Your husband will be Isaac, and we will announce your engagement at my own wedding next week."

Helen, now panicked, immediately sets off to track Aaron down at Max's farm. When she arrives, Max is working in the field. She waves to him, and he walks over to her, astonished.

"Helen? Is that you?"

"Yes. I was told you were here, and that Aaron stays here, too. Can you help me find him? It's urgent."

Max smiles. "What's he done now? Sold you diluted heating oil?"

"No. He proposed to me."

"And now he's run away?" Max asks.

"No, Max. It's my brother. He wants to marry me off to a man I don't even know, and he wants to do it next week. I couldn't bear for that to happen."

"Wolf? He won't let you marry Aaron? He practically worships Aaron—he loves him like a brother," says Max.

"No, Max. Meyer-Joseph has taken over as head of the family. Wolf died in Russia."

Max closes his eyes and lowers his head. "I'm so sorry, Helen."

"He refused to eat *traif* (non-kosher food), even in the snows of Siberia."

"True to his God to the bitter end," says Max, shaking his head.

"But Max," Helen says. "I heard you lost your wife and children. I'm so sorry."

"Thank you, Helen, it's true. So many of our loved ones lost. But we're still here, though you look tired and thirsty. Let me give you something to drink and we'll talk."

"Thank you, Max, but I don't want anything to drink. I want Aaron."

"Don't worry, Helen. Aaron has to stop in Bucharest for a couple of days to barter some goods for us—and for you, too," smiles Max. "I'll send my younger brother with a message for him to come back before it's too late."

A week later, Aaron hurriedly approaches Helen's now-familiar apartment house in Carlsbad. After everything he has endured, is he going to lose his love again, the woman whose memory has kept him alive? Aaron knows only one thing: he will fight for his love as he has fought for his life. No one is going to take his Helen away from him again.

As he opens the door to her home, he sees a bride and groom exchanging wedding vows. Frozen in fear for a moment, he then sighs with relief as he realizes the groom is Helen's older brother, Meyer-Joseph. When he spots Helen, he quickly maneuvers his way through the crowd and takes her in his arms.

"Thank God you came," says Helen. "Joe is trying to marry me off to Isaac."

"I heard," says Aaron. "You'll leave with me for Palestine tonight? I can only promise you a life of hardship and danger—but we'll be together."

"Because I love you, Aaron, I'll go anywhere with you." They embrace again, this time with tears of joy.

"Helen, what are you doing?" shouts Joe, coming toward them.

"I'm going to marry Aaron," says Helen defiantly.

"What about me, Joe? You promised Helen to me." It is Isaac, who has overheard the conversation.

Suddenly there is a cacophony of shouting as Michael cries out, "Meyer-Joseph! *I* want to marry Helen," and David screams, "Give *me* a chance, Joe. I'm as good a man as them—and I'm a Bilker!"

Realizing his predicament, Joe declares, "There's only one way to settle this!" He pulls the hat off Isaac's head. "She'll draw a name out of a hat."

"That's crazy!" shouts Isaac, trying unsuccessfully to snatch his hat back.

"It's the only fair way to decide," says Joe who quickly scribbles the suitors' names on four scraps of paper, crumples them up and places them in the hat, believing this scheme will diminish Aaron's chances.

But Aaron has not made this journey merely to succumb to Joe's trickery. No matter the outcome, Aaron intends to whisk Helen away and marry her. And in his heart, he knows this is exactly what she would want him to do.

Joe moves forward and presents the hat to his sister. All eyes turn to Helen, who has begun to shake her head 'no,' when a cheer rises up from the crowd, drowning out her objections.

Helen closes her eyes, takes a deep breath, and retrieves one of the pieces of paper. Before she can open it, however, Joe snatches it from her and opens it. He stares at it for a moment, then shows it to Helen.

"Aaron!" she shouts. The two lovers embrace and the crowd cheers. Pandemonium ensues, and Joe's wedding party transforms itself into an engagement party for Aaron and Helen.

But that is only the start of Joe's vexation.

"You may place the ring on her finger," says Joe.

It is three weeks later, and Aaron is back in Carlsbad, standing under the same *chupa* [wedding altar] that had served for Meyer-Joseph's wedding. Helen is at his side, looking radiant as ever, and their surviving relatives and friends are present. Joe is performing the wedding ceremony despite his objections to Helen's choice of husband. Because there are so few rabbis left in Europe at the time, any Jew who holds a position that is even vaguely "official" is deemed appropriate to perform a wedding ceremony; and as a notary public as well as a learned man of the *Torah*—holy Hebrew scroll—Joe fits the bill.

"The ring, Aaron. Please place it on her finger," says Joe.

Aaron hesitates. Preparations have been hectic, and at that moment, Aaron realizes he has neglected to get one.

Aaron shrugs. "Sorry, Joe, I'm going to have to borrow yours."

Joe sighs, removes the ring from his own finger, and gives it to Aaron, who places it on Helen's finger. And so the ceremony is brought to a successful cheerful conclusion, after which Joe immediately demands his ring back.

The swirl of the wedding celebration that follows exceeds any joy Aaron and Helen have ever known and will remain in their memories all the rest of their days as a feast of vast proportions, far more extravagant than it actually was or could have been. The liquor seems to flow as if from a limitless river; the music enraptures the crowd, and the dancing, laughter, good wishes and good will all seem to be flowing in boundless quantities. Is it possible there is actually enough joy in the universe to counterbalance the sorrow Aaron, Helen, and their loved ones have endured?

And yet, as the party winds down at last, a bittersweet feeling creeps over those who are present. This is also, after all, a going-away party for Aaron and Helen: They are about to leave for Palestine to make a new life for themselves. The Soviet takeover of the rest of Czechoslovakia is gaining momentum, and Aaron does not want his marital bliss to be interrupted by a long stay in a Russian gulag.

At last, as the musicians begin to pack their instruments, Aaron hears his name being shouted.

"Aaron Herskowitz!" cries an unfamiliar voice. "Is there an Aaron Herskowitz here?"

Aaron immediately senses danger—have the Russians come to take him? Have they just allowed him these brief moments of joy before arresting him? He spots a man in a uniform at the entrance to the house and instinctively shrinks back, but too late. Some of the guests are already pointing Aaron out.

The man walks across to Aaron, who holds Helen tightly.

"Aaron Herskowitz?"

"That's me."

"You're a hard man to find. This letter has been forwarded to you from Bielka. It is marked "urgent," so that's why I'm personally delivering it.

He smiles and holds out the envelope. Aaron approaches cautiously. Is it some sort of summons? An arrest warrant? He plucks the letter from the man's hand. It is postmarked New York City, from one Harry Herskowitz. Somehow, Aaron's letter addressed simply to "Harry Herskowitz, New York City, USA" had eventually reached its destination.

Aaron trembles as he rips it open. Inside are a hundred dollar bill and a note, which reads: "Aaron, we were overjoyed to get your letter. I would have responded sooner but New York City is a large place, and your letter was very small by comparison. We are working more hours in our business and will be able to send you more money soon, enough to get you out. We will borrow it if we need to. We have a plan to bring you to America quickly. Two of us, myself and Sam, married two Hungarian sisters. They have a third sister who is ready to marry you. She is very beautiful, and she will make you a good wife. We are told this is the quickest way to get you out."

Aaron is astonished with joy that his letter addressed to "Harry Herskowitz, New York City, USA" had found its way to Harry's home. When he writes back to Harry and his brothers Izzie and Sam, telling them that he has already married Helen and could never abandon her again, the brothers instantly understand. Instead, Aaron's brothers work hard to convince the American government that they are established U.S. citizens fully capable of supporting and sponsoring Aaron and Helen. They finally bring them out after two years of countless bureaucratic delays with a U.S. State Department that is still anti-Semitic, making it extremely harsh for the Jewish people to immigrate, even after the U.S. government knows all about the murders of six million Jews in The Holocaust.

While he waits, Aaron tries to work with Joe and Helen's younger brother, Ludwig, in the black market. But when the Czech government decides it's time to outlaw such enterprises, Aaron and his brothers-in-law are arrested and jailed. Luckily, Helen is able to find a lawyer to get them out. After that, Aaron realizes he'll have to adapt once more and returns to farming with Helen and her family.

At last, Helen and Aaron are permitted to immigrate to America. Aaron's reunion with his brothers is joyous beyond words. They tell him they had tried in vain to get the family out of Bielka before the war, but the anti-Semitic American government, with the approval of President Roosevelt, had thwarted all their efforts by raising their quota and financial requirements for immigration of Jews to impossibly high restrictions. Afterward, Aaron often wonders how many innocent Jewish lives might have been spared if America and the nations of the world had opened their doors to Jewish people before World War II and The Holocaust.

A chilly wind is blowing in off the Hudson River and across the busy streets of Manhattan when Aaron Herskowitz and his bride step out of the subway at 50th Street and Broadway in the spring of 1948. In Bielka, seven thousand miles away, it is time to plant the last of the crops, repair the roof, and mend the fences. But Aaron is no longer the young man who felt trapped in that small village, tending the fields and caring for his mother and younger sisters, fantasizing about what life in America would be like. A great catastrophe had stripped him of his family and home and had nearly taken his life, but it has freed him to live this other dream. Inevitably, the pain of the past begins to loosen its grip, and his sense of possibility soars to match the skyscrapers around him.

He knows that he will come to embrace this nation as his own in a way that his older brothers, whose transit had occurred under much less difficult circumstances, would never understand.

For the man who had endured Novyi Oskol, Vóronezh, Davidóvka, three Russian winters, the deaths of Eisler, Kimlit, Foeldish, and Shmiel, his mother and sisters, and the anguish of countless others, the spring wind cannot possibly hold any chill. It can only fill his lungs with the hopeful breath of life that will vault him into the birth of the richest, most prosperous days of his time on earth.

CHAPTER 20
AARON RETURNS TO HIS FAITH

SOON AFTER THEY ARRIVE in New York, Aaron and Helen stay with Harry's family in Miami, Florida where Aaron starts working in his brothers' laundry and dry cleaning business. Once their lives are settled, they begin a family, which grows to include two sons and a daughter, and then grandchildren. Eventually, all four brothers settle in Florida where their business prospers.

In 1990, at the urging of their now adult children, Aaron and Helen return for the first time to Bielka.[13] They'd been reluctant to make the trip, fearing that the visit would stir horrific memories, but finally agree when their children explain they'd longed to see for themselves where their roots lay; and to experience a glimpse of the magical place about which their parents had told them captivating stories since childhood. As it turns out, instead of the sorrow they had feared, the once familiar hills and streams—and many of the good Christian neighbors who still remember them—bring tears of joy to Aaron's and Helen's eyes.

Aaron asks where he might find his loyal neighbor Ivan Kwok, who not only welcomed him home at the end of the war, but who also told Aaron that he brought food to Aaron's family with a satchel on his back, walking to the ghetto in Béregszas a few times every week. Unfortunately, Aaron is told that Ivan is no longer alive.

However, a special journey awaits Helen in Bielka and her family as they walk down the street from her former property to climb up the hills to try to visit Mihai Barzoún, the kindly Ukrainian Christian who had pleaded with Helen and her family to allow Helen and her two younger siblings to hide in his barn from the Hungarian Nazis, trying to save them from deportation to the death camps.

To Helen's joy, Mihai and his wife are alive and well, and they greet Helen and her family with great happiness. They invite family and close friends to host a "welcome home" party for Aaron and Helen that very same afternoon filled with cakes, liquor and music. They treat our family as kings. Mihai asks about the fate of Helen's parents and siblings, as he remembers all of them quite well. He expresses sorrow upon hearing that so many of them didn't survive.

Somehow, as a master linguist, Aaron remains completely fluent in the Ukrainian language after forty-five years of never speaking it, and he helps facilitate conversation between Helen and the Barzoúns and their Ukrainian family and friends.

The Barzoúns and Aaron's neighbors Ivan Kwok and his wife would all be forever remembered by the Herskowitzes amongst "The Righteous Gentiles."

Unfortunately, Bielka's Jewish cemetery had been so unkempt that Aaron is unable to find his father's grave, but he does discover his grandfather's. Standing there in the cemetery, he is overcome with emotion and says *Kaddish* (the mourner's prayer) for his lost family. In the years that follow, he would reaffirm the Jewish faith he had abandoned in the horrors of those times. With the wise counsel of his rabbi and other holocaust survivors in America, he would come to believe it was God's plan for Aaron to abandon his belief in the Almighty during the war, giving him the unshakable avowal to believe only in himself that was so crucial to his survival.

Harder for him is reconciling some of the violent acts of retribution he had committed with the moral strictures of Judaism. In time, however, along with the wisdom and guidance of his rabbi, Aaron also comes to believe that God would forgive him those transgressions, because God knew well the horrors that had brought them about, and it was God's plan that Aaron's unleashing of punishment against the savage persecutors of the Chosen People were acts of justice.

Aaron's mother and five sisters are assumed to have perished in the death camps. Of the one hundred thousand Hungarian Jewish slaves taken to Russia, only about six thousand survive. Aaron never sees nor hears from Sax again, and no trace of him is found. Aaron supposes that his violent temper may have been his undoing during the dangerous, lawless time just after the war.

However, Aaron's best friend Max eventually immigrates to America and Aaron convinces him to settle in Miami, Florida. Max had taken a bullet for Aaron in Russia, and Aaron would never forget it. The two men joyfully reunite, and Aaron helps Max in every way possible to go into business. The two remain best friends and confidantes for the rest of their lives.

Helen wants desperately to bring her beloved sister Gitu, with whom she survived the concentration camps to live in the US, and after fighting years of bureaucratic red tape, Gitu finally immigrates along with her husband Joseph, also a survivor. The two sisters ecstatically reunite, and Gitu and her husband settle in Miami, Florida, so that Helen and Gitu remain very close and intimate sisters for the remainder of their lives.

Throughout his life in America, Aaron remains keenly aware of the dangers posed by fanatical, racial or religious extremism, as history continues to repeat itself with more genocide, whether manifested in violent form; or in the passive fanaticism of the Eastern European rabbis of Aaron's youth who had refused to allow the Jewish people to either resist the Nazis or flee to Palestine. The spiritual descendants of those rabbis survive to this very day. Following World War II, many of them ironically protest angrily against the movement to establish the state of Israel out of the ashes of the Holocaust, arguing again that only the Messiah had the authority to re-create the Jewish homeland. To Aaron's joy, however, the surviving Jewish population sweeps aside these fanatical protests and fight to see their dream of the nation of Israel come true.

A staunch supporter of Israel from the moment of its birth, Aaron is also a great patriot of the United States of America. In an echo of his own father, who had kept a portrait of Emperor Franz-Josef in his home, Aaron displays a portrait of President Ronald Reagan in his living room to honor the man who had vanquished the Soviet Union, in whose prisons Aaron had suffered betrayal, brutal interrogation, and torture.

Aaron is overjoyed that in the crumbling of the Soviet Union in the 1990s, Ukraine becomes an independent democracy. Aaron was always fond of his Ukrainian friends during his youth, and he felt a special bond with the Ukrainian soldiers he had fought with shoulder-to-shoulder during the war. He is pleased beyond words that his hometown Bielka is inherited into Ukraine from the Soviets, and that his former beloved Carpathian province is now located within the borders of Ukraine.

He would have been further amazed that the Christian nation of Ukraine, formerly a rabidly antisemitic province and/or country, would turn the page over its past, and the modern generations of Ukraine would eventually elect a Jewish president, Vlodomir Zelensky along with a Jewish vice president.

There is no doubt that Aaron would have been most supportive of Ukraine's stalwart defense of their nation from the savage invasion by Russia against Ukraine. Ironically, he was present on some of the same battlefields as in the Ukraine/Russia war. He would have been proud that the descendants of his Ukrainian friends thwarted Russia's initial attempt to seize the Ukrainian capital, Kyiv and topple President Zelensky's government to install a puppet regime under the thumb of Vladimir Putin. If Aaron would see the atrocities committed by Putin against Ukraine, he would have felt that history is repeating itself, except that Adolf Hitler and Josef Stalin have been replaced by Vladimir Putin.

Aaron lives a vigorous happy life in Florida with Helen. When the sun finally sets for the last time upon his life, Aaron is surrounded by his loving children and grandchildren until his death on December 29, 2003, at the age of 89.

---

13 See the maps on pages 301 and 302 (Europe 1945 – 1980s; Europe Mid-1990s – Today).

CHAPTER 21
A FINAL RECKONING

I, THEN, AM AARON Herskowitz, Beloved Son, *father, brother, husband; a farmer, horseman, patriotic son of Czechoslovakia, soldier, Jew, lover of God, slave laborer, hater of God, Russian partisan, persecutor, assassin, survivor, and now beloved grandfather and patriotic son of America. I have been a hard worker and good citizen who has counted among my closest friends both Jews and Christians, a man who broke no laws, who one day found himself enveloped by a storm of unimaginable magnitude; a storm that swept over a continent and snatched me away from the life and people I loved. I weathered that storm, in the only way I knew how, and I do not apologize for how I did so. I ask only that you consider my testimony before rendering judgment, and ask yourself, truly, what would you have done in my place?*

CHAPTER 22

WHATEVER HAPPENED TO SAX?

INITIALLY, MY FATHER DID not want me to write this book. He had never shared the darker side of his story with anyone—including my mother, his brothers, my siblings, nor most of his closest friends. He did not want any of us to know that he had taken the lives of others, no matter how justified.

Still, the question remains—*why didn't other Jews fight back during the war?* I often asked myself. Of course we have one important answer from Aaron Herskowitz in this book: the fanatical orthodox rabbis, urging their people not to resist—instead to wait and pray for a mysterious Messiah to descend from the heavens to protect them from such evil. But even when some of the victims of the Holocaust knew they were doomed, why didn't they try to take some of the murderers down with them? As I grew up and these stories of Jews failing to fight were again presented, I recall my non-Jewish friends also wondering why so many millions of Jews had failed to resist. I was often embarrassed, even ashamed, as such passivity went against the very fabric of my personal beliefs about defending oneself against such persecution. After all, the canons of Jewish history are full of tales of heroic uprisings in the bible: Didn't David slay Goliath? What about Judah Maccabee's epic revolt that led to the annual celebration of Hanukah? Didn't Samson exert his incredible strength and power over his nation's more numerous and formidable enemies? Didn't any of these stories mean anything? As a youngster, I had often fantasized myself as being one of these real-life heroes.

There were, of course, exceptions: The Warsaw ghetto uprising, the escape from the Sobibor concentration camp, and the story of the Bielsky brothers of the Byelorus province of the Soviet Union, hiding and protecting about 1,200 Jews in the Russian forests, among a few others. Yet, as brave as these revolts and actions were, most resulted with few survivors and limited retribution.

Ironically, as it turned out, my own father had struck a blow, not only for himself but for all those who were being persecuted—and delivered a measure of justice to their oppressors. Yet Aaron remained modest to the core, never boasting of his wartime accomplishments. Instead, he would dismiss his actions as purely necessary for survival, or due to incredibly good luck. He did not consider himself a hero, and in retrospect, he questioned the justification of some of his actions.

I'm quite sure I could never have survived were I in my father's shoes, let alone accomplish what he did after his escape from the Nazis. But *he* was suited to survive, as if he were born for it. He was certainly the toughest man I've ever known, a figure larger than life, no matter his short stature. It was as if everything he had learned and possessed as a youth groomed him for this ordeal: He was a man whose physical strength belied his size, a master horseman, a linguist, a master of self-defense, whether with a weapon or just his hands, a man of great charisma who could befriend anyone or charm his way out of danger. He was also a man who could instill fear with merely a stare and interrogate anyone out of whatever information he wanted. Yet when he immigrated to America, he somehow put much of his wartime past behind him, lived a peaceful life without ever owning a gun, and became a passionate American patriot.

I feel privileged and lucky that Aaron Herskowitz, my father, shared his story with me—the whole story—the good and the bad — and that he recognized my passion to consume it and eventually write about it, and share it with the world.

How could any man or woman who had been tortured and persecuted for years not be expected to react with a measure of retribution when given unlimited power and authority to be the judge, jury and executioner over their former oppressors? Under such conditions, brought by war, I believe my father's actions would garner an understanding and justification with those human beings who seek to understand the resourcefulness needed during this horrific time to survive. I am reminded of an old adage sent to me by the late Tom Lantos, the only holocaust survivor ever elected to the U.S. Congress, after reading the first outline for this book: "Don't judge a man until you have walked in his own shoes." The walk of Aaron Herskowitz through his cauldron of fire is a walk I hope none of us ever has to endure.

The words "Never Again" have been used to underscore the resolve of the Jewish people to the world to never allow another Holocaust against the Jews. And yet, on October 6, 2023 Hamas terrorists from Gaza invaded Israel, killing over 1200 people and dragging scores of hostages back into Gaza, committing atrocities and crimes against humanity. Aaron would have been disappointed that the world failed to heed "Never Again."

As a result of the Hamas terrorist invasion, antisemitism has broken out the world over. Aaron would have felt that history is repeating itself, and the world has not yet learned its lesson.

Whenever I've done speaking engagements about my father's story, I've been very often asked, "So whatever happened to Aaron's friend, the wild strongman, Sax?" I'd always responded that neither my father nor the rest of our family ever knew Sax's fate. My father did say that immediately after the war, when the Russians annexed his hometown Bielka with the entire Carpathian province into the Soviet Union, and the Russians were about to install a communist puppet regime in Czechoslovakia, that he was afraid to get in touch with Sax, because there could still be a Soviet price on each of their heads.

But after Aaron immigrated to America in 1948, he began asking anyone he could find who'd immigrated from the Carpathians and surrounding areas if they'd ever heard of Ignatz Sax, and if so, what was his fate? Unfortunately, no one my dad encountered ever knew of his old comrade. After my father passed away, our family continued the search to find Sax, but to no avail.

Then, many years later, a breakthrough occurred. I was presenting the story of Aaron's Reckoning to a group discussion of World War II and the Holocaust, when some members of the audience came forward and claimed to be relatives of the late Ignatz Sax, whom they advised had immigrated to live in Pittsburgh, Pennsylvania. Soon afterward, I was contacted by the two sons of Ignatz, Billy and Alex Sax, still living in Pittsburgh. We immediately exchanged information and the Saxes read the early working version of the manuscript, and they watched videos on the Aaronsreckoning.com website in which my father describes his old friend Ignatz. Following this, the sons of Ignatz Sax felt certain that their father was the Ignatz Sax depicted in Aaron's Reckoning. They were grateful to me for chronicling some of the war years of their dad, because Ignatz never wanted to talk about that horrific painful period in his past to his family. He understandably did not want them to know about his brutal torrent of revenge. After comparing all the provided information and materials, my family and I are convinced that we had found our father's old comrade at last, through his sons, Billy and Alex. The Saxes expressed their gratitude to me for advising them that Ignatz had a wife and two children who were murdered in Hitler's death camps. They were never aware of this.

We all realized that a plausible reason we'd previously failed to locate the correct Ignatz Sax was because in all our searches, we used the more widely known "Sachs" spelling, instead of "Sax," which would have been key to locating Ignatz while he and Aaron were both living. Billy and Alex described how their dad remained a champion of the Jewish community of Pittsburgh, and how he continued to stand up for his fellow Jews. They spoke about the many violent encounters he had against anti-Semites who might be committing violence upon a Jewish individual. Ignatz would come to their aid and take on two or three men at a time and fight them until they ran away.

Billy and Alex said that their dad had a temper and was quick to violence, consistent with the behavior of Aaron Herskowitz's old friend. Now that we have finally made this incredible connection, we shall continue to forge forward with these memories of the past, so that the tragedy that befell so many millions of innocent people during the Second World War shall never happen again.

Department of History

HISTORIAN'S COMMENTARY

*by Colonel David M. Glantz,
U.S. ARMY (Retired)*

This gem of a true historical saga describes the extraordinary journey, in reality, the epic heroic ordeal of Aaron Herskowitz, a young Czechoslovakian Jewish soldier who, caught up in the treacherously deadly currents of World War II, somehow survived and, with his son, Howard Herskowitz's brilliant assistance as the author of this magnificent work, now shares his harrowing experiences with posterity.

Few periods in modern history have been more complex, brutal, barbaric, and terrifying than the Russian Front of The Second World War, indeed a campaign of extermination. The author felt that it was his mission to document the horrors of war experienced by his father, as a reminder to future generations of the evil inherent in man and to further chronicle how this one man heroically achieved the ultimate reversal of fortune from lowly Jewish slave to master of his former persecutors. The result is a gripping page-turning thriller set against the background of the vast geography of the Soviet Union, and the brutal war fought on its territory.

It has been my great privilege to serve as historian for this story of Aaron Herskowitz's death-defying journey across the Russian Front during World War II. The author apparently felt I was uniquely qualified upon his review of my career, where I ended my active service in the U.S. Army at the rank of Colonel, and then beyond as a history professor and author of numerous books and treatises, the focus and specialty of much of my work centering on the conflict between the Soviet Union vs. Germany, including Germany's Axis partners (Hungary, Italy and Romania) during the War. I am honored to be considered by many as the world's leading expert on this conflict, and I have lectured frequently about it, not only as a history professor, but at many other venues. I am also privileged to have prepared the maps for Aaron's Reckoning, to which I worked with the author to align these maps as to where Aaron Herskowitz was located at various events during his harrowing nightmare across Eastern Europe.

The author, Howard Herskowitz, stressed to me at the outset of this undertaking that the only way he was comfortable telling the epic story of his father's journey in the nonfiction narrative he was writing, was to obtain as much historical verification as possible of the trials and tribulations experienced by his father, Aaron Herskowitz. I advised Howard that I would be honored to research and authenticate his father's epic journey and the military history surrounding it that covered thousands of miles throughout the former Soviet Union and other sectors of Eastern Europe. In addition to my own research, I also reached out to my counterpart military historians in Ukraine, Germany, Hungary, and other parts of the former Soviet Union. I had previously cultivated relationships with several of these historians in order to assist me with my own books and treatises about the war fought on the Russian front during World War II.

Thus, with the able assistance of my counterpart historians and their works, I have been able to verify the locations where the book has indicated Aaron Herskowitz to be present at the various battle scenes, locations and times described in his journey, based in part on whether Aaron was under the control of the German-Hungarian army, or later, after he had escaped to join the Russian Army.

Hitler had rewarded his ally Hungary with Aaron's Czechoslovakian province of Transcarpathia, but when the Fuhrer needed reinforcements to bolster his armies in Russia against unexpectedly fierce Russian resistance, Hitler called upon his Axis allies to send their armies to serve with the Germans on the Russian front.

Because he was Jewish, Aaron was dragooned into the slave labor battalions of the Hungarian 2nd Army to march toward the battlefront. As the Axis tide flowed eastward into the Soviet Union, the Hungarians dragged along their Jewish slaves, drifting eastward in the German army's wake, in a seemingly endless and increasingly senseless Nazi crusade. The slaves were always stationed at the very front lines of battle to serve the German and Hungarian soldiers, placing them at very high risk of death from the crossfire.

My European counterparts and I have reviewed and studied the events of the battle of Voronezh on January 13, 1943, especially because Hitler had issued one of his suicidal "No Retreat!" commands to the Axis position, no matter whether the Axis or the Russians attacked first. Apparently, an individual ostensibly acting as an officer in the Hungarian sector, issued an order to "Retreat!" in violation of Hitler's orders, causing the Axis Army in that sector to flee to the rear, followed by the rest of the Axis army, as they assumed that the Fuhrer had reversed his previous "No Retreat!" orders. As a result, the Axis lost this major battle. I have verified from my military historian counterparts in Hungary and Germany that thorough investigations were undertaken by the Axis armies to identify and punish the "traitor" who issued the command for the Axis to retreat from the battlefront. That individual has remained unidentified—until the revelations in this book. Thus, it becomes most plausible that the bold actions taken by Aaron Herskowitz at the Voronezh battlefront substantially contributed to the Axis defeat, handing the Russians a major victory, and saving the lives of countless thousands of Jewish slaves.

During the early spring of 1944, Aaron Herskowitz escaped from the Nazi-Hungarian forces to join the Russian army. Per my research with my military historian counterparts in Europe, we have confirmed that Aaron Herskowitz, while acting as a Soviet secret agent, crossed back over enemy lines to arrest and capture hundreds of Nazi and Hungarian soldiers and spies, bringing them back to the Russian positions. Because he was multi-lingual, Aaron interrogated his captives, extracting high-level military intelligence, all of which played a notable role in assisting the Soviet armies to drive the Axis forces out of southern Russia.

In further research together with consultations with my European counterparts that followed, it has been confirmed that Aaron Herskowitz was appointed by the Russian Army to serve as overlord of the conquered Nazi-Hungarian town, Gérjen, in late 1944 through early 1945. He captured and interrogated hundreds of German and Hungarian soldiers and spies from this sector and punished those who could be identified as war criminals, sending others to imprisonment in Soviet gulags.

In early 1945, per our research, Aaron Herskowitz suddenly came into disfavor with the Russians, when an unidentified whistleblower wrongfully advised the NKVD (the Soviet secret police and precursor to the KGB) that Herskowitz was a German spy. Notwithstanding Herskowitz's protests that the charges were absurd, especially since the Germans would never appoint a Jew to be their spy, he was arrested and imprisoned in Soviet gulags. He was then shipped in a truck to another location to be executed when he escaped to the woods. The infuriated Russians announced 50,000 rubles in reward money to anyone giving the NKVD or the Russian army information leading to the arrest of Aaron Herskowitz.

There are certain scenes of dialogue in the story that occurred without the presence of Aaron Herskowitz. Though these conversations cannot be confirmed as verbatim, my European counterparts and I have agreed that the actions that subsequently occurred strongly suggest that these or similar conversations would have taken place. This book offers the unique perspective of a class of men whose ethnic or religious origins rendered them as undesirable and cursed amidst the struggle on the Eastern Front of World War II. Aaron would thus be deemed among the least likely to survive, let alone succeed, to the unimaginable heights of power he ultimately achieved against his former persecutors. Poignant and often as "raw" as the times it depicts, this memoir stands as a monument to this one remarkable man who somehow succeeded by luck, courage and ingenious imagination, to survive and triumph over the horrific ordeals inflicted upon him by his mortal enemies.

Social history at its best, this book is a must-read for anyone hoping to gain a deeper and more profound understanding of war and its effects on mankind.

David M. Glantz

Colonel David M. Glantz, US Army (retired)
Mark W. Clark Visiting Professor of History
The Citadel (Military College of South Carolina)
Charleston, SC

INDEX OF PHOTOGRAPHS

Aaron Herskowitz's Parents 1924
Emperor Franz – Josef (1830–1916)
Aaron's family 1924
Aaron Herskowitz 1936 – Czech Army
Max, Aaron's best friend, late 1930s
Samuel Zvi, son of the Cantor, mid-1930s
The Rabbi of Bielka
Ignatz Sax
Field kitchens, Russian Front 1941–1945
Aaron 1945
Helen 1946
Aaron and Helen's wedding 1946
Aaron and Helen on farm 1948
Aaron on horseback 1970s
Return to Bielka 1990
Aaron and Helen's family 1996
Aaron and equine friends, 1990s

Aaron Herskowitz's Parents 1924

Paula and Jacob Herskowitz (shortly after the creation of Czechoslovakia). Jacob was a loyal citizen of the Austro-Hungarian Empire. He continued to display a portrait of the esteemed Emperor Franz-Josef in his home until the day he died.

Emperor Franz – Josef (1830–1916)

Revered by Aaron's family and nearly all his subjects as a kind and benevolent monarch during his reign and long after his death, Emperor Franz-Josef and his predecessors were the first European monarchs to emancipate their Jewish citizens. A blessing for the emperor remained in the prayer books of synagogues throughout the former Austro-Hungarian Empire long after Franz-Josef's death.

Aaron's family 1924

Seated front row: Grandmother Reisel Klein, mother Paula and father Jacob. Standing behind: older siblings Bela, Harry and Hannah, young Aaron is on the right. In the foreground: Aaron's younger sisters Rachel, Leah and Sarah. Rachel and Leah were still living at home when Aaron was taken to Russia.

Aaron Herskowitz 1936 – Czech Army

An optimistic Aaron Herskowitz in his Czech army uniform seated between two comrades.

Max, Aaron's best friend, late 1930s

Max took a bullet for Aaron in Russia while they were both in a Nazi-Hungarian slave labor camp. Max eventually immigrated to America where the two men reunited and remained best friends for life.

Samuel Zvi, son of the Cantor, mid-1930s

Zionist son of Bielka's Cantor, and Aaron's friend. His father disowned him and declared him dead for immigrating to Palestine in defiance of the orthodox religious laws of that era, which also decreed that the Jewish people must not organize to fight the Nazis, but instead wait for God to send the Messiah to arrive and lead them out of danger to the Promised Land.

The Rabbi of Bielka

Rabbi Naftali Weiss, on the left. Ironically, he was one of Aaron's greatest adversaries, because he preached prayer instead of resistance. This photo was taken at his arrival at Auschwitz in 1944.

Ignatz Sax

After immigrating to America, Aaron searched in vain for his old comrade Sax. It was not until after the deaths of both men that members of the Sax family by chance attended a live presentation of "Aaron's Reckoning" and then stepped forward with the amazing news that their relative was the late Ignatz Sax of Aaron's story. This photograph was taken in the mid-to-late 1940s.

Field kitchens, Russian Front 1941–1945

Military Field Kitchens on the Russian Front during World War II. Aaron first met his friend Ignatz Sax when they volunteered to retrieve a field kitchen that had become deeply embedded in snow, a task that required Sax's remarkable strength. For this, they were rewarded with jobs in the kitchen, which became their lifeline to survival. Despite all the innovations in the field of mechanization, the Germans and Hungarians could never supply enough motorized vehicles for the whole army, and horse-drawn vehicles were used right up to the last days of the war on the Eastern Front.

Aaron 1945

A world-weary Aaron Herskowitz after fighting for the Russian Army at the end of World War II.

Helen 1946

Helen: "The most beautiful woman in Czechoslovakia," according to Aaron.

Aaron and Helen's wedding 1946

Aaron and Helen's wedding took place in Carlsbad, Czechoslovakia. Quite the romantic soul, Aaron had written Helen beautiful poetic love letters during their engagement. However, shortly after they were married, when he learned that Helen was showing the letters to her girlfriends, he burned them.

Aaron and Helen on farm 1948

Aaron shows off his farm skills for the camera as Helen watches, circa 1948. Location: Carlsbad, Czechoslovakia. Ironically, in the midst of the most mechanized war that history had known, it was Aaron's knowledge of horses and farms that played a crucial role in his survival.

Aaron on horseback 1970s

After the war, Aaron returns to one of his favorite pastimes in North Carolina.

Return to Bielka 1990

Aaron and Helen reunite with old friends from before the war on their return to their hometown, Bielka in 1990. The tool in the gentleman's hand is a kossa (hand-plow/scythe).

Aaron and Helen's family 1996

Aaron and Helen, with their children and grandchildren.

Aaron and equine friends, 1990s

INDEX OF MAPS

(PER FOOTNOTES)

1 Europe in 1871
1 Europe in 1914 – Outbreak of World War I
1 Europe 1918–1938
1 The Bielka Region
1 Jewish Escape Routes to Palestine—1930s
2 The Partition of Czechoslovakia 1938–1939
3 Axis Europe July 1940
4 Axis Europe June 1941
4 Axis Europe 1942
4 Russian Front June - October 1942
4 The Peak of Axis Power October 1942
5 Russian Front November–December 1942
6 Russian Front January 1943
7 Southern Russian Front February–March 1943
8 Southern Russian Front April–July 1943
9 Russian Front July - December 1943
10 Russian Front June–October 1944
11 German-held Territory January 1945
12 Defeat of Germany
13 Europe 1945–1980s
13 Europe Mid-1990s -Today

EUROPE 1871

Though Bielka belonged to the Austro-Hungarian Empire during this historical time, the primary language of many townspeople was Ukrainian.

EUROPE 1914 - OUTBREAK OF WORLD WAR I

This map depicts the opposing sides during World War I. Bielka is still part of the Austro - Hungarian Empire.

EUROPE 1918 - 1938

After World War I, Aaron's hometown Bielka belonged to the new nation of Czechoslovakia, carved out of the erstwhile empires of Germany, Russia, and Austria-Hungary.

THE BILKY REGION 1918 - 1938

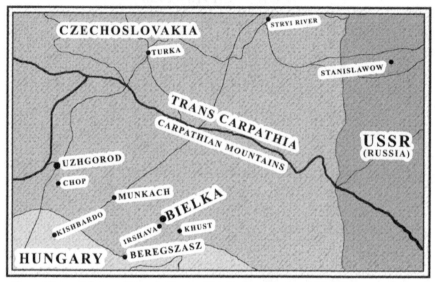

Trans-Carpathia was the province in Czechoslovakia in which Bielka was located.

JEWISH ESCAPE ROUTES TO PALESTINE - 1930s

THE PARTITION OF CZECHOSLOVAKIA 1938 - 1939

After land-grabs of vulnerable Czech border territory by Poland and Hungary in 1938, Hungary then seized Bielka's Trans-Carpathian province and Germany seized the rest of Czechoslovakia (the clear section) in March, 1939.

AXIS EUROPE JULY 1940

Bielka at this time belonged to Hungary, Germany's ally.

AXIS EUROPE JUNE 1941

On the eve of Germany's invasion of Russia, the Axis conquest of Southern Europe was complete.

AXIS EUROPE 1942

284

RUSSIAN FRONT JUNE - OCTOBER 1942

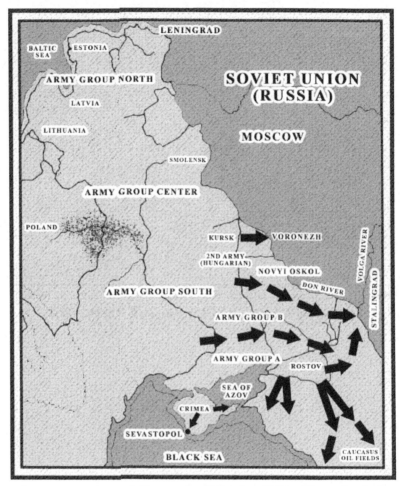

Arrows represent the main thrusts of the German-Axis 1942 offensive campaign.

THE PEAK OF AXIS POWER OCTOBER 1942

Hitler at the peak of his power, along with his Axis satellite allies, controlled nearly all of Europe and North Africa.

RUSSIAN FRONT NOVEMBER - DECEMBER 1942

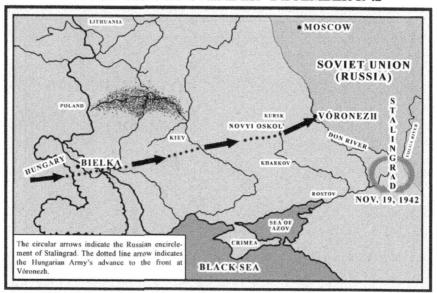

During the battle of Stalingrad, eventually resulting in the Russian encirclement of Germany's 6th Army, Aaron and his fellow slaves were forcibly taken to the front, from Hungary to Vóronezh in order to bolster the German forces.

RUSSIAN FRONT JANUARY 1943

Following the Russian breakthrough on January 13, 1943, at Aaron's location at Vóronezh, the German garrison surrounded at Stalingrad surrendered on Feb. 2, 1943. Aaron fled on foot with the German-Hungarian Army far to the west all the way to Davidovka.

SOUTHERN RUSSIAN FRONT FEBRUARY - MARCH 1943

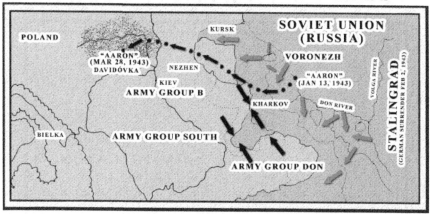

Red arrows indicate the Russian advance following their Stalingrad and Vóronezh victories. Black arrows surrounding the Kharkov area represent German counter-offensive, February-March 1943. Meanwhile, the remnants of Aaron's slave battalion under the Hungarians and Germans retreated all the way from Vóronezh, reaching Davidóvka on March 28, 1943, identified by the dotted black arrows from Vóronezh.

SOUTHERN RUSSIAN FRONT APRIL - JULY 1943

Red arrows represent the Russian spring offensive, 1943. The dark green arrows north and south of Kursk represent the last great German offensive on the Russian Front, July 1943.

RUSSIAN FRONT JULY - DECEMBER 1943

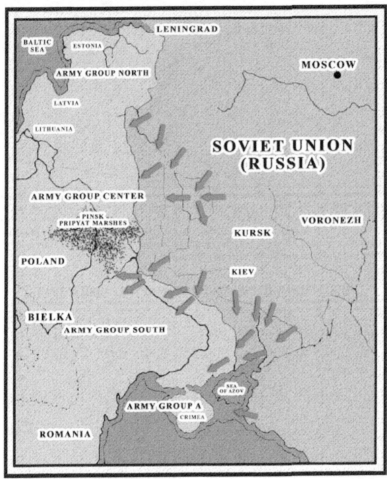

Arrows indicate the Red Army's thrusts during its great post July 1943 offensive.

RUSSIAN FRONT JUNE - OCTOBER 1944

Arrows indicate the Red Army's thrusts during its summer and fall campaign of 1944. Päks and Gérjen are located to the far west.

GERMAN - HELD TERRITORY JANUARY 1945

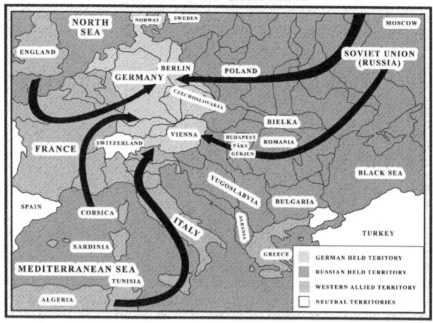

Arrows summarize Western - Russian Alliance advances, 1943 - 1945.

EUROPE 1945 - 1980s

After World War II, the Soviet Union seized Bielka and its province, claiming many inhabitants were of Ukrainian-Russian descent.

EUROPE MID-1990s - TODAY

Today, after the Cold War and the demise of the Soviet Union, Bielka belongs to Ukraine. Czechoslovakia divided itself into the Czech Republic and Slovakia.

ACKNOWLEDGEMENTS

THERE ARE SO MANY fine people to thank for their contributions to this immense project, I may have unintentionally left out some. I apologize if that occurred, for everyone deserves to be recognized. In their own way, they have all been instrumental in bringing this book to fruition.

First, to the late Congressman Tom Lantos, who provided powerful support for this true story. He understood only too well the struggles of Aaron Herskowitz, for he too, suffered under the Nazis and Hungarian fascists and was the only survivor of the Holocaust ever elected to the US Congress. The eloquent and distinguished Congressman had offered to write an Introduction to Aaron's Revenge, after reading the initial manuscript, but to the detriment of his family, his constituents, and our nation, he unexpectedly passed away.

Colonel David Glantz, US Army (retired), professor at the Citadel Military College, as well as other institutions and academies, and considered an outstanding historian, now recognized by many as the world's top military and historical expert on the Russian Front of World War II, who contributed extensive research and maps and was able to verify the historical accuracy of this true story, so as to ensure that my facts were as correct as possible. The Colonel has written a powerful Historian's Commentary for this book.

General Albin Irzyk US Army (retired), who heroically served our country in various conflicts around the globe over several decades. He is author of the book, "I Rode Up Front With Patton," among several others. He generously fact-checked Aaron's story and remarked that Aaron's transformation from lowly Jewish slave to master of his former tormentors was "one of the greatest turn-around sagas" he had ever known of during wartime.

To Paul Gulino, a fabulous professor of Literature and Film at Chapman University in California, who made splendid contributions, providing ideas for narrative formats and special assistance to contribute to my understanding of the writing of dialogue.

To Jay Koren, a gifted thinker and one of my finest friends, for his passion, intellect and insight, who reached down deeply into his mind and soul to provide phenomenal guidance and instrumental suggestions with consistent candor, from the inception of this undertaking.

NEXT GENERATIONS (www.nextgenerations.org): an organization of children, grandchildren, great-grandchildren, relatives and friends of Holocaust survivors, including a special acknowledgement to its amazing founder, Nancy Dershaw, and so many of its members. This organization provided invaluable support for this book.

My dear friend Harold Lovell and his marvelous family, whose passionate support for this book will always be remembered.

Magno Rodriguez, a wonderful friend and tireless worker, a gifted and talented IT expert as well as a unique artist, has dedicated much of his time and energy to finely tune technological and digital aspects of the presentation of this story. He is passionate about the story and wants the world to access it in all forms of media.

To journalist Ron Ishoy, who triggered ideas to help me plant the initial seeds for writing this book; Moshe Avital, a survivor, scholar and author who provided the use of valuable personal photographs and has given me encouragement and support to pursue completing this book as an important part of history; to close and dear friends, for their unswerving faith and work, some of whom are: Teressa McDavitt, Pam Franciscus and contributing editor Sand Sinclair; Billy and Alex Sax; to Paulette Fein and Mendy Lieberman.

To my brother Dr. Louis Herskowitz, and his wife Enid, and my sister Philis Edelman, and her husband Dr. David Edelman, who have provided unwavering faith and support as well as helpful suggestions and ideas; and the special support and dedication of my niece, Andrea Herskowitz.

To my phenomenal son, Hunter Herskowitz: Hunter contributed some incredibly helpful editing and opinions for the manuscript; and to my son Blake Herskowitz for his inspiration.

To my late and loving mother and my best friend, Helen Herskowitz, a survivor of Auschwitz, Bergen-Belsen, and other Nazi slave labor camps, for her unconditional love and support, and her personal contribution of countless hours of her time, heart and soul, to describe valuable aspects of this memoir. It had been her undying hope that Aaron's story be told to the world. She was the kindest person I have ever known, and she spoke with ease to all groups of people to educate them about the greatest tragedy of the twentieth century.

And finally, to my late father, Aaron Herskowitz, the modest hero, who spent countless hours allowing me to audiotape and videotape him, describing memories filled with laughter as well as dark times, revealing secrets that he had kept private for nearly his entire life. I thank him for letting me inside his heart and his soul. From this I am able to share his story with the world.

ABOUT THE AUTHOR

Howard B. Herskowitz

Howard Herskowitz has been a practicing trial lawyer for over twenty-five years. He received his law degree from Nova University in Fort Lauderdale, Florida. Mr. Herskowitz was raised by European Jewish parents who both experienced and survived The Holocaust and World War II. His upbringing fostered a career in fighting for the rights of injured victims, often the underdogs, against adversaries superior in numbers and power. He has developed and nurtured a life-long interest in history and the study of war, with a passionate curiosity about the lack of Jewish resistance during the Second World War. Mr. Herskowitz's continued attempts to learn everything possible surrounding his father's experiences of escape and retribution allowed him to capture the intriguing elements and facts which are portrayed in this compelling true story. He spent several years verifying all the essentials to convey Aaron's Reckoning accurately. Mr. Herskowitz's passion for relaying his father's struggles illustrates his love for communicating truths never previously revealed during a significant and tragic period in history.

Phone Number: (954) 303-7821
E-Mail Address: howardherskowitz@gmail.com
www.howardherskowitz.com

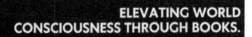

ELEVATING WORLD CONSCIOUSNESS THROUGH BOOKS.

PIERUCCI PUBLISHING

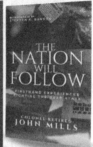

More Info

www.PierucciPublishing.com

855-720-1111

Made in the USA
Columbia, SC
28 May 2024

36040800R10173